The
Farther
Shore
· · · · · ·

THE FARTHER SHORE

**A Natural History of
Perception, 1798–1984**
· · · · · · · · · · · · · · · · · · · ·

Don Gifford

THE ATLANTIC MONTHLY PRESS

NEW YORK

♦

Published simultaneously in Canada
Printed in the United States of America

Library of Congress Cataloging-in-Publication Data

Gifford, Don.
    The farther shore : a natural history of perception, 1798–1984 / Don Gifford.
    Includes bibliographies.
    ISBN 0-87113-335-0
    1. Senses and sensation—History.   2. Perception—History.
    I. Title.
    QP441.G54   1990   153.7—dc20   89-34456

Design by Laura Hough

The Atlantic Monthly Press
19 Union Square West
New York, NY 10003

Second printing

To Honora, with emphasis and insistence

· ·

Then we have insistence insistence that in its emphasis can never be repeating, because insistence is always alive and if it is alive it is never saying anything in the same way because emphasis can never be the same not even when it is most the same that is when it has been taught.

Gertrude Stein, *Lectures in America*

As works of the imagination, the historian's work and the novelist's do not differ. Where they do differ is that the historian's picture is meant to be true.

R. G. Collingwood

Contents

. . . .

Acknowledgments
· ·

The subtitle and central theme of these overlapping essays had their origin in conversation with the late Edith and Boughton Cobb in the early 1960s. He had a few years earlier accomplished *A Field Guide to the Ferns* (1956) for the Peterson Field Guide series. She was at work on *The Ecology of Imagination in Childhood* (1977). "What we need in ecological studies," they said, "is a natural history of perception." So the attempt.

As the essays evolved from a series of three lectures delivered in an alumni seminar at Williams College in 1984, I began to realize my indebtedness to my undergraduate students in English and American literature. So many of the slants and observations derived from and expanded upon things I had had to urge on them so that we could resist the impulse to confuse the worlds—and languages—of Wordsworth and Ezra Pound, Jane Austen and Joyce, Melville and Faulkner.

Peggy Brooks read the first complete version of the manuscript and responded cogently. As it finally stands, the book has found its proper title and is leaner and much less capricious thanks to Gary Fisketjon's patience and his nimble blue pencil. It's been an interesting reversal of roles: as he suffered my running commentary on his writing a decade or so ago, so now I benefit from his.

Introduction

· · · · · · · · · · · · · · · · · · ·

The center around which these overlapping essays rotate and upon which they seek to focus is perception: in Coleridge's phrase, "the outward Beholding"[1]—our ways of preconfiguring and thus intuiting what we perceive, both literally with the physical senses and figuratively with the senses of the mind. That is, how we look things over and size things up.

In Neoplatonic tradition, sight was enthroned as queen of the senses, the comprehensive metaphor for all visionary experience: sight, understanding, intuition, spiritual vision. Today, sight is the neurophysiological queen of the senses, its electrochemical highways and byways, its procedures and capacities exhaustively explored in and for themselves and as guides to the neurophysiology of the other senses and of the brain. During a thorough physical examination a few years ago, my doctor looked into my eyes with an orthoscope and remarked that he was looking into the brain itself—not into that elusive thing, the mind, but into the brain. As Oliver Sacks and Robert Wasserman have observed,

> Though one may separate out a small part of the visual cortex as an isolated unit as is necessary in a physiological

1

approach, the visual cortex is part of the brain, and the brain is part of the organism, and the organism—every organism—has a world of its own in which perceptions become infinitely more than information carriers, become an integral part of the subjectivity, the feeling, the style of the individual.[2]

And that is what I want to explore: perception as an integral part of the subjectivity, the feeling, the style of individual experience.

The natural history of this book's subtitle is meant to suggest my method of exploration, implying (as it now does) the descriptive and fragmentary approach of the amateur rather than the analytic and comprehensive procedures of the professional. In the eighteenth century, natural history comprised the scientific study of all aspects of the natural world and its three kingdoms: animal, vegetable, and mineral. It was not only science, but also the great hobby of the English, and its heyday lasted from the closing decades of the eighteenth century through the middle of the nineteenth.[3] By the beginning of this century, natural history had been displaced by the ologies it had spawned: geology (1795), mineralogy (1796), biology (1819), zoology (1818), paleontology (1838), and the rest. To be called a natural historian was to be dismissed as superficial, a dilettante who rhapsodized and generalized about the natural world instead of cultivating the rigorous discipline of scientific specialization. And it may be just as well for this attempt to trace the shaping and reshaping of perception between 1798 & 1984 if I invite an echo of that note of disparagement at the same time that I hope for some of the integrity and probity that characterized many natural historians when the calling was still amateur and respectable.

The tentative approach of the amateur natural historian may also be appropriate to these essays because we are generally so accustomed to the shapes and patterns of our ways of perceiving that we inhabit them unaware of having participated in their origins. It is as though our perceptions are a continuous flow of a priori intuitions, instant recognitions about which we are for the most part unself-conscious. We select and frame our percepts without monitoring that process, just as we are not conscious of the neurophysiological processes that sort out, integrate, present, and sustain the images that constantly bombard our senses.

We frequently use words such as *ideas* and *concepts* in speaking of our modes of perception, implying that as ideas they would be available to consciousness in the ways that, for example, the timespace of relativity theory is available. But our modes of perception remain creative filters, bents of the mind that change by osmosis rather than by the processes of grasp and argument and choice that we associate with ideas. The creative filters are built into the given rather than consciously put in place, and to trace the natural history of those filters may be to discover a sort of double vision: the possibility of perceiving and of being aware of how we are perceiving at the same time.

The dates that bracket these essays are both arbitrary and pivotal: any year toward the end of the eighteenth century would do as well as 1798, but that was the year of Wordsworth and Coleridge's *Lyrical Ballads,* a volume that the lens of retrospect has pronounced revolutionary. It was also the year of Thomas Malthus's *Essay on the Principle of Population* and Aloys Senefelder's invention of lithography. Any of the later Reagan years would do as well as 1984, but that was the year George Orwell's chilling vision half faltered, half came true.* The real significance of those arbitrary years is that between them what has been called the break occurred, or rather, has continued to occur. As the Anglo-

---

*So many commentators have said of George Orwell's *1984* (1949), "Yes, prescient, but he didn't really get it right!" as though the "point" of writing a utopia was to present a viable program for reform or the point of a dystopia was to predict how things really would be—that is, ghastly.

Welsh poet, painter, watercolorist, and engraver David Jones has put it,

> In the nineteenth century, Western Man moved across a rubicon which, if as unseen as the 38th Parallel, seems to have been as definitive as the Styx. That much is I think generally appreciated. But it was not the memory-effacing Lethe that was crossed; and consequently, although man has found much to his liking, advantage, and considerable wonderment, he has still retained ineradicable longings for, as it were, the farther shore.[4]

Jones's emphasis is on the break in the realm of ideas, the subsidence of what Matthew Arnold called "the sea of faith." I want to explore aspects of this break that are more elusive, less available to analysis and codification.

Obviously, there must be constants through time in the ways human beings perceive. We assume that Wordsworth and Coleridge and their contemporaries saw and heard, touched and tasted and felt much as Shakespeare or Homer and their contemporaries did. Human perception must have remained constant through the genetic time of recorded history. Conversely, Homer and Shakespeare and Wordsworth and Coleridge could not have foreseen how very different the modern world and our ways of inhabiting it were going to be. But they must have assumed a correspondence between their ways of perceiving and ours, a seamless human continuum. Yet in many ways there have been such discontinuities that it seems farther from this shore to 1798 than it seems from 1798 to the farther shores of Shakespeare and Homer. The natural history of perception since 1798 presents an accelerating dance of contraries: the seamless continuum of human perception in the embrace of increasingly striking historical discontinuity.

For the purposes of this history, the closing years of the 1980s are the near shore, but even as I rewrite, I am aware of the undercutting current, the riverbank about to give way. Having my feet firmly planted on this shore is a necessary fiction, but the two natural historians I want to use as benchmarks to help my triangulation are fixed in realms of historical fact: Gilbert White (1720–93), safely on that farther shore, and Henry David Thoreau (1817–62), uncomfortably in midstream.

In the last half of the eighteenth century, natural history at its best involved both science and poetics. The history of natural history begins with an unself-conscious fusion of the two in the person of the father of English natural history, Gilbert White. White was not only a scrupulously observant pioneer among natural historians; he was also a master of what literary historians call the eighteenth-century common style, and consequently one of the great prose stylists of English literature. We admire White's style primarily for its restraint and cadenced clarity, but there is also Flaubert's dictum that "style is a way of seeing." At its best, style is verbal precision and felicity combined with disciplined and well-coordinated modes of perception. Style isn't just a matter of verbal fashion but of a fashioning and a shaping that makes it, as Brecht said, "an active aspect of meaning."

White was born in 1720 in the vicarage of Selborne, a Hampshire village and parish, eighteen miles east and slightly north of Winchester in south-central England, where his family was temporarily residing with the vicar, his grandfather Gilbert White, Sr. About ten years later, his family settled permanently at Selborne in a house called The Wakes, one hundred yards across the village green from the vicarage. With brief interruptions, White was to live in The Wakes (which he owned after 1763) for the rest of his life.

In 1743, he was graduated from Oriel College, Oxford, into the clergy, apparently with some distinction. Exactly what distinction isn't clear, but it was enough to merit a graduation award of Alexander Pope's six-volume translation of *The Iliad,* presented by the poet's own hand. In 1751, White settled down in Selborne to become what he called "a stationary man," the curate in charge of a neighboring parish and eventually of the parish of Selborne, but never vicar because the living (the vicarage rent-free and a secure income for life) of Selborne was in the gift of Oxford's Magdalen College, and White was Oriel. Traditionally, the Oxford colleges jealously guarded the livings at their disposal. White was offered several livings by Oriel, but he turned them down for a variety of reasons, all of which now seem to add up to his profound preference for Selborne. He was a bachelor, comfortable on what is now frequently misrepresented as a slender annual income of three hundred pounds, which is hardly slender when we realize that the annual rent of The Wakes was five guineas and that his income enabled White to support a sizable house with several servants, a modest stable, and a well-provided and hospitable table. His income (not counting salaries for the servants or rent for the house) would approach fifty or sixty thousand dollars a year in modern currency.

The parish of Selborne in the second half of the eighteenth century included an area of thirteen square miles. According to White's census of 1783, it had a population of 676; 313 in the village of Selborne, 363 in the rest of the parish. It was an ideally sequestered niche for the stationary man. The landlocked parish could only be reached by one narrow and difficult cartway and three hanging or hollow lanes, narrow paths overhung by steep banks, more suitable for pedestrians and pack-animals than for carts. In some places, the paths had been worn as much as sixteen feet down into the freestone by traffic and erosion. White's lifelong friend John Mulso complained that the access was "inscrutable" and, whenever he came to visit, insisted on being provided with a guide to meet him in Alton, four miles to the northwest.

White did travel more than the word *stationary* suggests— to Oxford, fifty miles to the north, at least once a year; up to London, fifty-five miles northeast, to see his brothers two or three times a year; he once journeyed as far as Shrewsbury in the Midlands, 150 miles to the northwest. He usually traveled on horseback, because he suffered terribly from coach-sickness. He traveled less as he grew older, and, I suspect, as he grew more involved in the rhythms of the natural history of Selborne. For White, the human and natural history of his parish comprised an organic whole. When, twenty years after White's death, the word *biology* made its first appearance in English, it didn't mean the science of life processes and of living organisms but was firmly attached to its Greek root and was used to mean the study of human life and character. Only later (circa 1819) did it shift to Lamarck's 1802 meaning, our present sense of the word.

White's contemporary, the German philosopher Immanuel Kant, enjoyed reading fictions of sea adventure, though he had never seen the sea, which was only some thirty miles to the west and north of Königsberg in Prussia—now Kaliningrad in the U.S.S.R.—where he lived. When a friend urged him to make the trip to the sea, he replied, "I have traveled much in Königsberg." White could similarly have said, "I have traveled much in Selborne"; Thoreau was to quip in *Walden,* "I have traveled a good deal in Concord."[5]

To White, natural history meant not only the study of the animal, vegetable, and mineral kingdoms; it also included some attention to meteorology and astronomy and to what White called antiquities, namely archaeology and cultural anthropology. The separation of natural history into the professional fields of study so familiar to us dates from the closing decades of the nineteenth century. Charles Darwin, for example, called himself a naturalist, that is, a natural historian, as much geologist and paleontologist as biologist. When he joined the HMS *Beagle* in 1831 at the age of twenty-two, Darwin was a refugee from a brief and uncongenial encounter with medical studies and from a career in the clergy, which seemed to his family the only other alternative. Darwin wasn't a professional natural historian but a promising amateur who lived into the twilight of the great age of amateurs.

White lived at the height of that age, when intellectual curiosity and creative energy could determine their own horizons instead of being forced into the straitjacket of predetermined professional boundaries. Amateur or preprofessional, White was nonetheless determined to practice natural history as a scientific discipline, founded on the principle that, as Kant said, concepts without percepts are empty. White described himself as an "outdoor naturalist, one who takes his observations from the subject itself, and not from the writings of others." When one of his correspondents caught him making an unverified statement, White responded,

> You put a very shrewd question when you ask me how I know that the [ring-ousel's] autumnal migration is southwards? Was not candour and openness the very life of natural history, I should pass over this query just as a sly commentator does over a crabbed passage in a classic; but common ingenuousness obliges me to confess, not without some degree of shame, that I only reasoned in that case from analogy. For as all other autumnal birds migrate from the northwards to us . . . so I concluded that the ring-ousels did the same.[6]

It was White whom Darwin praised for the inspiration of his example, for his way of seeing, for the precision of his observations and the felicity of his expression. It is one of the ironies of the history of science that Darwin, as much committed to direct observation and outdoor natural history as Gilbert White, had the effect of driving everyone who followed him back into the laboratory.

White's landmark book, *The Natural History and Antiquities of Selborne*, was published in 1789. It is presented as a collection of 110 letters, dated between August 1767 and June 1787, polished and updated in 1787–88. White describes it as a "humble attempt to promote a more minute inquiry into natural history; into the life and conversation of animals," that is, into ethology. In 1788, he added an Advertisement, or preface, in which he suggests that if other stationary men "would pay some attention to the districts in which they reside," they could produce comparable "parochial" histories, which, compiled and coordinated (411 parishes for White's county, Hampshire) would become county histories, and in the fullness of time those county histories would constitute "a full and complete natural history of these kingdoms." The idea is as lucid as the eighteenth-century common style in which it's proposed but flawed in that there was only one Gilbert White.

The epistolary form of *The Natural History of Selborne* is peculiarly appropriate to White's perspective as pioneer natural historian. Letters are open-ended; they imply the possibility of dialogue and seem to invite a response in turn. White exploits these implications to emphasize the communal nature of the study of natural history. The goal is not personal knowledge but a community of knowledge that White calls "a universal natural history." Conversely, this form also allows White to emphasize the limits of his local and personal perspective. He grounds his observations and generalizations in the particulars of his own experience as a stationary man. By definition, those particulars are fragmentary and local, suggestive of more to come.

There are two sequences of letters: forty-four dated between 1767 and 1780 and addressed to the naturalist Thomas Pennant and sixty-six between 1769 and 1787 addressed to the lawyer and antiquary, the Honourable Daines Barrington. The temporal sequence of the letters, traced and retraced, implies that the same ground of experience can be explored again and again because natural history is both open-ended and cumulative in time. White also kept day-to-day records of the natural world of Selborne: the *Garden Kalendar* (1751–68), superseded by the more detailed and discursive *Naturalist's Journal* (1768–93). Those records provided White with an elaborate bank of information on which he could draw when subsequent observations revealed the significance of earlier entries.

The Natural History of Selborne, for all its importance to Coleridge, Darwin, Thoreau, and others, tends to prove troublesome to readers in the closing decades of this century, as do the almost ten thousand entries in the *Naturalist's Journal*. White's simplicity and his exceptional clarity (which the Victorians patronized as his quaintness) are apparent, but his observations seem more poetic and episodic than scientific and encyclopedic. A common stumbling block for the contemporary reader of White is the vast quantity of random information and apparently irrelevant detail in the journals and letters. In part, that quantity is the result of fieldwork itself. Stephen Jay Gould quotes a friend as saying,

> Fieldwork is one hell of a way to get information. All that time, effort, money, often for comparatively little when measured against the hours spent.[7]

But the fundamental reasons for the frustrating quantity of apparent trivia in White's letters and journals lie deeper than the hazards of fieldwork. By the middle of the eighteenth century, Carolus Linnaeus's revolutionary classification system had been established as the universal language of speciation, and White's contemporaries were in a rage to classify. White wasn't immune to this enthusiasm, but he was more interested in studying the habits and behavior of plants and animals than in hunting for and classifying new species. In this realm of natural history, there was virtually no precedent. White undertook to extricate the observations of the naturalist from the accumulated lore of folk wisdom, legendry, fable, and heraldry, from medieval bestiaries and scholastic authority.

In effect, White's perspective differs radically from our own because he had no a priori basis for distinguishing between trivial and significant things. Each day he faced the recurring problem of deciding which bits of data were worth recording. The problem could be solved only from the vantage point of retrospect, and forty years of retrospect count for very little at the beginning of natural history. The amateur naturalist today can go into the field with a comprehensive library of field guides and handbooks, which not only enable him to identify and classify but which also outline habitat and behavior; in effect, they tell the amateur what to look for, what to see. And behind the field guides and handbooks is a vast and growing literature, so overwhelming that it almost inevitably dictates the specialization of the professional— or the superficialization of the amateur. No such head start was available to White, and he habitually treated the reference works of his day with courteous skepticism. He encouraged his eye and ear in the discipline of turning his back on the wisdom of the closet naturalists and starting from scratch—a discipline akin to what Keats called "negative capability, that is when man is capable of being in uncertainties, Mysteries, doubts, without any irritable reaching after fact and reason."[8] John Mulso summed up his friend White with the finest of compliments: "You are more able to see with your own Eyes than any man I know."[9] But in addition to seeing with his own eyes, White also had to see cumulatively, a second order of seeing that led Mulso, among others, to accuse him of dragging his feet, procrastinating instead of speeding his natural history into print. White did delay for almost two decades, well aware of the limits on his cumulative seeing.

> If a man was never to write on natural knowledge 'til he knew everything, he would never write at all.[10]

Coleridge, who called White's *Natural History of Selborne* "this sweet delightful book," reports that it took Wordsworth, Wordsworth's sister Dorothy, and himself several months in 1797–98 to learn to take field notes "with the object and imagery immediately before my sense"—notes relevant, of course, to poetry as well as to the natural world and its history. Thoreau, another field-naturalist with notebook and pencil in hand, reduced his friend young Ellery Channing to tears because, as Channing admitted, he knew so little about what merited recording that he returned home from his nature walks day after day with an empty note-book. The trouble late-twentieth-century readers have with White and *The Natural History of Selborne* is not unrelated to Channing's tears. It is the difficulty we have in seeing from a perspective far removed from our own. In White's case, the perspective was original in the sense of at the beginning of things. Half a century later, Thoreau's perspective would have its similarities to White's when he was in the field with his notebooks, but at the worktable what might have been entitled *The Natural History of Walden* became instead the pursuit of a comprehensive metaphor for a new way of asking questions about and undertaking the history of individual human consciousness. The world of Walden Pond and Concord wasn't as insulated as White's parish of Selborne. Thoreau punned Walden as Walled-in Pond, but the walls came down as he watched some workmen cutting ice on the pond. He realized that the ice was destined for China via the railroad that crossed the southwest shore of the pond and the clipper ship waiting in Boston Harbor. That mind's-eye glimpse of the ice trade with China, which then called itself the Celestial Empire, reminded Thoreau of his own business with the celestial empire of transcendental vision—the macrocosm of mind reflected in the microcosm of the pond.

The distance from White's worktable to Thoreau's is instructive. White never questioned his personal perspective as letter writer, as the "monographer" of his "province," and his perspective is matched and balanced by that of his correspondents. Together they constitute a community confident of their pursuit of natural history and of the "candour and openness" of their method. Letters, selected and revised, are the obvious literary form, the ideally transparent medium for their open-ended community of enterprise. No such comfortably appropriate literary form was available to Thoreau. He had practiced the process of distillation from the field notebooks to the journals to the text of a lecture, essay, or book; that process had become habit by the time he sat down to write *Walden.* But the choice of overall form, the genre or literary family that would unify those materials, was not as simple or as natural as a cluster of letters or sequence of journal entries.

The overall pattern of a book of hours had served Thoreau in *A Week on the Concord and Merrimack Rivers* (1849), and it was summoned again in *Walden* to structure the opening and closing sections. But other principles of organization are also invoked, including natural history itself. There is descriptive study of the three kingdoms of nature as they intersect at Walden Pond, but the scientific and poetic phases of natural history jostle each other with a self-consciousness that isn't present in White's Selborne. At Walden, science measures and quantifies the configurations and depths of the pond and the undulation of its ice; poetry celebrates the pond as a well, an eye, a heart, a mouth, a "perfect forest mirror." But each defers to the other; science stands aside to let poetry have its day, and the poetry of microcosm/macrocosm intrudes when the surveyor's instruments determine that the ice undulates on the pond. "Who knows but if our instruments were delicate enough we might detect an undulation in the crust of the earth."[11] The elaborate delicacies of modern instruments agree that his poetry was scientifically correct.

The how-to-do-it book, with its suggested program for action, is invoked in the first chapter of *Walden* to provide an ironic backdrop for a running critical commentary on how not to do it, how not to live the life of the mind. The epic is summoned to render everyday reality fabulous, as it must be if it is to activate and sustain the eye of a wide-awake consciousness. A principle of dialectical opposition structures other parts of the book; solitude vies with society, "higher laws" with "brute neighbors." Nature that "smiles on him as in the plains" vies with "vast, Titanic, inhuman Nature" that gets man "at a disadvantage . . . and pilfers him of some of his divine faculty."[12]

The book of hours with its interlocking temporal metaphors (the round of a day is like the round of the week, is like the round of a year, is like the round of a life) activates spatial metaphors: the macrocosm of nature is at hand in the microcosm of Walden Pond; the human community is at hand in Concord, and civilization is present in the solitary man and his consciousness. But the man is solitary, not stationary as he was in Selborne, and he is no longer the comfortably unself-conscious letter writer but a persona, a sharp-edged self-caricature of the village eccentric who insults in order to speak as and for everyman.

Gilbert White's ideal was to observe and record what was there; Thoreau's was to "live deliberately," to achieve an intensity of consciousness that he likened to being perpetually awake, and he expropriated all that was there for that enterprise. The distance between the two natural historians could be summed up as a matter of character, the distance between the objective and the subjective, if those terms weren't so evasive, and if there weren't more to the difference than character. White's sense of the personal and communal stasis available to him as stationary man contrasts quite sharply with Thoreau's view of himself as "sojourner" in several senses, including the archaic sense of a student temporarily lodging in the house or school where he is taught. The world of difference between the two men comes down not to a difference in character but to the distance between a world that can house a stationary man and his community and a world that offers so little hospitality to things stationary that the best one can hope for is a sojourn.

When I reflect on how far it is from my world to Thoreau's of 130 years ago, I am floored by the magnitude of the difference until I raise my sights and consider the order of change that took place during the sixty-five years between Thoreau and White. The order of magnitude is staggering: there was more change in that sixty-five-year span than there was between Gilbert White's Hampshire and Homer's Greece. Clearly, the distance from our perspective to Thoreau's involves more than just a few steps from here to the world next door.

I'm aware that the seismic shift between the 1798 and 1984

of my title has been so overimpressed upon us that we have had to dull it down to cliché. Most of our attempts to understand this change have focused on the radical alteration of the physical world achieved by science and technology and on the radical alteration of the world of ideas and their history associated with names such as Darwin, Marx, Freud, and Einstein. But the history of perception offers a third possibility that mediates between change in the physical world and change in the realm of ideas. I assume that perception takes its shape from the givens of the physical world while creatively shaping the physical world in turn. I also assume that the capacity of perception to shape and reshape is both influenced by and gives rise to those more formal historical presences we call ideas. In an elaborate choreography of turn and counterturn, perception functions as both foretaste and aftereffect in our physical and mental worlds.

I once imagined that it might be possible to relive a life like White's in Selborne or Thoreau's at Walden Pond, to retire to a relatively closed ecological niche such as the cul-de-sac in the village of Williamstown, Massachusetts, where my worktable now sits; to live there as perceptively as possible and to practice in notebooks and journals en route to assembling a natural history of this town. But there are revealing obstacles to this pastoral fantasy. White was born in and to Selborne; Selborne, so to speak, had chosen him. Thoreau chose Walden because it was a limited and readable environment, handy to Concord and conversation, on land belonging to Emerson and therefore economically available for the asking. The world of eighteenth-century Selborne was closed, to the satisfaction of a stationary man. The door into the world of Walden was ajar for the sojourner, although Thoreau put a good deal of comic energy into the pretense that it was closed and that he was inside and stationary. But whatever place I chose—unless I outpretended Thoreau and imposed an artificial ban on all media, electronic, print, the works—could never seem a comfortably closed world. We are, as Diderot observed, "our contacts," and the rings of my late twentieth-century contacts are too expansive, too inclusive to allow the fiction of closure. The natural history of this cul-de-sac becomes, at a touch, the natural history of perception.

Over my desk is Yeats's exhortation, "Hammer your thoughts into unity."[13] But the calendar of my contacts jostles into expanding rings of parentheses, footnotes, and asides; my categories (the realms of eye and ear, of timespace, of quantity and scale, of personal worth and self-esteem, of *ecos)* overlap and turn in kaleidoscopic interchange as the history of perception becomes personal history and vice versa.

1.
The Mighty World of Eye
· · · · · · · · · ·

> *all the mighty world*
> *Of eye, and ear—both what they half create,*
> *And what perceive*
> Wordsworth, "Lines / Composed a Few
> Miles above Tintern Abbey / On
> Revisiting the Banks of the Wye /
> During a Tour. July 13, 1798"

Commentators on this near shore of the 1980s proclaim that the mighty world of eye is all-dominant, the eye gratified, dazzled, distracted in the flood of print, film, and electronic media. By contrast, they complain, the mighty world of ear fades toward obscurity. But on the farther shore of 1798, Wordsworth even-handedly regards those two once-mighty worlds as in balance, equally accessible, equally nourishing. It now seems that in the long, slow progress of the ferry from that shore to this, the eye crossed a Rubicon while the ear crossed a Rubicon that has proven to be Lethe.

*   *   *

Wordsworth's lines announce not only a balance but also an insight and an excitement that was new in 1798: that the act of perception is in part an act of creation; that perception involves not just passive receptivity (the stylus of the objective world writing on the tabula rasa of the mind) but the active participation of what Coleridge called "the Primary IMAGINATION" and defined as

> the living Power and prime Agent of all human Perception, and as a repetition in the finite mind [of man] of the eternal act of Creation, in the infinite I AM.[1]

Coleridge assumed that for God, outside of time, the act of creating and the act of contemplating the thing created were one and the same. Thus, for the human being inside time, the act of perceiving and the act of creating the thing perceived would be simultaneous and continuous, at once active-creative and passive-contemplative.

Even as Wordsworth and Coleridge were exploring this new concept of perception, there was a growing popular fascination with optical instruments and a growing interest on the part of painters in achieving objectivity, a goal that they assumed could be facilitated by the use of mechanical and optical aids. A quiet revolution was taking place in the way the eye was being trained to see. In a little more than two decades, this sort of painterly objectivity would triumph in the invention of photography, which until the early twentieth century was regarded not as an art, shaping the images it presumably fixed, but as arguably the ultimate in objective documentation of the visual world.

All through the eighteenth century and into the nineteenth, sketching was a fashionable pursuit for the leisured classes. Tourists, amateur sketchers, and more than a few professional painters, turned to mechanical aids, chiefly the camera obscura and the

Claude glass, the latter named after Claude Lorrain, a much-admired French landscape painter. Initially, these aids were used to isolate and enhance the picturesque in a scene rather than to develop its objectivity.

Available in England by 1700, the portable camera obscura is a lightproof box with a lens at the front that produces an image reflected by an inclined mirror onto a glass screen on top. The image can then be traced onto light translucent paper and transferred to heavier paper or canvas, or it can simply be appreciated for itself.

The Claude glass was used primarily for on-the-spot appreciation of images. It's a hand-held, slightly convex blackened mirror, usually carried in a protective case. It afforded the viewer in search of the silver-toned picturesque "low-key images of supposedly Claudian character."[2] The person using the Claude glass usually turned his back to the view; thus, use of the glass was not without risk. The poet Thomas Gray reported that while on a walking tour of the Lowlands, he had been so taken with a prospect in his glass that he had backed up to improve the frame and had tumbled into a ditch. Pratfalls aside, there is a studied indirection in this use of aids, as though a scene viewed with the unaided eye would be aesthetically inferior to the scene composed by the mediating presence of an optical device. This reliance on optical aids also reflects the way the eighteenth-century eye was nurtured—on portfolios of prints, black and white or sepia engravings of the great masters, most notably Raphael and his imitators whose draftsmanship translated well into engraving. Sir Joshua Reynolds summed it up in 1771: "Claude Lorrain . . . was convinced [rightly so from Reynolds's point of view] that taking nature as he found it seldom produced beauty."

The tourist (the *Oxford English Dictionary* dates the word from around 1800) in search of beauty or the picturesque sought to compose and experience landscape as though it were a sequence of prints in a portfolio or of paintings hung on a gallery wall. By the 1730s, designers of gardens and parks, anticipating and reflecting these preoccupations, had begun to organize circuits, series of vistas to be viewed from predetermined vantage points, eventually to be marked by elaborate guideposts such as "temples, obelisks, seats, pagodas, rotundas, and so on."³ The concept of circuitry became so refined that Lancelot "Capability" Brown would design circuits (such as the one around the lake at Claremont in Surrey) that would unfold their prospects only if one walked or rode in a given direction (counterclockwise at Claremont). The concept of landscape organized as a sequence of prospects spread to include the experience of wild landscape. In his *Guide to the Lakes,* Thomas West, a proponent of the Claude glass, had proposed looking at the Lake District

> from certain pre-ordained viewpoints or Stations so that the experience of tourism, instead of a jumble of impressions should be a series of properly composed and memorable tableaux.⁴

West's *Guide* was immensely popular; it had the effect of standardizing the experience of the Lake District for generations to come. It was also widely imitated by guides to other picturesque districts and thus encouraged the tourist to experience landscape not as a continuum through which he moved but as a sequence of static compositions. Presumably, the tourist could close his eyes in between.

At much the same time, Wordsworth and Coleridge were turning away from the reliance on fixed prospects and stations toward a more fluid experience of the natural world, itself perceived as organism in motion. Meanwhile, the pace of invention sped up, mothered not by necessity but by the excitement of new ways of seeing. William Hyde Wollaston's camera lucida in 1807 and Cornelius Varley's Patent Graphic Telescope in 1811 were considerable improvements over the camera obscura for use in the field. The camera lucida is a system of eyepiece, prism, and lens mounted on a rod that can be attached to a drawing board or table. By careful adjustment, the scene or object in view and the hand on the paper can be seen simultaneously and the object or scene traced. Varley's Graphic Telescope also produces a traceable image with the added advantage of telescopic magnification (up to nineteen times, his patent claims).

These two instruments, particularly the camera lucida, enjoyed instant and sustained popularity among amateurs and professionals alike, and their popularity confirmed the preference for a visual reality with the object centered and isolated, its edges sharpened by the defining presence of a lens. When looking at an object, the human eye shifts focus between telephoto and wide-angle something on the order of twenty times per second, but we see the object as fixed and centered in the field of vision. The way the mediating presence of the lens sharpens edges enhances that sense of fixity and centrality—frequently in ways that are exciting and instructive. One witness described the sensation: "The world I saw through [microscope and telescope] seemed particularly beautiful, crystal clear and sharp." He goes on to describe "the feeling of magic and beauty I associated with optics."[5]

After its introduction in the early ninteenth century, the camera lucida didn't remain a tool for the professional painter and the plaything of leisured sketchers such as Queen Victoria. In the 1820s, technological innovation made it possible to run wood engravings and a body of type at the same time on high-speed printing presses. This resulted in the sudden proliferation of the so-called fully illustrated books and magazines that were to be tremendously popular for the rest of the century and into the next. These publications played a key role in the education of the vernacular eye, and the camera lucida was central in the preparation of wood engravings until both were superseded by the combination of the camera, halftone printing, and photoengraving in the 1870s and 1880s.

The career of the American illustrator and popular historian Benson John Lossing provides a glimpse of how the camera lucida informed the nineteenth-century eye. By the age of twenty-three, with the aid of three years of formal education, Lossing was editor of the major newspaper of Poughkeepsie, New York, as well as editor and publisher of the *Poughkeepsie Casket,* a little magazine devoted to the arts. To better illustrate his magazine and to prepare his *Outline History of the Fine Arts* for publication by Harper's in 1843, Lossing apprenticed himself to learn wood engraving in New York City. By that time, wood engravers were trained to use the camera lucida to transfer images from the illustrator's watercolors or sketches to the woodblock. The technique Lossing subsequently developed involved three stages: he used the camera lucida to make pencil sketches in the field; he used it again back in the studio to reduce the field sketches to small watercolors (usually smaller than six by nine inches); and then he, or one of the employees in his wood-engraving business, would use it a final time to reduce the watercolors to engravings on woodblocks.

Thus by 1850 in America, England, and Western Europe, the reader's visual expectations of everything from fine arts to new inventions, from battlefields and cityscapes to haystacks, farms, and villages were being shaped by the camera lucida.

Photography came along at about the same time. It didn't begin the process of training the eye to the mediating presence of the optical instrument, but speeded it up. Photography further encouraged the eye to accept the lens as the mediator of objectivity and to expect an optical clarity of edge and a fixity of the image within its frame that, unaided or untrained, the human eye, itself constantly in motion and constantly changing its depth of field, simply cannot convey. By the 1860s, the magic of that mediating presence was so indispensable that Albert Bierstadt, when he showed his ten-foot canvases of vast Rocky Mountain scenes, encouraged viewers to scan the paintings with the aid of binoculars in order to experience the scene as though they were on-site and to improve the sense of sublimity and scale. The actual effect was that the viewer with binoculars couldn't see the whole painting at once, just as the viewer at a vantage point in a mountain landscape can't take in the whole scene without moving his eyes or head.

The lens hasn't slackened its grip on our preferences. In the 1950s, I was involved in a series of experiments designed to test the commercial viability of pinhole cameras. Our test cameras produced fascinating soft-edged images that were rejected out of hand as crude by the evaluators because they didn't look like images produced by the camera lens. As visual images, those pinhole photographs were certainly different but hardly crude (the pinholes had been drilled with the precision required for the apertures of electron microscopes). The photographs were unacceptable because they didn't conform to the modern eye's expectation of sharp-edged optical images. Only the exceptional image, blurred by oil or gauze in special-effects photography, can be tolerated as acceptable; no such tolerance would cover the everyday use of a pinhole camera.

Photography was to retrain and change the eye in other ways as well. In 1844, William Henry Fox Talbot—the English inventor of calotype, one of the early processes of fixing visual images on light-sensitive paper—put the desire for this change poignantly, and with a measure of self-pity, in his publication *The Pencil of Nature*. Talbot was something of a muff with the camera lucida, and his failures led him, he says,

> to reflect on the inimitable beauty of the pictures of nature's painting which the glass lense of the Camera throws upon the paper in its focus—fairy pictures, creatures of a moment, and destined as rapidly to fade away . . . how charming it would be if it were possible to cause these natural images to imprint themselves durably, and remain fixed upon the paper.

As Talbot wished, photography has converted the visual image into a permanent creature of the moment, an accident in visual time, but fixed and framed in time just as paintings are. In a photograph, however, there is always an indeterminacy, always a tincture of chance. Between the triggering instant and the flick of the shutter, a subject or object can move, an eye close, a hand twitch; light can shift and play its tricks. Chemical and electrical presences in the darkroom can produce all sorts of accidents—from subtle improvements to outright ruin. The instant of a photographic glance is not necessarily the same as the contemplative time in which the painter moves and which is shared by the trained viewer of paintings. Degas implied a definition of this contemplative time by saying "I don't paint what I see but what would enable others to see what I see," and it is that dimension that has been altered by the camera. As a result, we are now in the habit of assuming that we can read all visual compositions at a glance. In museums, I frequently catch myself thinking and moving that way, having fallen into a glance-and-move-on pace that has become the norm.

This is not to say that photography can't be art or that the serious photographer doesn't work in a contemplative time similar to the painter's. Nor am I suggesting that photographic images won't reward the viewer who moves in contemplative time. But we do tend to read photographs—and all the other visual images introduced to us through photographic reproduction—as though we were reading in passing, in a way epitomized by the new language *Life* magazine taught us in the 1930s and 1940s—to scan sequences of small black-and-white photographs as though we were rapidly scanning lines of print on a page.

Our experience of photography oscillates between two orders of time, glance or contemplation, just as the photograph itself is ambiguously private mirror and public image. There is reason to suspect, for example, that the snapshots taken on family occasions ostensibly to fix the moment for the family archives are at least in part taken to call attention to the moment itself—as though the click of the snapshooter's camera were admonishing the family to commemorate the gathering with a moment of silence. The private mirror of the snapshot calls for a glance; to contemplate the image it offers is to transform it into an anachronism or a memento mori. "What strange clothes people wore in those days" or "How funny Uncle George looks with all that hair on his head." And, on the other hand, "How sad it is, that world of cars with fins and plump smiling faces, forever lost to us."

The public image of the documentary photograph presents itself as a permanent record that we can store and consult in historical time, but those images are frequently posed as photo opportunities or selected because they flatter or demean. I recall a page of snapshots of Harry Truman at a state banquet that *Life* published in 1948 in an all-too-obvious effort to make the eating president look vulgar. A classic in this ambiguous realm of the historical record is the photograph of the Americans planting the flag on the crest of Iwo Jima. Was that heroic gesture caught in passing or staged for effect? In either case the effect is there, but, as the argument about the validity of the photograph continues, the record remains inconclusive.

The camera also enables us to achieve new realms of narcissism. "These photographs are my vision." "This is how I saw the people of Morocco, the architecture of France, the gardens of Britain." The camera can also turn its mirror-eye on the photographer, offering new and ever-changing occasions for self-consciousness—"Which is the better side of your face?"—as well as the possibility that one could film (and thus have available for constant review) one's whole life. Another dimension of memento mori: I too "had pretty plumage once."

The photograph further alters visual time by providing the possibility of endless replication: "I can always have it at hand; if it wears out, I can get another," or, "I don't have to look closely now because I can return to it at any time and look closely at my leisure." And with the development of halftone printing and photoengraving in the 1870s and 1880s, there was the advent of endless reproduction of photographs in print. Wood engraving was superseded as the medium of illustration by processes far less labor-intensive, and there was immediate popular prejudice in favor of photographic images, which were read as so much closer to the thing itself than the images produced by wood engraving. And, whereas the size of a wood engraving was relatively fixed, the size of a photoengraving reflected the flexibility of the size of the photograph, which could be enlarged or reduced optically instead of manually. The photograph thus offered both endless reproduction of its fixed image in time and radical flexibility in scale and in its suggestion of space, since the same negative could be used to make a postage-stamp miniature and a photomural. With the advent of Wirephotos in 1935, the photograph could transcend time as well as space. The frame of the photograph is also flexible. The photograph can be cropped; images on the periphery of the original negative can be isolated and enlarged. The original subject framed in the photograph can be cut out and replaced with an infinite range of actual subjects. Virtually anyone can be photographed, or rather can be seen in a photograph, shaking hands with the president.

The history of the reproduced images available to those interested in the history of art outlines the change effected by the camera and its forerunners. In the eighteenth and early nineteenth centuries, reproductions of paintings for study were commonly black-and-white or sepia prints, widely available thanks to the rapid growth of the print trade in eighteenth-century England. This growth was spurred by William Hogarth's achievement of the Copyright Act of 1735, which meant that the artist or craftsman who produced the original could continue to profit from the sale of reproductions. Prints became so popular that by 1800, print shops were prospering in every major town in England.

By the 1840s, wood engravings of the world's great paintings were available in widely circulated magazines and books, such as the *Family Magazine*, the first fully illustrated American periodical, and Lossing's *Outline History of the Fine Arts.* At the same time, lithography (invented in 1798, followed by chromolithography in 1837) had come to dominate printmaking and, once adapted to the power press, made inexpensive reproductions of paintings an overnight popular success under the aegis of the American Art Union* and Currier and Ives. By 1900, color illustrations were available in magazines and books, as were color prints made from photographs (but these were relatively expensive and were to remain so until midcentury). For the student with an empty purse, there were the University Prints, four-by-six- and five-by-seven-inch black-and-white photoengravings of the "fine art of the world." Since World War II, lavish color-illustrated books, inexpensive color reproductions in a variety of sizes, countless color slides, and, most recently, a proliferation of well-designed posters—truly the arts of the world, in color reproductions of all sizes—are at the student's fingertips.

The modern visual world is superanimated by sophisticated reproduction** and skillfully designed presentation of all sorts of visual images in all sorts of contexts. Always present is the possibility of visual surfeit, visual overload, as counterpoint to the satisfaction and excitement of our riches. There is the blurring of scale that miniaturizes the twenty-eight-foot Jackson Pollock painting to postcard size and gigantizes the four-by-six-inch Paul Klee watercolor to cover a wall. Everywhere we encounter the ambiguous tension between the reproduction of the photograph and the photographic reproduction of images from painting and the other arts. And there is the luminosity of images presented by slide and movie projector and television screen, which frequently

---

*Founded in 1844, the Union's annual membership fee was five dollars, for which the subscriber received a premium of an engraving or a color lithograph of a famous contemporary painting (by such artists as Thomas Cole, William Sidney Mount, and George Caleb Bingham) and a lottery ticket chance to win an original painting. Membership in the Union peaked at sixteen thousand, and its reputable board of directors included among others William Cullen Bryant, but the lottery was nevertheless illegal and proved to be the Union's undoing, by court order, in 1852.

**So sophisticated, in fact, that the United States government has been forced to protect its paper currency from photoreproduction by interweaving the paper with a special chemically treated plastic thread.

challenges the painting or photograph, making the real thing seem opaque, dull. Always present are the raveling questions: Is that the thing itself? Is that an image of the thing itself? Is that the image itself? Is that a reproduction of the image itself? Is that an imitation of an image, or is it a billboard? A sculpture in plastic wrap or a T-shirt? Always present is the photo image's reassurance that this is the once familiar that we can always have at hand, the camera always ready as the "invaluable assistant" in the "defamiliarization" of the all-too-familiar everyday world.[6]

Yet even as I puzzle these much-puzzled questions, I am reminded of Stephen Crane, whose only exposure to war before he wrote *The Red Badge of Courage* (1895) was the chatter-stories of veterans and the war photographs prepared by Mathew Brady's teams, which were widely published after the development of photoengraving in the 1880s. Tableaux from some of those photographs are explicitly described in scenes from Crane's classic war novel. This should serve as a reminder of the paradox that Crane, for all of his subsequent experience as war correspondent, would never see and focus the psychological experience of war as clearly again.

Much of this revolution in how the eye would half-create, half-perceive—thanks to the mediating presence of optical instruments and the technologies of reproduction—was well under way during the period between Gilbert White's death in 1793 and Wordsworth's in 1850. But Wordsworth, in the starting gate when the new technologies were beginning to retrain the eye, was among the least visual of poets—generalizing the visual world so that it became a sustained "true metaphor" (true to him, metaphor to us) for

A motion and a spirit that impels
All thinking things, all objects of all thought
And rolls through all things.[7]

In "I Wandered Lonely as a Cloud," the "host of golden daffodils" he sees from the helicopter perspective of the lonely cloud are not there for the camera's quick glance but to "flash upon that inward eye / Which is the bliss of solitude." When Wordsworth supplied (anonymously) a text for Joseph Wilkinson's *Select Views in Cumberland, Westmoreland, and Lancashire* (1810),[8] he advocated a nonpictorial, flow-through method of looking at landscape—in search not of views but of what he called "unity of impression," "grandeur" undiminished by painterly "intrusion of shade," nature without the intervention of the Claude glass.

Coleridge was the more visual of the two. He shared Wordsworth's determination to immerse himself in the flow of landscape, though he still tended to see (as though with an eighteenth-century eye) sequences of framed visual compositions; for example, "a painted ship / Upon a painted ocean" from "The Rime of the Ancient Mariner." And Keats's overripe tableaux—such as the bejeweled supper Porphyro sets for Madeline in "The Eve of St. Agnes"—are not so much visual as they are exercises in synesthesia, as much perfume, touch, taste, and dance as they are sight.

Gerard Manley Hopkins, on our side of the watershed, was so intensely visual that it worried the priest in him: "dangerous; does set danc— / ing blood."[9] He was adept with pencil and sketchbook into the bargain, and he has taught generations of twentieth-century readers and poets to catch a glimpse of what seeing intensely might mean. The natural history of the eye has not been all technology by any means, even in this period of technological ferment. Indeed, the scope of the change wasn't as apparent in the 1850s as it can be to us in the 1980s, even though we may have to make a special effort to defamiliarize our eyes, since we have long-since ceased to be aware of the new ways in which we have been trained to see. In retrospect, many twentieth-century claims of technological revolution in the way we see deserve to be tempered with modesty. For example, Harold Edgerton's claim for the high-speed photography of the stroboscope (1931) holds while the rifle bullet slices through the playing card and until we recall its preimage: Eadweard Muybridge's twelve stop-action photographs of a galloping horse (1878). His photographs present the flow of motion as a sequence of fixed, analyzable moments and challenge the eye: "No, a galloping horse never has all four feet off the ground."

The alteration of the creative practices of the eye from 1798 to 1850 doesn't stop with optics and the technologies of reproduction. Those same fifty-odd years saw the advent of travel by continuous mechanical motion. The rhythms of passage through space and time, once the biorhythms of walking or riding a horse, became mechanorhythms. The eye, carried past the ever-changing landscape at steady speeds of twenty-five or more miles an hour, had to learn new techniques of composition, had to accommodate new and shifting relationships between foreground, middle ground, and background. The roadside, an intimate play of particulars when one is on foot or horseback, is homogenized by speed. Middle ground and horizon advance to lay claim to the eye. Henri Matisse, when taken for automobile rides through the Provençal landscape, insisted on speeds no greater than five kilometers per hour—slightly more than three miles per hour, a walking pace—"otherwise you have no sense of the trees."

But, once again, these new motion perspectives had been anticipated by Louis Daguerre's invention (with Charles Bouton) in 1822 of the diorama, a mode of presenting scenes in which a series of paintings (some opaque, some translucent) are seen at a distance through a sequence of openings controlled by screens and shutters. A considerable range of semianimated visual effects became possible. Dioramas took as their subjects sweeping scenes: geographical and historical travelogues, decisive battles, the careers of great men and women, and so forth. They were enormously popular from the start and remained so until they were superseded by the motion picture early in this century.

A further plot of the differences between Gilbert White's eyes and our own would have to include all sorts of optical experiments and inventions from toys such as Sir David Brewster's kaleidoscope in 1816 to more serious tools such as the stereoscope invented by Sir Charles Wheatstone in 1838, which was improved from mirrors to lenses by Sir David Brewster in 1849, and completed the following year when Brewster developed a camera to take stereoscopic pictures. The stereoscope gives the viewer the illusion of a three-dimensional photograph by focusing, through a binocular eyepiece, two photographs of the same scene taken from slightly different angles. The images rendered by the stereoscope were advertised as more real— particularly in their presentation of perspective—than those of the photograph. In fact, stereoscopic images tend not to emphasize perspective but to render objects in high relief, the optical delineation of edge much more pronounced than in two-dimensional photographs. In stereoscopic images, foreground, middle ground, and background are separated in sharp outline. The human eye, as it constantly oscillates between wide-angle and telephoto vision, produces no such sense of optical outline, no such sharp succession of planes, though such visual phenomena can occasionally be experienced in a misty landscape and can readily be imagined and depicted in sketches, stage sets, and paintings.

Stereoscopic images don't present objects and scenes as in ordinary vision but as cardboard cutouts mounted in a fictional or stage space. The illusion of heightened optical realism was not there at a glance but had to be learned, in effect more than half created before it could be half perceived. One giveaway is that one frequently has to cross one's eyes to encourage the binocular image of the stereoscope to swim into focus. Another is that stereoscope cards commercially available in the nineteenth and early twentieth centuries tended to feature exotic places like Egypt and Japan or dramatic views with unusual and striking perspectives.

At the same time that the stereoscope was being developed, the binocular telescope and microscope were being reinvented, in 1823 and 1852, respectively. They had been invented by the Dutch in the early seventeenth century, but apparently there was little interest in them as tools for the study of objects in spatial relation and depth. When that interest arose in the nineteenth century as a result of widespread public and scientific fascination with the natural history of microscopic plants and animals, the binocular microscope offered the depths of a drop of water, while the binocular telescope made it possible to explore the spatial depths of the surface of the moon and the nearest planets. The hand-held monocular telescope—what the Dutch general who first promoted its battlefield use in 1603 called his "looker"—was adequate to Napoleon's needs in the shallow spaces of the battle-scape at Waterloo, but binoculars were indispensable to artillery observers on the Somme one hundred years later.

In the course of the nineteenth century, the eye was being elaborately prepared for the advent of the motion picture: by the diorama, by the revival of interest in the magic lantern* (the grandparent of the slide projector), and by the continuous me-chanical motion of the railroad carriage with the relatively smooth flow of the landscape in the picture frame of the window. At the same time, the introduction of gas and then electric light in the theater made it possible to create the illusion on the stage that all could be seen in the full light of day, nothing left in the shadow of the imagination—and as light went, so went stage effects. The realism of furniture was first introduced to the English-speaking stage in the 1820s. By the 1880s, real locomo-tives puffed onstage on real tracks in a New York City theatre;

---

*The magic lantern was invented in 1600 by the German Athanasius Kircher and was much improved in the nineteenth century by the development of electric light for projection and by the use of photographic processes for the preparation of slides.

stage-set houses went up in real flames combatted by real water from real fire engines in the popular series *Mose, the Fireman.*

The first kinetoscopes were regarded as toys, though in the hands of Eadweard Muybridge (aided and abetted by Thomas Eakins) their sequences of stop-action photographs could become a scientific tool for the study of animals and human beings in motion. Not until Edison's kinetoscope (1891) was combined with the magic lantern by Woodville Latham in 1895 was the modern motion picture born—on its way with the luminosity, optical clarity, and images-in-motion that were to give the impression of extraordinary documentary verisimilitude. But even as it promised to tell it like it is, the motion picture was serving an improbable range of fictions, from the quasi-fiction of objective documentary to the full range of real fictions, from the starkly mimetic to empty melodrama and romance.

The illusion of verisimilitude toward which the nineteenth-century theater so eagerly aspired has, from the beginning, been the motion picture's great appeal, and that illusion has effectively masked the distinctive ways in which the motion picture as medium alters our ways of seeing. The illusion of verisimilitude leaves out of account the scale and luminosity of the images—the way they seem larger than life, more beautiful, more sinister, or more ugly. Also left out is the magnifying power of the motion-picture image and what it does to the smallest flick of gesture. Beyond the optical phenomenon of the infinitely reproducible visual image-in-motion, there is the motion picture's plasticity in both space and time: from long shot to close-up in one jump cut and back again in an instant. In a film version of Tolstoy's *War and Peace,* one now sees the whole battlescape of Borodino; then Prince Andrew's face in pain; Napoleon's face in bewildered half victory, half defeat; Kutuzov's imperturbable scarred face; and once more the battlescape, the Russians in retreat. The shooting of this sequence isn't fixed in time; scenes can be shot in any order and rearranged in the cutting room. Nor are they limited in space—the close-ups can be done on location or mocked up in a studio. Even the battle can be faked by pretending an overview by helicopter and substituting a quick sequence of close-ups like those booted feet descending the Odessa steps in *The Battleship Potemkin*.

When color motion pictures were first promoted in the 1930s, they were advertised as the ultimate in realism. Instead, they had the paradoxical effect of undercutting the impression of objective documentation established by black and white, because the synthetic and unreal colors of early color processes read as illustrations from fairyland, and the relatively immobile color cameras all but eliminated the dimension of camera movement. Actors continued to move, but the picture had gone static, fixed in its frame. Technological advances in color photography have of course achieved the supermobility of hand-held cameras and colors our eyes have learned to accept as true, so that color has almost come to rival black and white in its ability to assert the reality of the visual image—until, of course, experiments in computerized colorization demonstrated just how improbably unreal color could make *The Maltese Falcon* and *The Third Man*.

At its advent, television seemed to promise the domestication of the documentary verisimilitude of the motion picture, but that has not been the case. The differences in image, scale, and context are crucial.

IMAGE. In the motion-picture theater, the screen at rest is a neutral, shadowy blank; at rest, the fish-eye lens of the TV screen mirrors the room over which it presides. In both, the images are luminous, lighted as though from within, but the motion-picture images hover on or just in front of the surface of the screen. The viewer moves toward inclusion; no need for those movie-palace stunts, those three-dimensional experiments when, bicolored glasses in place, we ducked the baseball flung at us or were frozen in our seats by the locomotive that roared out of the screen and over our heads. The TV image, by contrast, recedes into its box and includes us out. If, as Daniel-Henry Kahnweiler observed, the painted image in cubism projects forward to float in front of the plane surface of the canvas, the motion-picture image exists in a muted cubist space. The TV image returns us to the old-fashioned space of classical perspective, plane behind plane behind the looking-glass surface of the tube—only Alice admitted here. At the movies, the eye's oscillating telephoto/wide-angle focus enables us to read the subtitles and watch the image at the same time. The much smaller TV screen forces us to shift our eyes to read the bottom of the page and thus to miss the image being captioned. The contrast in image is most striking when the object on the screen is superspatial—fireworks, for example. The TV images seem Lilliputian and remote, as though dimly perceived through oil and water. Motion-picture fireworks soar by contrast. Neither medium can compete with the spatial excitement of the real thing, but the motion picture can recall that excitement, while television miniaturizes and distances it to the point of denial and mockery. In addition, the visual quality of the TV image is poor (terrible, really) in contrast to the visual quality of a well-made motion picture.

SCALE. The motion-picture screen consistently shows images larger than life, more real than life. The television screen's scaled-down images threaten to undermine and trivialize reality. Images of elephants, humpback whales, cheetahs, gophers, the hand-sized fishes of the coral reef, and microscopic shrimp are all a standard three-by-four-inch size. The caterpillar and the python blur in monoscale. And there is little readable depth of field in television imagery. Heads and faces crowd forward to dominate the screen and compensate for the shallowness of field. The limited number of camera angles and setups in everyday use combines with that shallowness to threaten an insidious uniformity, a homogenized visual space. This tendency encourages occasional and spectacular quantitative attempts to achieve variety and animation—as when ABC deployed seventy-two cameras and crews to cover the extravaganza of the rededication of the Statue of Liberty in July 1986. Partly successful in suggesting the scale of the celebration, this over-animation had the effect of translating the occasion into the media event we expect from a well-staged rock concert or football game.

CONTEXT. Most television is viewed in the familiar and immediate setting of the home—not in a darkened theater with an audience for reinforcement. And most television interrupts itself every few minutes with advertisements that remind us of everyday realities and return us for a moment to our living rooms and kitchens.

This is not to suggest that television can't impress us with its documentary verisimilitude. It can and does; particularly, I suspect, those of us whose eyes were trained to the big movie screen and who therefore automatically upscale documentary TV images. But I wonder whether a generation trained to the scale of television will have learned to downscale the images on the movie screen? Many filmmakers, whether consciously or not, have already adopted an emphasis on close-ups and a visual format and composition more appropriate to the TV screen than the motion-picture screen. In the cramped, new-look movie houses, TV scale asserts itself. The six or eight screens offered are smaller and less commanding than the single screen of the old Bijou.

Television has not only profoundly altered our sense of visual space, it has also profoundly altered our experience of visual time. Documentary films and, before television, movie newsreels are comfortably after the fact—time out for developing, editing, printing the film—whereas television can have us right at the event and can itself be a participant. The students at Concord High School in New Hampshire gather to watch Christa Mc-Auliffe's part in the *Challenger* disaster, except that for seventy-two seconds after lift-off they don't know it's going to be a disaster. They, too, are being watched, monitored, by TV editors in their control rooms. There is a satelite hookup between the high school and the Shuttle. The plan is to show them talking to their astronaut teacher. Where are we in visual time? Where is the before, during, and after? After the fact of disaster, the students can be watched before, during, and after by the rest of us, over and over again until confusion becomes timeless and there is no more to say.

In addition, the centrality of ads in television threatens to reverse the temporal focus so that our attention span is timed not by the stretch of program between the ads but by the punctuation of ads between the stretches.

Television's impact on verbal time has been, if anything, more profound than its impact on visual time. It is as though the visual image must be superanimated toward restlessness itself to sustain its presence on the screen and hold our attention there, as though it dare not pause for contemplation or sustained speech. Erwin Panofsky observed that continuity in film is visual, while continuity in drama is verbal.[10] His assertion can be substantiated by the observation that most good movie scripts are verbally rather thin. The verbal density of Shakespeare, imposed on films of his work by audience and directorial reverence for the foreign language of that blank verse, strains the scriptwriter to find some busy work for the camera—a quick rummage through Elsinor's closets, anything to animate visual time, while Hamlet's soliloquies drone on. But the visual time of a motion picture is, thanks to its command of scale, slow to the point of stasis compared with the visual time of television.

The impact of television on the news and on political discourse can focus the point. The basic structural unit of the evening news is the ninety-second spot; two-plus minutes is a long segment; four minutes, extremely so, reserved for spectaculars and blockbuster news items. If at all possible, the images must be sufficiently animated or violent to hold the visual attention over short bursts of words. Lebanon in ninety seconds with 165 words. South Africa in 185 words, the two-minute visual complete with necklace and torch. When the anchors and reporters take over with what the trade calls tell items, the news goes preternaturally calm, as though violence were in recess while the talking heads read their lines for the allotted minute or minute and a half. The president speaks to the nation: fifteen minutes, twenty at the very most. The average press conference, twenty minutes; time for less than twelve hundred words of response, five or six typewritten pages. Commentators mock Gorbachev for his five-hour speech to the Supreme Soviet ("that must have put them to sleep"), and all are expected to smirk in derision at Fidel Castro when he speaks for two and a half hours on the twenty-fifth anniversary of the Bay of Pigs. Such performances would be unimaginable in the context of television today—as would be the Lincoln-Douglas debates of 1858, which were programmed for three hours,* though they repeatedly spilled over toward four. And there is the reminder that Lincoln's Gettysburg Address, at less than two and a half minutes, was considered an oratorical disaster by many of his contemporaries. "Some remarks by the president," one newspaper reported, overshadowed, if not blacked out, for that audience in the gray rain of 19 November 1863 by Edward Everett's oration of two hours and fourteen minutes that preceded it.

Commentators, circa 1984, complain to the point of cliché that television has had a cataclysmic effect—the demolition of political discourse. Television obviously rewards the genial face, the casual aw-shucks manner, the facile quasi-slogan one-liner. In the short run, beyond discontent with the present political scene, television can be regarded as a further and radical tipping of the

---

*A one-hour introductory speech, answered by a one-and-a-half-hour speech, answered by a half-hour speech. Political handlers in our midst suggest that we should regard the hit-and-run exchanges of thirty-second TV political ads as our version of the Lincoln-Douglas Debates, as though those debates were simply an exchange of slogans and mud balls!

verbal/visual imbalance in favor of the visual, an imbalance that has been steadily increasing over the last century.

The presidential campaigns of the 1980s are conceived as daily symbolic television opportunities in which the candidates strive to impersonate a president for ninety-second items on the evening news. In the '88 campaign, Candidate Dukakis, wearing protective headgear, smiles at us and salutes from the open driver's hatch of an M-1 tank on a test range. Candidate Bush laughs and waves from a motor launch in Boston Harbor. Is that a real tank or a studio mock-up? Is that really Boston Harbor or a photomontage? Both are stunts with props and a symbolic message. In that tank, Candidate Dukakis is in the driver's seat. He is in control of a sound defense policy. Nowhere is there any symbolic hint of how effective tanks are at putting down civilian uprisings and controlling urban riots. Candidate Bush is happy and laughing because Boston Harbor is polluted and Candidate Dukakis hasn't cleaned it up; maybe it's even Candidate Dukakis's fault that it's polluted in the first place. What a happy thought. All this requires the complicity and inattentiveness of the viewer. Radio-news addicts need not apply. There are no smiling and cheering backdrop crowds on radio, just the devastatingly hollow voices, "Headpiece filled with straw."

The proverbial wisdom that one picture is worth a thousand words* may reign unchallenged as long as no one thinks to say, "True enough, if you expect words to *depict.*" But what of all the things that can't be depicted, such as poetry or political debate? Television's tyrannical exploitation of that proverb may yet excite a reaction that redresses the balance, a reaction similar to Goethe's revolutionary delight when, upon reading Lessing's *Laokoon,* he found himself released at a stroke from what he called

---

*Altered by ABC's Sam Donaldson to fit the Reagan years: "This administration has discovered that one picture is worth a thousand facts."

the "tyranny" of Simonides's dictum that a poem is a painting in words. Perhaps we can expect redress of that thousand-word imbalance from Richard III's complaint:

> *My conscience hath a thousand several tongues,*
> *And every tongue brings in a several tale.*

And there is always the story of the child who preferred the radio to television because he could see the picture so much more clearly.

But hooked on television and film, the military eye anticipates the battlescape of the future as media event. The United States Army trains troops for "mobile operations in urban terrain" by using a full-scale model of a war-torn German village—in central Texas. "Eye-media training" is the point of this set on location, with appropriate sound effects. But does that mean training troops for urban warfare or training troops to demonstrate for videotape and training films how to "fight" a Bradley Fighting Vehicle "forward" past the rubble and assorted antitank dangers of a ruined town? Is the soldier in action really in action or only watching himself on film? Philip Caputo reports several instances of this ambiguity in his descriptions of combat experience in Vietnam: "We are starring in our very own war movie," playing the part of "John Wayne," or having the recurring sensation "of watching myself in a movie."[11]

I have only just begun to sketch the fantastic development of eye extenders and modifiers over the last 150 years. The flood of new technologies has been impressive, enormously exciting, and frequently threatening: x-rays (1895) and, more recently, sonic probes enable us to see through solids; radar and infrared technology enable us to see in the dark. Polaroid gives us instant photographs. Military satellite cameras (we are told, though we can't see because such images are classified) have achieved resolution fine enough to read license plates from a hundred thousand feet. Electron micrographs and thermographs join the array, and holography surprises us with its three-dimensional illusions and promises hard copy holography that will present the image in three dimensions, projected in front of the computer instead of inside its screen. The computer is doing extraordinary things to the images developed by other visual technologies (microscopy, telescopy, photography, television, etc.) with the range of visual enhancement and improvisation of which it is capable. And I have yet to dwell on the fabulous libraries of visual images that those technologies are enabling us to accumulate, store, and retrieve.

If I imagine myself writing a natural history of Williamstown, using only my eyes, I would have to take into account my access to those libraries of visual images in my home and community. Without leaving my house and its books, I can travel the world, seeing its landscapes, its architectures, its peoples, and their visual arts. My eye can range from the finches on the bird feeder, identifiable from the color plates in field guides, to probe via television and its libraries into almost any of the ecological niches of the biosphere, watching penguins in the Antarctic, three-toed sloths in the Amazonian rain forest, the mountain gorilla in Kenya, the round of the year on the Illinois prairie. Gilbert White found it almost impossible to trace the flight paths of migratory birds, limited as he was to a few observant and trustworthy correspondents in the British Isles and one on Gibraltar, his brother John. My eye suffers no such limit. With help from the television screen, it can follow, by pickup truck and small plane, the migratory flight of three whooping cranes as they make their way from southeastern Texas along their flight corridor east of the Rockies to their nesting grounds in Canada. And my eye doesn't stop there: it can swim underwater with humpback whales off Bermuda, with sharks in the Red Sea and off the Great Barrier Reef. It can probe into the microworld of plankton and into the depths of the Galápagos Fracture Zone to discover bloodred mussels a foot long and six-foot sea worms, nurtured on emissions of volcanic gases. My eye can venture into outer space for satellite views and moon views of the earth, for close-ups of the surface of the moon and Mars and Venus, for middle-distance views of the sun and Jupiter and Saturn and Uranus. All that, and I haven't even moved out of my house to consider access to visual experience in the museums and libraries of this village—130,000 slides in the slide room of the college art department; thousands more in biology, geology, astronomy. And thousands upon thousands of picture books. And libraries of videotape and film. And. . . .

The quantitative point is so easy to make that it's easy to forget how distant we are from that farther shore on which Gilbert White stood. Once again, his experience can provide an instructive contrast. In 1783, he was puzzled by a particularly oppressive summer,

> a period when the wind varied to every quarter without making any alteration in the air. The sun, at noon, looked as black as a clouded moon, and shed a rust-coloured ferruginous light on the ground, and floors of rooms; but was particularly lurid and blood-coloured at rising and setting. All the time the heat was so intense that butchers' meat could hardly be eaten on the day after it was killed; and the flies swarmed so in the lanes and hedges that they rendered the horses half frantic and riding irksome.

In a letter written in 1787, he recalls this summer from his *Journals* and adds what he came to know later, that that was a summer of severe earthquakes in Calabria and Sicily and "a *volcano* sprung out of the sea on the coast of *Norway*" (by which he meant Iceland). We can complete the causal connection for him: the great eruption of Skaftárjökull on 11 June 1783 resulted in a lava flow the size of the Mont Blanc massif and filled the upper atmosphere with a cloud of volcanic dust that accounted for the greenhouse effect and White's oppressive summer. White notes the coincidence but says only that it aroused "superstitions." As a disciplined natural historian, he didn't make the connection because he couldn't see it. We can, of course, see: our eyes can have Mount Saint Helens for breakfast the morning after the night before, have it now and record it on our VCRs for comparative study at our leisure.

In 1884, Sir Charles Parsons developed a steam turbine that would drive constant-output dynamos to generate electricity. Parsons's turbine-driven dynamo was the other half of Edison's invention of the incandescent light bulb in 1879. Parsons said that his turbines would turn night into day, and they and their descendents have, to the vast advantage of our eyes in our homes and workplaces and cities and their surround and to the disadvantage of eyes that search the light-brushed night sky for a glimpse of the Milky Way or of Halley's comet.

On the farther shore of 1798, night was quite a different experience from what it is today. Traveling on foot or horseback was by no means impossible at night, but it was slower and less certain than by day, and difficult enough to encourage the English country gentry of Jane Austen's experience to schedule their balls and other evening entertainments at the time of the full moon when, even on a cloudy night, coachmen could see their way to strange houses. Once indoors, producing light in an emergency could be a time-consuming and frustrating business—at least until the invention of the Lucifer friction match in 1827. Even then, Emily Dickinson was apparently sufficiently impatient with the procedure of lighting a lamp or a candle that she scribbled many of her late-night quatrains in the dark.

One moment of midnight crisis in Tolstoy's *War and Peace*[12] makes the point beautifully. On 12 October 1812, the Russians are surprised by the French army's sudden retreat from Moscow and by the southwestern course the retreat initially takes. The commander in chief must be alerted. The midnight messenger arrives at the all-dark quarters of the general staff and is delayed while an orderly and then an adjutant and then a candle are awakened. Sparks were obtained by striking flint against steel; the sparks were caught in tinder, which began to smolder; then a splinter that had been dipped in sulphur was applied to the tinder and a light was obtained. The fumbling about at a moment that Tolstoy presents as one of great Russian success is intolerably comic in its tension.

Gas light anticipated electricity by more than half a century in homes, factories, theaters, and streets (in London from 1807, Baltimore from 1819, Boston from 1822), but electricity after Edison-Parsons quickly proved itself much cleaner, safer, and far more flexible than illuminating gas. I'm not sure that the general illumination made possible by electric light has had consequences as far-reaching in the home as it has in workplaces and schools and marketplaces, in sports and entertainment venues, and in the special applications of electric light in the other technologies of the eye. After all, jobs and chores can be done by lantern light; books can be read and letters written by oil lamp or candlelight. Streets, roads, and paths can be navigated. The ease of electric seeing is a pleasure and a comfort but hardly an eye-transforming necessity. There is always the proposition that the candle and the electric desk lamp are equally and indifferently friendly to the composition of poetry.

But perhaps the change has been more sweeping than I allow. The omnipresence of electric light has eroded the diurnal rhythms that were once so much more apparent in our lives. In the home there is no longer a noticeable transition from daylight to dark, no making ready. In the 1790s, dusk meant laying out rushlights handy to the kitchen fire, squills ready to light candles or oil lamps. In the 1850s, after the invention of matches and kerosene, it meant lighting the lamps and lanterns to warm their chimneys. There is now no sharp sense that daylight must be obeyed before it wanes. We can effortlessly turn on lights in the corners as they darken in the late afternoon without even noticing what we're doing, practicing a general and constant level of illumination in our homes. And that practice is the domestic counterpart of what has been happening in the public spaces of our world, where the general levels of illumination have leapt upward, urged by illuminating engineers such as those at General Electric who have trebled their recommendations for light levels over the past forty years. The result may well be overillumination of workplaces and stores and classrooms and, as a consequence, heightened levels of nervous irritability. A team of researchers at Albany Medical College has come to the tentative conclusion that one cannot harm one's eyes by reading in dim light but can certainly do so by reading in too much light. And the shadowless over-illumination of public spaces is a bore and an irritation, as one can discover in a quick descent into the softly lit underground stations of the subway in Washington, D.C. But many object to low levels of illumination, and more and more of our workplaces and public areas are being designed without windows for round-the-clock illumination, Muzak, and occupancy in airless, air-conditioned spaces. Games such as baseball and football that were once played on daylit fields are now played at night (and for television) in what amounts to electrically lit studio space, with artificial turf whose colors don't fade and brightly colored uniforms that speed the miniaturized action.

A recent advertisement for light bulbs promises, "So that you can see the world the way *you* want to see it." No dark corners, no ghosts in the attic or cellar, no night watch, all chiaroscuro gone, all colors bright, flat, acrylic, up-front, and the line that Adolphe Appia* tried to draw between something being illumi-

---

*Appia (1862–1928) was a French-Swiss artist and stage designer who regarded "light [on the stage] as an expressive medium," akin to music in its emotional and aesthetic plasticity, in its ability to develop mood and establish the actor and action in three-dimensional space. "We shall seek no longer to afford the illusion of a forest, but only the illusion of a man in the atmosphere of a forest." The stage-presence of light that he envisioned in *Die Musik und die Inscenierung* (1899) was twenty-five years in advance of the technology that was to make it possible and still lurks as the underlying ideal for designer and audience.

nated (for the eye to possess physically) and something being seen (conceptually encountered) blurs toward indistinction.

In this transformation of the mighty world of eye, our eyes are under siege, overloaded with visual riches until we're in danger of being distracted into a sort of visual paralysis, our ability to discriminate homogenized and dulled by surfeit. The corollary symptoms are all around us. Advertising and the arts are dominated by visual stunts designed to override our distraction, and the critics among us compensate for the homogenization with a rage to discriminate, a rush to judgment and an abrupt stridency of tone that announce the poverty that threatens us in the midst of plenty.

Afterimage: When Gilbert White was preparing *The Natural History of Selborne* for publication, he sought the help of the Dutch illustrator Hieronymus Grimm, who came down to Selborne as guest and employee. He spent four leisurely weeks with White and prepared twelve views, which became the basis for the engraved illustrations of the first edition of White's book. White described Grimm's method.

> He first of all sketches his scapes with a lead-pencil; then he *pens* them all over, as he calls it, with indian-ink, rubbing out the superfluous pencil-strokes; then he gives a charming shading with a brush dipped in indian-ink; and last he throws a light tinge of watercolours over the whole.[13]

A modern photographer could document Selborne in a day, providing the author with hundreds of images from among which to choose, the size and patterns of the illustrations to be determined. Or, in a day, we could produce a continuous helicopter overview of the parish of Selborne and capture some of White's extraordinary excitement about the manned hot-air balloon that traversed the parish from northeast to southwest in October 1784, a passage White had to observe from the ground.

But those late-twentieth-century photography sessions would have the pace of a flyby, skimming the visual surface with little of the penetration that four weeks' leisurely drawing in the midst of White's household and conversation would have provided for both illustrator and patron.

2.
The Mighty World
of Ear
· · · · · · · · ·

The transformation of the mighty world of ear has, of course, been corollary to the transformation of the world of eye. The change may at first appear more subtle, less sweeping, thanks in part to the verbal/visual imbalance that has been developing so radically in favor of the visual since 1798, thanks in part to the fact that we still talk to each other in words and sentences, endlessly and in detail, just as Gilbert White and his contemporaries did. Appearances to the contrary, the pace of invention, development, and exploitation of new technologies and practices in the world of ear was far more rapid and sweeping in the two decades after 1845 than anything that happened in the realm of the eye. At the beginning of the nineteenth century Napoleon heard about events much as Caesar and, one assumes, Alexander the Great had: by word of mouth or from hand-carried message, or by someone signaling within the line of sight.*

---

*Napoleon had one advantage over Caesar: the carrier piegon, introduced to Western Europeans by the Saracens during the eleventh century in the course of

In March 1865, on the eve of Appomattox, Grant, the commander in chief of the Union armies, could, from his headquarters before Petersburg, Virginia, "hear" and "talk" by telegraph to President Lincoln in Washington, Sherman in the Carolinas, and Union army commanders at their posts almost anywhere on the North American continent. Out of sight was no longer out of earshot.

Historically, the changes in the worlds of eye and ear have been born of the same great upwelling of impulse. In many cases, the people whose scientific and technological explorations transformed the world of eye researched and experimented in the world of ear as well. Sir Charles Wheatstone, the inventor of the mirror-stereoscope, was also deeply involved with research on sound—to the point where the eleventh edition of the *Encyclopaedia Britannica* praises him as the "practical founder of modern telegraphy." Samuel F. B. Morse, Wheatstone's American counterpart and competitor, was a professional easel and mural painter as well as an amateur inventor. And while Edison gave the eye electric light, the mimeograph machine, and the kinetoscope, he gave the ear the phonograph and improved the telegraph and telephone. His 1883 discovery of the Edison effect (that electric current could be sent through space) was to provide the basis for radio and television. The eye and ear were caught up, modified, and extended by that historical transformation that Alfred North Whitehead identified: "The greatest invention of the nineteenth century was the invention of the method of invention."*

---

the First Crusade. The Chinese had used pigeons (and signal kites) as early as the eighth century. In 1588, the English used a sequence of bonfires along the Channel coast to announce the Spanish Armada's advance up the Channel. But kites and bonfires are line-of-sight signals, and a carrier pigeon is limited to flights destined for a well-fixed home that can't move as flexibly as a military campaign might demand.

*Whitehead's paragraph continues: "A new method entered into life. In order to understand our epoch, we can neglect all the details of change, such as railways, telegraphs, radios, spinning machines, synthetic dyes. We must concentrate on the

The extension of the ear's capacity to hear began with experiments in telegraphy in the closing decades of the eighteenth century. The experiments were inhibited because the only electricity available was static electricity produced by friction machines. The numerous and simultaneous inventions of the electromagnetic telegraph in the 1830s and 1840s depended on the invention of the voltaic cell, or battery, by Alessandro Volta in 1800 and the discovery of electromagnetism by the Danish physicist Hans Christian Oersted in 1819. Setting aside the controversy about who invented the telegraph, the impressive thing in retrospect is the enterprise and speed with which the telegraphic network was expanded and elaborated. The English had adapted the French invention of a mechanical semaphore system in 1792 to link key coastal stations and naval bases to London during the Napoleonic Wars, but that system was labor-intensive and only the London-to-Portsmouth line was useful enough to survive after Waterloo.

At first, the railroads and their need for rapid communication provided the spur that transformed the electric telegraph in England from a twelve-mile Paddington-to-Drayton line for the Great Western Railway in 1836 into a network that spanned England, Wales, and southern Scotland by the early 1850s. In America, Morse's Baltimore-to-Washington line of 1844 had expanded to crisscross the country east of the Mississippi by the early 1850s and had gone transcontinental by 1861. Three years before that, the first transatlantic cable had been completed—and had lasted for only one-hundred-plus messages. But two more cables were laid, with enduring success, in 1866. The rapid

---

method in itself; that is the real novelty, which has broken up the foundations of the old civilisation. The prophecy of Francis Bacon has now been fulfilled; and man, who at times dreamt of himself as a little lower than the angels, has submitted to become the servant and minister of nature. It still remains to be seen whether the same actor can play both parts." In *Science and the Modern World* (1925; Reprint, New York, 1948), 98.

growth of this communication network is usually attributed to national and international commercial interests and to the time-table and safety needs of the rapidly expanding railroads, but those attributions oversimplify and underestimate the public's excitement about high-speed communication and its fascination with what the extended ear was doing to the news from distant places and how that news was understood.

Dispatches from the American forces in Mexico during the Mexican War (1846–48) took two to three weeks to reach Washington; dispatches from Civil War fronts could be received within minutes, though Sherman could still be lost to Washington for over a month during his march from Atlanta to Savannah in late 1864. Recipients of telegraphic dispatches, both in Washington and in the field, still tended to bide their time, to make decisions and to act on the old timetable of at least days if not weeks, rather than on the new timetable of minutes. But the new timetable was, within the decade of the 1860s, to revolutionize the way the news was phrased and understood. The reporter in the 1840s had the essayist's leisure to ask himself and others about what he had seen and heard. The detailed and discursive news dispatches he wrote were designed to be read with the leisure of retrospect, several days or weeks after the event. The news in the 1860s was infected with the piecemeal phrases of telegraphic transmission and full of confusions and contradictions—or, rather, the impressions of things reported minute by minute.

The telephone (1876) and Marconi's wireless telegraphy (1890s) may seem radical alterations of the electronic network, but the principle of near-instantaneous communication by electric signal had already been established, and the rate of its expansion into new technologies in the early twentieth century was to match the rate of expansion of the telegraph itself in the two decades after 1845. Today, the electronic network continues to expand to include signals not just from Voyager II as it swings past Uranus but from nonhuman sources, from quasars (quasi-stellar radio sources) at immense distances from earth. Soon, the navy keeps hinting, we'll be able to communicate to and from the ocean depths.

Our capacity to store and retrieve sounds and signals has been transformed by Edison's phonograph (1878) and by all its technological siblings—reproducible records (1887) and even-tually wire-recordings and tape recordings and electronic repro-duction of higher and higher fidelity—to the point where our libraries and airwaves and homes are full to overflowing with the world's talk and music. Their broadcast availability reaches to-ward the paradoxical result of perpetual sound that blurs into white noise and goes unheard.

In the early decades of this century, recorded music was a squeaky and attenuated approximation of the real thing. The ear had to learn to compensate, to remember and add the color and timbre of live performance. In the last thirty years, electronic approximation has become better and better, still an approxima-tion but requiring less and less compensation. During that same period, recorded sound has so conditioned the ear that many people, perhaps a majority, prefer music that has been electroni-cally processed and amplified; then, they say, it sounds real. The real thing has, in its turn, become pale, an approximation. An electronic lens must be interposed between the instrument and the ear if the ear is to be satisfied, in the same way that an optical lens has come to seem necessary to satisfy the eye.

Just as visual reproductions can be transformed and orches-trated, so recordings can be mixed and remixed, becoming new compositions during the transition from studio or concert hall to published recording. As a result, the success of a popular musician or group can depend as much if not more on the mixers at their computer keyboards as on the musicians. The recording musician can also correct his performance by computer, replacing notes, phrases, and passages until the final disk or tape displays instru-mental or vocal skill at near perfection—an order of skill impossible in the living, transient space of music room or concert hall. The well-trained critic's ear may reject these technological orchestrations and editings as canned and sterile, but most of us cannot make that discrimination. Electronically edited recordings can, however, do more than impress or depress our ears with musical perfection and elate or deafen them with hard rock. Recordings can extend our ears, projecting them beyond their normal thresholds. We can speed up seismograph tapes to hear the echoing reverberations of earthquakes as they pass through the earth's mantle and core. We can go underwater for the songs and soundings of whales and dolphins and for the snap and crackle of shrimp. We can reach below the threshold of our ears to overhear the subsonic (communicative?) rumblings of elephants and blue whales. And we can rise above the normal lintel of our hearing to hear the response of the ionosphere to sunrise, to distinguish the cry of a bat's sonar in the incredible buzz and din above (blessedly above) the twenty-thousand cycle limit beneath which our ears are trapped.

In contrast, Gilbert White was, he reports, "much entertained" in the summer of 1767 "with a tame bat which would take flies out of a person's hand."[1] He was closely observant of bats as his journals and the *Natural History* demonstrate. He knew that they fed on insects, drank on the wing, and hibernated in a "torpid state" but

> come forth at all times of the year when ye Therm^r is at 50, because at such temperament of the air Phalaenae [Obs. for all moths] are stirring, on which they feed.[2]

White did note about several bats that he examined,

> Within the ear there was somewhat of a peculiar structure that I did not understand perfectly; but refer it to the observation of the curious anatomist.[3]

White would have been staggered to know that bats navigate and locate their insect prey by sonar. That is of course an irresponsible observation, but it provides a measure of the distance from here to 1787. Gilbert White couldn't have known bat sonar as a single, isolable fact. For that one fact to be known requires as context the whole transformation of the mighty world of eye and ear that has taken place since White's time; it requires "the invention of the method of invention." Sonar and radar were invented and elaborately deployed for war before the reverse metaphor of the bat's predatory accomplishment was discovered. We didn't invent echolocation in imitation of bats, but we could understand their echolocation thanks to models of our own invention.

Aristotle made two observations about seeing and hearing that have some bearing on this discussion of the mighty world of ear. He pointed out that we can choose to see or not to see. We can turn our heads or close our eyes. But we cannot as easily choose not to hear. The ear is always in touch. Further, he said, the loss of sight is a calamity for which we can compensate, but the loss of hearing is an irremediable calamity because it cuts the individual off from discourse and thus from participation in the cognitive life of the community. Hearing aids have alleviated the plight of many who suffer from loss of hearing, but by no means all, and the present preoccupation with miniaturization of hearing aids for cosmetic purposes has distracted manufacturers and their researchers from the goal of enabling those suffering from hearing loss to continue to participate, to follow the metaphoric leaps and darts of conversation. As Victor Hugo wrote to his deaf friend Ferdinand Berthier;

> What matters deafness of the ear when the mind hears? The one true deafness, the incurable deafness, is that of the mind.[4]

Technology has radically extended our ears (and the reach of our voices and musical instruments), and it has banked our libraries with sound. But what of the changes in our modes of discourse, the ways in which we participate in the cognitive life of the community, the ways in which our minds hear, during the last two hundred years? In his *Confessions,* written in the 1760s when he was in his fifties, Jean Jacques Rousseau says that he learned to read at the age of five or six and remarks, "It is from my earliest reading that I date the unbroken consciousness of my own existence."[5] He reports that at first he read aloud with his father; subsequently, he read to himself, though in the presence of members of his family (whom he would occasionally shock with outbursts triggered by emotional identification with a character in Plutarch). Later, Rousseau developed the habit of reading alone, in camera, and says that he came to loathe interruptions or distractions. In effect, what Rousseau describes is the transformation of the act of reading from what had traditionally been a shared social experience into a private and personal experience, which he identifies in retrospect as the origin and sustenance of an interiorized self-consciousness—the self defined not through the play of its contacts with others but through internal dialogue with itself, metaphorically represented as the self reading to itself.

What happened to reading in Rousseau's personal experience seems to have happened in a less idiosyncratic (and less Romantic) way to reading in general in the course of the eighteenth century. At the beginning, reading was something one did aloud and shared with others; by the end, reading had become a private act. The effect was to interiorize and emotionalize the experience. Dr. Johnson told Mrs. Thrale that

> he was just nine Years old when having got the play of *Hamlet* to read in his Father's Kitchen, he read on very quietly till he came to the Ghost Scene, when he hurried up Stairs to the Shop Door that he might see folks about him.[6]

The impulse to escape from the inner tension of reading by seeking the company of others reflects the older communal style of reading. A hundred years later, it would apparently have been easier to let the flesh creep in solitude. The novel as an English literary form comes of age in the course of the eighteenth century and seems peculiarly adapted to reading in camera. Henry Fielding's *Tom Jones* (1749) behaves as though it were at the watershed between prose fiction designed to be read aloud in company and that designed to be read to oneself. For reading aloud, a series of playlets and farces; for reading to oneself, short narratives and chatty essays to be read silently, interiorized.

The tradition of reading aloud did not of course die a sudden death in 1750; it continued alive and well through the nineteenth century, thanks in part to the daily family Bible readings, which metamorphosed and expanded to include the family practice of reading the serial installments of popular fictions (particularly Dickens's novels) as they were received. This practice was reinforced by the immense popularity of Dickens's public performances of passages from his novels, and he seems consistently to have tuned his prose for performance. But interiorization, the sound of the voice heard in the privacy of the ear, became more and more the rule as Romantic and Victorian poets (pace Robert Browning) developed styles imitative of the rhythm and turn of interior thought/feeling, giving the impression that the reader is overhearing the poet's contemplative interior voice. Corollary to this interiorization of voice was the rise of the assumption, or prejudice, that, as John Stuart Mill put it,

> Lyric poetry, as it was the earliest kind, is also . . . more eminently and peculiarly poetry than any other: it is the poetry most natural to a really poetic temperament.[7]

Clearly, Mill assumes that lyric poetry is private, interior, personal to the poet, confessional. Wordsworth wrote of the sonnet, "with this key / Shakespeare unlocked his heart."[8] This exaltation of the short lyric was radically overstated by Edgar Allan Poe, who argued that a long poem is a contradiction of terms.[9] His championship of the brief lyric (as a poem of effect) was a marked shift away from the pride of place previously granted epic poetry from Milton through the Romantics. Clearly Wordsworth intended *The Prelude, The Excursion,* and *The Recluse* as a three-part epic. Coleridge regarded Wordsworth's enterprise as such, and Coleridge's deprecation of his own poetry isn't just another of his self-deprecatory tics; the poems he had accomplished were, from his point of view, small-scale "occasional" poems, not the high poetic accomplishment of a sustained epic work. And Keats's chronic ambition, more or less frustrated, was for epic achievement.

A comparable interiorization of voice was taking place in prose fiction with the retreat from the convention of the omniscient narrator and development of the techniques (limitation of narrative perspective, placement of point of view, control of tone and diction) that cluster around what Henry James was eventually to call "the center of consciousness." From James's perspective, the center is that character (or characters) through whose consciousness the language and action of the novel are refracted. For example, we witness the action of *The Ambassadors* (1903) from the perspective of an anonymous narrator who speaks of the center of consciousness, Lambert Strether, as "our friend," and who can comment on Strether's mental state and processes from a perspective, which while at times more knowing than Strether's, is far from omniscient, close to but not locked within Strether's consciousness.

Stream of consciousness* in the early twentieth century extends, or rather limits, by heightening this emphasis on center of consciousness toward exclusive focus on and through the

---

*"Consciousness, then, does not appear to itself chopped up in bits. Such words as 'chain' or 'train' do not describe it fitly as it presents itself in the first instance. It is nothing jointed; it flows. A 'river' or a 'stream' are the metaphors by which it is most naturally described. *In talking of it hereafter, let us call it the stream of thought, of consciousness, or of subjective life."* William James, *The Principles of Psychology* (Boston, 1890), 1: 239.

subjective life of one or more of the central characters. "Consciousness" may not be quite the right term here. The complex of mental processes that, for example, Joyce seeks to imitate in the presentation of Leopold Bloom in *Ulysses* includes not just conscious thought and awareness (consciousness as Thoreau and Henry James meant it) but also half-perceived sensations, half-formed memories, half-conscious or prereflective thoughts, half-suppressed recognitions—psychic blips that could be fully developed by being brought forward in a character's consciousness but that aren't in the interest of psychic realism. Joyce does this by establishing the characteristic self-countering rhythms of Bloom's mind and by loading particular details with significance and resonance personal to Bloom. Once this characterization is accomplished in the course of episodes four through six (Calypso, Lotus Eaters, Hades), Joyce can increasingly shorthand the imitation of Bloom's mental stream.

Stream may be as much a misnomer as consciousness in this discussion because our experience of consciousness as flow may well be an after-the-fact reading of discontinuous bits of awareness. Similarly, the literary techniques that suggest the stream present a sequence of fragments that we're encouraged to read as flow. Julian Jaynes suggests that "consciousness knits itself over its time gaps and gives the illusion of continuity."[10] William James was also aware of this knitting over; his argument is that "within each personal consciousness thought feels continuous." There are "time-gaps" and "changes from one moment to another," but they are "never absolutely abrupt."[11] James's focus in the over-quoted stream passage is not on what consciousness is but on what it feels like. Regardless of whether that subjective continuity is psychological fact or illusion in consciousness itself, the imitation of that continuity, that flow, in literature is accomplished by the presentation of discontinuities that we as readers knit over and read as a stream.

* * *

While the voices of poetry and fiction were going private during
the nineteenth and early twentieth centuries, public voices were
also changing. Before the high-speed printing press (1819) and
the radical extension of the literacy franchise in nineteenth-
century England and America, popular poetry had its roots in the
oral and folklore traditions of songs and ballads and stories. Only
in the late eighteenth century did that tradition make its way into
print, thanks to a great heave of interest in literary antiquities:
ancient superstitions, early verse forms, medieval poetry, and
song.* This occurred not long before the shift from the listening
and remembering ear to the reading eye began to erode the oral
tradition and usher in the tin-ear age, when popular poets and
their publics began to assume that poetry wasn't poetry unless
written in an English that struck the ear as a foreign language,
unless the meter thumped and the rhyme clanged and the senti-
ment roared or simpered.

By the early nineteenth century, theaters had been transformed into great barns from the relatively intimate spaces they
had been from Shakespeare's time until the Licensing Act of 1737
silenced satire and protest by shutting down all of the small
theaters in London by licensing at first only one and eventually
two patent theaters. In Shakespeare's theater, with a sharp-eared
audience in place, language could move one and a half to two
times faster than we could tolerate in today's theater. In the
echoing halls that were called theaters in Victoria's time, the by
then foreign language of Shakespeare's lines could no longer be
spoken rapidly and "trippingly on the tongue." Actors performed
as though the plays were oratorios, Hamlet's soliloquies and Lear's

---

*This rage to collect and preserve we associate with Thomas Percy's *Reliques of
Ancient English Poetry* (1765), with Thomas Warton's *History of English Poetry*
(1774–81), and with the antiquarian interests of poets such as Thomas Gray.
Exemplary among these collectors was Robert Burns, who regarded the preserva-
tion of songs from the oral tradition as so important that he gave his collections
to a song publisher for nothing, even though he was strapped for money at the
time.

ravings to be belted out as though they were written for Wagner-ian heldentenors. Too much of this operatic tradition is still with us, but, as inhospitable as film generally is to elaborate and sustained speech, the close-ups of which it is capable have had the effect of returning Shakespeare to a measure of theatrical immediacy.

Public oratory was undergoing a similar change as it adapted from the intimate spaces of eighteenth-century legislative and meeting houses to the large-scale outdoor gatherings of the newly enfranchised electorates in the United Kingdom and in the United States. In Ireland in 1843, Daniel O'Connell addressed a series of monster Sunday-morning meetings designed to demonstrate the unanimity of Irish support for Home Rule. The most impressive of those meetings was held at the Hill of Tara; conservative (English) estimates put the crowd at 250,000; patriotic (Irish) figures range from 750,000 to one million, with the added assertion, or fantasy, "and I heard every word." Much the same was said of Daniel Webster when he went down to Nantucket to give a speech to commemorate the whaling industry. In a splendid dramatic ges-ture, he turned his back to an audience estimated at three thousand and addressed himself to "the whales of the sea." "And I heard every word." Similarly, many among the fifteen thousand gathered at Gettysburg testified that they heard every word the president spoke in his high-pitched and unmusical voice. Realisti-cally, Edward Everett, the most famous orator of his time, found that the site, the audience, and the weather taxed his oratorical powers to their limit—but not his ability to hear. He seems to have been one of the few to have appraised Lincoln's "brief remarks" as the brilliant speech we now cherish.

The theater and popular oratory were preparing the public ear for amplified speech. Even when that speech first penetrated into the home with Franklin D. Roosevelt's fireside chats of the 1930s, it retained the orotund cadences of nineteenth-century political rhetoric.

* * *

In the early years of this century, most people regarded the telephone as a medium for messages that were rather more urgent than casual talk. Technological change improved the fidelity of the telephone's reproduction of voice in the 1920s and 1930s and increased the carrying capacity of telephone lines to the point where more and more subscribers could switch from party lines, with their obvious public dimensions,* to two-party and private lines. The result was that the telephone became increasingly capable of creating the illusion of private and intimate conversation. As we have become habituated to this electronic intimacy, personal correspondence has been replaced by the spoken word. Business and professional correspondence in recent years has also shifted in favor of telephone conversation, the change urged by the relative expense of writing, copying, and filing correspondence compared to telephoning, which is therefore cheaper and also offers the presumed advantage of immediate dialogue. Some of the problems and dangers that arise when telephone conversation takes the place of business and personal correspondence are obvious. First and foremost, such conversations are for the most part unrecorded and thus irretrievable. As Stephen Jay Gould has written,

> The telephone is the greatest single enemy of scholarship;
> for what our intellectual forebears used to inscribe in ink
> now goes once over a wire into permanent oblivion.[12]

But there are other and related hazards: preparation for the business or research conversation is liable to be less disciplined,

---

*The party line that linked us to the outside world from Ballston Lake, New York, in the 1920s counted twenty-three subscribers and functioned as newsletter and a public forum, since each subscriber could hear the call signals of all the others. Ours was two long and three short. The minute one answered, the click of one or two other receivers lifted was an obvious invitation to discreet and brief utterance.

more relaxed and improvisational (often, in fact, sloppier) than
the composition of a letter or memorandum. And the fact that the
correspondence won't be on record makes it easy for the conver-
sationalists to drift toward vagary and unintentional compromise
or misstatement, only to misremember and misreport their posi-
tions and statements as much firmer and tougher after the fact
than they actually were during the call. The rash of reinterpreta-
tions and reformulations that frequently follow that sort of con-
versational drift are outstanding symptoms of the unconscious
compromises that prevail.

The widespread anxiety during the last few decades about
the bugging or clandestine recording of telephone conversations
and private meetings suggests further uncertainties, continuously
exacerbated by fabulous and widely rumored (because secret)
improvements in eavesdropping technologies. The letter writer's
use of the written word is not subject to just one hearing but is,
by virtue of its physical presence, subject to precise recall and to
the responsibility entailed by publication.* The telephone conversationalist's use of words is apparently assumed to be much looser
and more flexible—a privileged use of language for which, short
of criminal activities, the conversationalist shouldn't be held as
publicly responsible as he would be for a published statement.
That habitual sidestep is spreading everywhere in public life as
spokespersons agree to speak only with some guarantee of the
anonymity that mysteriously enables one to speak authoritatively
while disavowing forthright responsibility.

The transformation of the mighty world of ear since 1798
presents us with the ambiguity of incalculable advantage and
incalculable anxiety. That transformation has encouraged an in-

---

*An awareness of the danger implied by that responsibility can help explain why
the Elizabethans, for all their fascination with words, were not very prolific or
confiding letterwriters or diarykeepers. They were anxious not to be on record,
given the unpredictability of the succession to Elizabeth and the religious and
political changes that might ensue.

creasing separation between the private interior voice and public, publishable speech to the point where the assumption of radical discontinuity is widespread. One now expects private truths (greed, the hunger for power) to be masked by public lies, and private lies (what Auden called "morning vows": "I will be true to the wife")[13] to be masked by public images of sincerity. At the same time, all sorts of electronic devices for bugging and eavesdropping threaten the privileged status of private speech by making its publication possible. "BIG BROTHER IS LISTENING, and even if he isn't, he damn well could if he wanted to." Public speech, cowed by the omnipresence of recording devices and their capacity to spread local speech worldwide, aspires toward the impenetrable mask of the politician's and the bureaucrat's safe-speak, a self-protective variant of George Orwell's Newspeak, speech so stripped of nuance that it will at once sound benign, optimistic, guiltless, well meaning, inspired, and prophetic but be virtually without content when published, "clarified" by spokespersons and reviewed by the relatively uncritical news media.

The technologies that extend and modify our ears not only invade our privacies and intercept our privileged communications; they also jam both public and private communications so that we can't hear. The ear can be assaulted, its privacy invaded by the Muzak, the sound truck, or the ghetto-blasted rock, the ear reduced to captive audience. Conversely, the ear can be sealed off from all outside interference so that we can walk or jog or drive or daydream enclosed in a bubble of recorded sound, the buzz and din of the city blocked out in favor of benign internalized melody; the ear of the jogger on a Nantucket beach can be shielded from the easy sound of wind and wave.

In the shifting imbalance between aural and visual—the mighty world of eye threatening to eclipse the world of ear—there is still the stuff of dreams. For most of us, dreams are (or are recalled as) primarily visual experience. In *The Interpretation of Dreams,*

Freud assumed that dreams were primarily visual, and contemporary dream researchers tend to follow his lead. Historically, the association of dream with the visual experience of theater has been well established and, in the twentieth century, heavily reinforced by the asymmetrical emphasis on visual over verbal continuities in film. Most of us, brought up on film as the dominant dramatic form in our lives, tend to "see" our dreams (and our visual memories) in filmic terms. To dream is like being at the movies, and vice versa. Jean Cocteau called film "the great machine of dreams"; Orwell suggested that films show us our dreams; and there is the everpresent cliché of Hollywood as the dream factory.

But this widely perceived dream/film linkage has its ambiguities and excites a number of questions:

Do films show us our dreams? That is, do they somehow do the dreaming for us and leave us only the effort of bearing witness, as Hollywood once provided us with our daydreams of glamour and success, escapist dreams of what Ogden Nash called "a life of nonchalance and insouciance"?

Or does the concentrated visual imagery of which film is capable resonate with the intense visual condensation we experience in dreams? Does the imagery of film go beyond showing us our dreams to penetrate and infect them?

Why is it that so many of us experience the presence of film in our dreams (or in our recall of dreams) but so few report a similar presence of television? Is this because film seems all around and within us, as our dreams do, whereas television confines its imagery within that box, walled securely away from us, its perspectives perpetually in retreat on the other side of that curved glass, the glass itself returning us to the mirror image of ourselves seated in the viewing room?

Is Cocteau suggesting that film manufactures dreams for us, or is he suggesting that film is the ideal medium for the imitation of dream? But if so, why do films imitative of dreams (including Cocteau's) present dreams as narrative or as complex choreographies of surreality and symbol? Dreams are rarely inherently narrative until we translate them into narrative in the process of recalling and telling or recording them. Dreams become symbolic not necessarily in and of themselves but in our experience of interpreting them, whether in the classical and biblical tradition of reading them as omens (gate of ivory, gate of horn) or in the Freudian and post-Freudian tradition by assigning them "to a specific place in the psychic activities of the waking state."[14]

If dreams are predominantly visual for most of us, what about the rare few who report to researchers that their dreams are predominantly verbal, more like listening to the radio than like being at the movies? If our impression is correct that historically the mighty world of ear was once in the ascendant, as in Shakespeare's time, did many more people then dream *listening* instead of *looking?*

The climactic question is why is Joyce's *Finnegans Wake* the finest, overwhelmingly the finest, "imitation of the dream-state"[15] in our heritage? Joyce did say to Arthur Power, "Indeed, you can compare much of my work to the intricate illuminations [in the *Book of Kells*]."[16] Joyce's intricacies are, of course, verbal, not visual, and when the *Book of Kells* makes its appearance in *Finnegans Wake,*[17] the suggestion is that one of its most famous illuminated pages has been inspired by a passage in *Finnegans Wake,* which, as universal dream, has its being from the dawn of prehistory and thus predates the eighth-century *Book of Kells.*

In the absence of firm evidence, it's idle to speculate that Joyce dreamed in verbal rather than visual imagery, but Richard Ellmann reports that Joyce was fascinated by other people's accounts of reading and vocables in dreams and by dream language. A year before I encountered *Finnegans Wake,* I had and recorded a couple of language dreams that were composed of strange amalgam words, English/French/German/pidgin Arabic. That sort of dream-amalgam-language, remembered and elaborated into a principle of language making, could be the basis for the creation of a whole lexicon of language for the imitation of dream. The extraordinary verbal tapestry of *Finnegans Wake* is, I suspect, woven that way from sixty-five "foreign" languages that make up the weft worked into the hard warp that underpins the tapestry—English, with its vast vocabularies, including archaisms, dialects, and slangs.

Just as Lord Rutherford split the atom in 1919, so Joyce achieves *"The abnihilisation of the etym,"*[18] e-t-y-m, to the roots of etymology and beyond. Many commentators (extracting one pun from the word *abnihilisation*), maintain that Joyce (as intransigent Irishman) is revenging himself on English, that his night language annihilates the word. But Ellmann records Joyce as saying, "I made it [*Ulysses*] out of next to nothing. *Work in Progress* I am making out of nothing."[19] That remark encourages the suggestion that this is a language created *ab nihil,* from nothing (as only God can create), a suggestion that may be even more fruitful. In *Finnegans Wake,* language is born again so that it can become a medium for the imitation of dream—not imitation through narration or symbolic interpretation but of what our dreams would be like if we could witness them as they unfold in the present tense of sleep instead of in the past tense of awakened recollection. What would it be like to be in the bleachers watching the event itself and to imitate the event from that perspective? That is, to imitate it in what seems to be Aristotle's sense of the word in the *Poetics* when he says that drama is the imitation of an action, thus implying that the action is being translated into and reproduced in a medium other than that in which it occurs. And so with the imitation of dream in *Finnegans Wake*—translated and reproduced in a medium other than that in which the experience of dream itself occurs.

One more question: In spite of what so many commentators see as the sad decline of the verbal and the ascendency of the visual in our eye-minded age and culture, is it still possible that the dominion of the ear lurks just beyond the range of our peripheral vision, ready to slip through the gate of horn "whereby the true shades pass with ease?"[20] Could *Finnegans Wake* enable us to redress that imbalance through the discipline of a verbal tapestry so dense that most of it cannot be read aloud as a linear thread of vocables; so dense that it can constitute the most extraordinary imitation of what is for most of us the visual rather than the verbal density of dream? Once again: is it still possible that the ear will be reborn to, realize again, something like the Shakespearian ascendency it might once have had? If we assume that *Finnegans Wake*, that impossible book, may one day be assimilated as other impossible works such as *Ulysses* have been, then some renaissance of the ear may just be on the way.

3.
The Mighty World
of Timespace
· · · · · · · · · · · · · · · · · ·

Space is really an indeterminate vastness.

William James

Consciousness is a space of time, filled, always filled with moving.

Gertrude Stein

You don't have to accentuate time to be in time.

George Balanchine to Stravinsky

By 1798, the Newtonian constants, absolute time and absolute space, had been comfortably in place for over one hundred years without appreciably altering the time and space in which people went about their daily lives. Everyday rhythms had changed little in the twenty-one centuries since Aristotle puzzled over the divisibility of time and motion and his contemporary, Euclid, undertook a diagrammatic clarification of space. The eighteenth century did evolve the capacity for much more precise measurement of time and calculation of celestial distances. John Harrison's highly accurate chronometers tamed longitude in the 1760s so that navigators could finally know where they were at sea. Sir William Herschel and other astronomers began to suspect the immensities of intergalactic space. And there was the birth of fascination with historical time, which climaxed in Edward Gibbon's *Decline and Fall of the Roman Empire.* But the everyday rhythms of human life remained much the same as they had been in the classical world: there was the diurnal round; the flow of fire and water, of winds and tides and currents, and of the biological rhythms of human beings and the animals on which they depended for food and labor and transport.

After 1798, and in ways that Wordsworth and his contemporaries regarded as singularly abrupt, "Time" triumphed "o'er his brother Space" thanks to "Steamboats, Viaducts, and Railways." Ever since, we have been sorting out ways to attune ourselves to the new rhythms that continue to derive from the always accelerating technological triumphs over time that have given us timespace. During the same period, through a historical process of osmosis, our intuitions about timespace have been shifting and changing, thanks to the geology and biology of evolution in the nineteenth century; thanks to Freudian and post-Freudian psychologies, and to physics and its exploration of those still-fabulous realms, intergalactic and submolecular timespace, in the twentieth century.

In book 3, chapter 1 of *Finnegans Wake,* Shaun, the son with the shopkeeper's mentality (or rather the world-keeper's mentality), redreams, reworks, retells one of our most seminal parables about time, Aesop's "The Grasshopper and the Ant." That fable from the sixth century B.C. has been retold in a variety of ways. In the middle of the spectrum are versions that end with a flat moral tag, pointing out that when he became winter-hungry, "the grasshopper knew it was best to prepare for the days of necessity." At the twentieth-century end of the spectrum, the ants are said to take pity on the grasshopper and keep him warm and well fed so that he is fit to fiddle all winter for the comfort of the children of a consumer society. At the seventeenth-century end, the ants tend toward the sarcastic: "Since you sang all summer, you may as well dance all winter to the tune you sang all summer." Shaun's version of the fable in *Finnegans Wake* is told in a manner we associate with that of his brother, Shem the Penman, sympathetic to the grasshopper's mentality and behavior and tolerant of the ants. The fable also evokes biographical associations: Joyce with the irresponsible grasshopper; the prudential philistines (brother Stanislaus and Wyndham Lewis among others) with the ants.

Shaun's version of the fable is entitled "The Ondt and the Gracehopper." *Ondt* in Norwegian means hard, ill, or mean (in the Irish-English sense of stingy, tightfisted, frugal) as the ants in the fable are; for them, time is money, as it is in Benjamin Franklin's *Advice to a Young Tradesman* (1748). Joyce's word *Gracehopper* is close to the Norwegian for grasshopper, but it also puns on the various graces*—spiritual, musical, and physical—with which the artist, for whom time is music, hops, dances, and hopes. Shaun's fable ends with the Gracehopper's song as addressed to the Ondt mentality but celebrating both Ondt and Gracehopper, moneytime and dancetime.

The last four lines of the song:

> *Your feats end enourmous, your volumes immense,*
> *(May the Graces I hoped for sing your Ondtship song*
>   *sense!),*
> *Your genus its world wide, your spacest sublime!*
> *But, Holy Saltmartin, why can't you beat time?*[1]

---

*Plus the three Graces, the daughters of Zeus and the sea-goddess Eurynome: Aglaia (Brilliance), Euphrosyne (Joy), and Thalia (Bloom, Luxuriance). They represent everything that lends charm and beauty to nature and to human life.

Enter Fats Waller's voice ("Your Feet's Too Big") plus praise for
the prodigious "feats" and "volumes immense" (presumably of
the Gracehopper's accomplishments, *Ulysses* and *Work in Progress*). In Italian, a *saltamartino* is literally an acrobat or tumbler,
figuratively, someone with a giddy head. And Saint Martin of Tours
is the patron saint of all drinking and joyous occasions, of grasshopper (Gracehopper) behavior.

"Why can't you beat time?" Why can't the frugal ant mentality, which can plan for and beat winter famine and for which time
is money, triumph over time? Answer: If time and money are the
same, it is metaphorical suicide for one to beat the other. They
can't beat each other because both are laying up "treasures upon
earth where moth and rust doth corrupt" (Matthew 6:19).

"Why can't you beat time?" Why can't you get with the music
and dance to the poetry of time? Art beats time as in the *volta* of
Shakespeare's sonnet 65. In answer to the question who or what
can prevent time's conquest, pillage, and destruction of the
citadel of beauty:

> *O none, unless this miracle have might,*
> *That in black ink my love may still shine bright.*

I want to explore these two dimensions of time-serving (if
not time-beating), the poetics of time and the economics of time,
and their interweavings.

THE POETICS OF TIME. From the Middle Ages through the
Renaissance, time might be beaten "in black ink," but time was
first and foremost accepted as the medium of mutability through
which all human beings moved, in Joyce's phrase, "from infancy
through maturity to decay."[2] In Joyce's twentieth-century version,
that movement is "vital growth, through convulsions of metamorphosis." In Renaissance terms, time wasn't open-ended but rather
the closed medium in which events in succession were domi-

nated by the specter of human mortality; in Sir Thomas Browne's words,

> Think not thy time short in this world, since the world itself is not long. The created world is but a small parenthesis in eternity, and a short interposition, for a time, between such a state of duration as was before it and may be after it.[3]

From Browne's point of view, time and eternity are mutually exclusive modes or states of duration, as mutually exclusive as the mind of man bound by "the created world" and the mind of God. Twentieth-century definitions of eternity (the totality of time without beginning or end; infinite time) tend to define eternity in terms of time and blur the sharpness of that mutual exclusivity. From Browne's perspective, located within the "small parenthesis" of time, eternity is all but unimaginable, radically other than any imaginable extension of time.

In the course of the eighteenth century, thanks to the impact of Sir Isaac Newton's theoretical model of the universe and the general secularization of thought, time began to edge out of that small parenthesis and to expand toward and include some of the nearer zones of what Browne called that "state of duration as was before . . . and may be after." In 1650, eight years after Newton's birth, Archbishop James Ussher unwittingly contributed to this expansion by translating the myth/metaphor of the Creation into the literal realm of calendar and clock time. In *Annals of the Old Testament,* he published chronological calculations that pinpointed the beginning (Genesis 1:1) of that small parenthesis at 9 A.M., 26 October 4004 B.C. By the end of the eighteenth century, a few natural historians, those whom we would call geologists, had begun to imagine a parenthesis enlarged to include hundreds of thousands of years of steady, uniform geological process before 4004 B.C.

This linear extension of time was accompanied by a metaphoric mechanization of Newtonian space and time. The Reverend William Paley's much quoted metaphor—the universe a vast watch perfected by God the watchmaker[4] and left to tick away until the God-ordained end of time—cuts both ways. The universe becomes admirable mechanism (and therefore proof of God's existence), but that mechanism brings in its train the mechanization of time. Since time is the medium of memory, the metaphor threatens the mechanization of memory; since memory, in the person of Mnemosyne, is the mother of the Muses, the mechanization of time threatens the mechanization of history, poetry, and the arts as well.

Mechanized, time is abstracted from the biological and intuitive rhythms of our lives and from the human scale of that unit of mnemonic time that is bounded by the grandparent's memories of childhood, as those memories are narrated for and changed in the memories of the grandchildren. In the direction of time-is-money, the mechanization of time obviously anticipated and reflected the needs of industrialized, televised, computerized society. But once mechanized, time begins to play strange tricks on memory, the medium of our poetics.

The unfinished Cathedral of Saints Peter and Paul in Washington, D.C., under construction since 1867, stands as a monument to those tricks. It has been conceived and built in a way that imitates medieval time. It took medieval masons and sculptors and glassmakers decades, even centuries, to achieve those great houses. Medieval time still obtains on that building site in Washington, except for the amenities of electric light, power tools, gantry cranes, and time clocks. Tourists come by charter bus and behave as today's pilgrim-tourists do all over Romanesque and Gothic Europe. The cathedral may be a little too clean and tidy, but the elevators are a comfort and it looks like the real thing. It has visual and conceptual authenticity, but it has slipped the notice of Clio, the Muse of history. It hasn't, in Philip Larkin's phrase,

> *held unspilt*
> *So long and equably what since is found*
> *Only in separation—marriage, and birth,*
> *And death, and thoughts of these.*[5]

So the pilgrim is faced with a disorienting temporal sterility—an authentic fake, a time capsule that has escaped from time.

Sir Isaac Newton stood—not that he meant to—as the great mechanizer of space and time for the eighteenth century, and for Paley, the watchmaker.

> *The noiseless tide of time, all bearing down*
> *To vast eternity's unbounded sea,*
> *Where the green islands of the happy shine*
> *He stemmed alone.*

These lines are from James Thomson's "To the Memory of Sir Isaac Newton" (1727). That image of Newton making headway against the inexorable tide of time informed in turn Wordsworth's recall of a moonlit vision of the statue of Newton in the chapel of Trinity College at Cambridge:

> *where the statue stood*
> *Of Newton with his prism and silent face,*
> *The marble index of a mind for ever*
> *Voyaging through strange seas of Thought, alone.*[6]

The image of forever-immersion in thought combines with Wordsworth's determination to immerse himself in what he called "the blood and vital juices of our minds"[7] to suggest a strong countercurrent that, during the last two centuries, has been sustained against the mechanization of time and memory, against what William Blake called "Newton's Sleep."

The contemplative ode "Tintern Abbey" explores that countercurrent through its deep concern with the dimensions of time and memory. Its full title is "Lines / Composed a Few Miles above

Tintern Abbey / On Revisiting the Banks of the Wye / During a
Tour. July 13, 1798." That title and the opening lines—"Five years
have passed; five summers . . . five long winters!"—work together
to emphasize time and occasion: a second visit to the Wye Valley
after a first visit five years before. The second visit was apparently
extraordinary. On that occasion, Wordsworth made a dramatic
discovery: that what he calls the "beauteous forms" of the valley
and the organic continuity of landscape, cliffs, and sky that
constitute those forms had been present, latent in his memory,
not in the sense that the forms were urging themselves on
conscious recall as visual memory, but present, nevertheless, as
active agents of

> *A motion and a spirit, that impels*
> *All thinking things, all objects of all thought,*
> *And rolls through all things.*

That agency has, he discovers, sustained him through five years of
"long winters," five years of "the heavy and the weary weight / Of
all this unintelligible world," the world of men in cities. This may
strike us as Wordsworth's comprehensive metaphor for the mind
distracted and imprisoned, cut off from its true source of nurture,
but what seems metaphor to us was, for Wordsworth, the existen-
tial state ("true metaphor").

Wordsworth's discovery of the source of that nurturing
agency involves the realization that what had been active in
unconscious memory has now become available to conscious
memory in the present tense of the poem. That realization hasn't
been achieved without cost; the introspection* necessary to its
achievement has been attended by "somewhat of a sad perplex-
ity" because the cost includes the loss of that rapturous and

---

*In a poem of 1814 now called Prospectus to *The Recluse,* Wordsworth described
this order of introspection as treading "on shadowy ground" and as breeding "fear
and awe."

appetitive immersion in nature that is characteristic of "thoughtless youth," immersion now replaced by thought informed by "The still, sad music of humanity." That cost may well be offset by the realization that the beauteous forms are, in the present tense of 1798, once again informing the unconscious memory with their impulsion, the batteries being charged for the next five years. Toward the end of the poem, he can read corroboration of that happening in his sister's voice and eyes because she is the living presence of his 1793 state; where he is now in 1798, she will be in 1803. There is further compensation in the active agency of the beauteous forms. That agency will not only be a nurturing presence in unconscious memory, it will also be available to conscious contemplation. The bright prospect is only slightly clouded by the possibility that the accession of self-consciousness may inhibit the natural and unconscious flow of his "genial spirits"—his creative powers.

What is involved in all of this is the faith that moments of visionary experience that seem to come unbidden and unannounced can, through mature and searching introspection, be traced to their source in impulses received from the forms of nature and felt through "the blood and vital juices of our minds." Once that psychological process is understood as organic blood-relation to nature, visionary experience will be available to conscious memory and thus become repeatable. Wordsworth describes the visionary, mystical experience of the flow of that blood as "the power / Of harmony and the deep power of joy"* that enables him "to see into the life of things." That way of seeing is both nutritive and therapeutic, and, once its sources are understood, it should be available on demand, to put it crudely. Time

---

*When Coleridge uses the word *joy* in "Dejection: An Ode," his answer to the joyless lament of the first four stanzas of Wordsworth's "Immortality Ode," he uses it to mean the experience of Christian beatitude, the earthly equivalent of beatific vision. Wordsworth, in what Coleridge called his "semi-Atheism," uses the word in 1798 to suggest a comparable but pantheistic beatitude.

will no longer be what Sir Thomas Browne calls "a small parenthesis" nor what David Hume calls "a succession of indivisible
moments" but a fully remembered, and therefore fully repeatable,
sequence of microcosmic visions of eternity.

This idealized (what I would call Romantic) concept of time
and of the perfectibility of memory was to be the source of
considerable depression to Wordsworth. Visionary experiences,
and what he called the light they promised, became less and less
available to him in the five years after 1798. When he speaks of
that light in the fifth stanza of "Ode: Intimations of Immortality
from Recollections of Early Childhood" in 1804, it is to lament its
loss:

> At length the Man perceives it die away,
> And fade into the light of common day.

But the Romantic expectation that memory of a transcendental experience in time-past can provide the conditions for an
identical experience in time-future was not to end with Wordsworth's qualified disillusionment after 1798. Others kept the faith
in spite of Wordsworth's pivot from optimistic anticipation of
future vision to stoic acceptance of what in the "Immortality
Ode" he calls "shadowy recollections" of past visions

> Which, be they what they may,
> Are yet the fountain light of all our day
> Are yet a master light of all our seeing.

A similar faith in the fully memorable, fully repeatable nature
of visionary experience led Ralph Waldo Emerson late in his life
to repeat a morning walk that he had taken and recorded in his
Journals almost forty years before. The earlier walk had coalesced
in a mystical experience of the sort he described in *Nature:* "The
currents of the Universal Being" had circulated through him, and
he had for the moment been "part or parcel of God."[8] He repeated

the walk at the same time of year, the same time of day, under the same weather conditions, in the hope, indeed with the faith, that the divine lightning would strike again. It didn't, but the end result wasn't so much a denial of faith in Romantic memory-time as it was a skeptical and depressing sense of his own inadequacy.

Some few complained against the Romantic faith in the fully memorable, fully repeatable visionary experience, Hawthorne among them:

> Let the past alone; do not seek to renew it; . . . and be assured that the right way can never be that which leads you back to the identical shapes that you long ago left behind you.[9]

Many commentators, beginning with Emerson, have complained that in the 1850s, Thoreau turned from the poetry of his life at Walden Pond toward a scribe's drudgery among the endless details of natural history. Thoreau's *Journal* does seem to reflect that shift, but it may be not so much a retreat into the shadow zone of particular and often apparently trivial observations as a defense against too heightened an expectation that each moment of perception would prove one of those golden moments so prized in poetic anticipation and recall. Thoreau's *Journal,* however, remains a journal—the day-to-day effort that, after the sojourn at Walden, increasingly mounts toward a strident determination to "take time by the forelock. Now or never!" Because, Thoreau continues, "take any other course, and life will be a succession of regrets."[10] Wordsworth discovered this between 1798 and 1804 and lived it to the hilt in the forty-five-year process of revising *The Prelude,* that epic celebration of the mind's growth to maturity during the years of light before the blinds came down in the slow years after 1798.

From Thoreau's point of view, moments of significant perception should be fully recoverable to consciousness through memory and thus fully repeatable in the time-future of the poetic imagination; yet, as he writes in his *Journal,*

It is impossible to remember a week ago. A river of Lethe flows with many windings the year through, separating one season from another.[11]

The difficulty, as Thoreau describes it, is that

a transient acquaintance with any phenomenon is not sufficient to make it completely the subject of your muse. You must be so conversant with it as to *remember* it and be reminded of it long afterward, while it lies remotely far and elysian in the horizon, approachable only by the imagination.[12]

Earlier, in *Walden,* he had announced with a flourish,

Time is but the stream I go a-fishing in. I drink at it; but while I drink I see the sandy bottom and detect how shallow it is. Its thin current slides away, but eternity remains.

And that eternity was to be sought with "divining rod," in the ground water beneath "these hills,"[13] in the reservoir of fully memorable, fully repeatable poetic (that is, transcendental) experience. By contrast, Gilbert White's distinction isn't between "transient acquaintance" and "the subject of your muse . . . far and elysian" but between "observation in the field of nature" (that is, casual contacts) and the focus of the natural historian, "investigation (where a man endeavours to be sure of his facts)."[14]

Ernest Hemingway tried the Romantic experiment with reentry on a much grander scale than Emerson or Thoreau and had his own depressing encounter with the unrepeatable nature of the past, that barrier to the Romantic imagination imposed by Thoreau's "river of Lethe." It had been what Hemingway called good for him on safari in Africa in the early 1930s.[15] That safari had supplied the raw materials and, if he hadn't been shy of the word, the inspiration for some of his better stories, notably "The Snows of Kilimanjaro" and "The Short Happy Life of Francis

Macomber," both written in 1936. Twenty years later, he went back on safari to those green hills, apparently in the hope that the experience would stir him out of a long and depressing period of artistic doldrums. That hope was frustrated, though an obscure small-plane accident did provide Hemingway with another sort of time-warp: the opportunity to read his own obituaries.

Hemingway and Emerson's experiments, together with Wordsworth and Thoreau's longings for sustained visionary consciousness, suggest attempts to reify memory in time so that the process of memory, fully contemplated in time-past, can be reversed, anticipated as a future experience to be reentered and fully realized in an ideal time-present. That is what I call Romantic time, and as a faith, or rather a desire, it seems tailor-made to be fulfilled by our vast technological capacity to record and reproduce the mighty world of eye and ear, our capacity to reify memory in the two-dimensional images of photograph and tape recording—though even those "true" images all too often strike us as foreign and strange, as images from those crowded lands of memento mori on the farther shore of Lethe. In attempting to cross that Lethe, one encounters Saint Augustine's unyielding triad.

> It is now plain and clear that neither past nor future are existent, and that it is not properly stated that there are three times, past, present, and future. But perhaps it might properly be said that there are three present times: the present of things past, the present of things present, and the present of things future. These three are in the soul, but elsewhere I do not see them: the present of things past is in memory; the present of things present is in intuition; the present of things future is in expectation.[16]

In another and related version of Romantic time, the work of art itself is regarded as the emblem of eternity. In Keats's "Ode on a Grecian Urn," the urn exists in "silence and slow time," a time

akin to (but not necessarily identical with) eternity in its extension. The images of a bacchanalia, carved in relief on one side of
the urn, are frozen in the stop action of slow-time. The poetic
imagination can release the stop action and animate the figures
on the frieze from anticipation through pleasure to fulfillment and
hangover in fast-time, the experiential time that the poet and the
reader share. The other side of the urn depicts a contrasting
scene, a religious procession suspended in slow-time between the
"little town" it has left and the "green altar" it approaches but has
yet to reach. The ode modulates toward a darker view of fast-
time: not the fast-time of one night of riot but of the more than
twenty centuries that have long since rendered the town "silent"
and "desolate" in history as well as in poetry.

Poet and reader share this historical dimension of fast-time
as they share the yesterday, today, and tomorrow of the baccha-
nal. The dilemma that swims into focus in the course of the ode
is that neither the slow-time in which the urn is frozen nor the
fast-time of centuries and days it has managed to survive are in
themselves emotionally or aesthetically satisfying. Experience in
fast-time ends in the mortality of hangover and the decline of
civilizations; experience in slow-time endures a forever of frustra-
tion: the cup in hand never reaches the lip, the propitiatory
sacrifice never gets made. A solemn act of worship in fast-time
couldn't save the little town from the desolation fast-time has in
store for it, and even in slow-time the little town is desolate,
undepicted, and permanently emptied of its population. The
cognitive and aesthetic excitement of the ode explodes when
slow-time (eternity) and fast-time (Browne's small parenthesis)
coincide in the last stanza:

> *O Attic shape! Fair attitude! with brede*
>   *Of marble men and maidens overwrought,*
> *With forest branches and trodden weed;*
>   *Thou, silent form, dost tease us out of thought*
> *As doth eternity: Cold Pastoral!*

When old age shall this generation waste,
Thou shalt remain, in midst of other woe
Than ours, a friend to man, to whom thou say'st
"Beauty is truth, truth beauty,"—that is all
Ye know on earth, and all ye need to know."

In logic, time and eternity are mutually exclusive, but from Keats's imaginative perspective they are mutually dependent. To evoke one is to invoke the other; the slow-time in which the urn exists becomes a metaphor for eternity in coincidence with the contrasting fast-time depicted in its friezes. Not that the urn itself can transcend time, except through what it excites in the imagination-as-witness, as the poem in turn can excite us. Thus, the closing lines of the ode suggest that the urn's (and the ode's) slow-time will survive to coincide with the fast-time of future generations ("in midst of other woe"). That coincidence will invoke that which transcends time.

Shelley's vision of the two tracks of time, the slow and the fast, is more awesome and potentially more terrifying. In "Mont Blanc: Lines Written in the Vale of Chamouni" (1816), Shelley confronts the overwhelming scale of the scene and rethinks the "faith so mild, / So solemn, so serene" that he associates with Wordsworth's "Tintern Abbey." The beauteous forms of the Wye Valley are what Shelley calls the "mysterious tongue" that teaches Wordsworthian faith and serenity, but the forms of the Wye Valley are what Wordsworth calls "sylvan," intimate and domestic in contrast with the mysterious tongue of Mont Blanc and its glacial offspring, the River Arve which flows through the Vale of Chamouni (Chamonix) where Shelley stands. Mont Blanc has its serenity, but it is the serenity of wilderness, remote, inaccessible* and

---

*Shelley and his contemporaries wouldn't have thought of Mont Blanc as an object accessible to the mountain climber's aspirations. Fascination of that sort was still a generation away. Mont Blanc had been climbed in 1786 by a guide named J. Balmat, who was motivated by a prize offered by the Swiss natural historian

forbidding in the fast-time of the immediate past and the immediate future. Mont Blanc exists, however, not only in the fast-time of human mortality but also in the contrasting fast-time of geological history.

The concept of geological time was born in the 1780s and 1790s of the assumption that the processes of geological change had been no faster or slower throughout geological history than at present. This theory of uniformitarianism had been published for only twenty-odd years and was not very widely known when Shelley composed his poem, but as a theory it was a clear outgrowth of the calm and detached modes of observation of the best of the late-eighteenth-century natural historians. Gilbert White, for example, observed that the Sussex Downs seemed to have been shaped

> by some plastic power; and so made to swell and heave their broad backs into the sky so much above the less animated clay of the wild below.[17]

As a consequence, the hills represent something he saw as "analogous to growth," though White characteristically refrains from any speculation about the time frame in which such swelling and heaving might have occurred. The following year, a spectacular slump of a hillside that impacted about fifty acres of land three miles south of Selborne confirmed White's suspicion that some sort of gradualism was at work,

> that though our hills may never have journeyed far, yet that the ends of many of them have slipped and fallen away at distant periods, leaving the cliffs bare and abrupt.[18]

Horace Bénédict de Saussure. Saussure himself made the ascent the following year, but his interest was not "the life of the High Alps," as the London Alpine Club would put it in 1857, or tourism, as it would be by 1900. Saussure's goal was to study atmospheric pressure and other meteorological phenomena at that altitude. The two hundredth anniversary of Balmat's achievement, celebrated in 1986, elaborately misstated the motivation as Alpinism *(pour le sport)* rather than as the scientific enterprise it was.

Shelley, and contemporary natural historians whom he might have read, didn't know the geological history of the Mont Blanc massif, but he envisions two alternatives that might have formed it: the earthquakes of a mountain-building revolution or the "sea / Of Fire" of the volcanic eruption that might have formed the massif. He then reflects, "all seems eternal now." The awe-inspiring thing, that "which teaches awful doubt," is the awareness that in geological time the "Power" that made Mont Blanc and that the mountain represents is not eternally at rest (even though the mountain seems eternal) but forever continuing its process of geological change in a fast-time that seems slow because it is of an almost unimaginable duration. The poet one obituary dismissed as "Shelley the Atheist" was still more mindful than many of his contemporaries of the mutual exclusivity of time and eternity—that which "seems eternal now" only seems that way because of the potential confusion of geological time and eternity.

The geological power that built Mont Blanc, given its awesome remoteness and inscrutability, may be indifferent to humanity and its fast-time concerns. Even so, and in spite of its apparent indifference, that slow fast-time force is available to the imaginative power of the human mind. Shelley would have anglicized the pronounciation of Mont Blanc as "Mount Blank," but, his ode concludes, "to the human mind's imaginings" the mountain is not "vacancy" but "Power"; more than power, it is at once a manifestation and an emblem of "the secret strength of things / Which governs thought."

Shelley may have been able to face those alternatives of "awful doubt" (his Mont Blanc) "or faith so mild" (Wordsworth's Wye Valley) with contemplative excitement and equanimity. Not so succeeding generations of Victorians, who were deeply disturbed by the conflict between the slow fast-time of geological history and the fast fast-time of human history on an earth presumed to have been created in six biblical days in 4004 B.C. That conflict threatened to undermine faith in historical Christianity and to call into question the medieval-Renaissance assumption that the duration of time in this small parenthesis and the duration of eternity were discontinuous and mutually exclusive. The publication of Darwin's *On the Origin of Species* in 1859 vastly increased the weight of slow fast-time and the intensity of the awful doubt that perhaps the universe in its millions of years of slow fast-time was at best indifferent, and at worst positively inimical, to human beings and the few thousand years of their history. Eight years before Darwin, Melville was to end *Moby-Dick* with a vision of the coincidence of geological time and biblical time: "then all collapsed, and the great shroud of the sea rolled on as it rolled five thousand years ago."[19] Most nineteenth-century family Bibles included a running chronology of biblical events. Melville is alluding not to Ussher's calendar but to the lesser-known one compiled by John Hales, which dates the Flood 5,005 years before 1850. From the beginning of his novel, Melville repeatedly refers to the new geological history: "The universe is finished; the copestone is on, and the chips were carted off a million years ago." In the light of that history, "Noah's flood is not yet subsided." At novel's end, the shroud of the sea can exist at once in the flexibilities of geological time (millions of years and still counting) and in the fixities of biblical time (Creation/ Crucifixion/Last Judgment).

Tennyson, speaking as he so often does (and felt he should) as the official voice of the Victorian world, tends to refocus the conflict between geological fast-time and human fast-time as a sense of something lost or wanting in the historical past—a lost Eden that will be found again, realized at last in the time-future of human progress, what Tennyson envisions at the end of *In Memoriam* (1850) as "one far-off divine event / To which the whole creation moves." On that eventful final occasion, gradual moral growth and development through historical time will modulate into the consciousness of eternity.

Meanwhile, Tennyson and his contemporaries were fond of citing the revolutionary transformation of the physical world being achieved by science, technology, and industry as proof positive, both literally and metaphorically, of the equally revolutionary moral and spiritual progress of humanity that was taking place in the nineteenth century. The new technology as rite of moral passage toward an ideal time-future is also Wordsworth's faith in the 1833 sonnet, "Steamboats, Viaducts, and Railways":

> *and Time,*
> *Pleased with your triumphs o'er his brother Space,*
> *Accepts from your bold hands the proffered crown*
> *Of hope, and smiles on you with cheer sublime.*

But this faith in progress in time-future was ambiguously balanced by a nostalgic longing for time-past. There was the sustained sentimental romance with Arthurian chivalry and the idealized realm of Arthur's kingdom of Logres and his capital, Camelot.[20] For many, that realm offered escape from the oppression of the new world born of the industrial revolution—escape from what William Morris saw as "six counties overhung with smoke." But there was also the desire to reify the past, to locate Arthur's Camelot in space and time, to locate Homer's Troy once and for all. Hence the credulous public fascination with Heinrich Schliemann's extravagant claims for his discoveries of the real Troy on the hill of Hissarlik (circa 1870), in the course of which many evidences of not-so-romantic settlements on the site were swept aside with a cavalier wave of the archaeologist's shovel.

The Victorian faith in the immediate possibility of moral and spiritual human progress, bolstered by the evidence of technological progress in the material world, had the effect of relegating time to an elsewhere in the future and of postponing any searching examination of time-present. There were, of course, Cassandras,* but their alarms did not prepare the Western world for the

---

*Notable among them is the Polish economist and military historian Jean de Bloch (1836–1902), who wrote *The Future of War in Its Technical, Economic, and Political Relations,* 7 vols. (St. Petersburg [Leningrad]: 1898); translated and abridged in English, *Is War Now Impossible?* (London: 1899).

rude disillusionment that occurred when World War I stopped time to deliver an alternate message about technological progress and the "inhumanity to man" that morally and spiritually progressive man, when armed with the new technology, could achieve. Ironically, the escapist code of Arthurian chivalry—inappropriate as courage, honor, bravery, and self-sacrifice are to the technological battlescape—made its contribution to the sustained popular delusion of the years 1914–18 and after. Mark Twain addressed this delusion when he quipped that the American Civil War never would have happened "if all those Southerners hadn't been reading Sir Walter Scott."

In spite of that first installment of international suicide, Yeats would carry into the 1920s the Romantic faith that art could, in his phrase, "break the teeth of Time."[21] But by 1935, faced with the ominous portent of World War II, Yeats's faith became bleaker. In "Lapis Lazuli" (1938), art won't itself break the teeth of time because "all things fall and are built again." All works of art fall and so do the civilizations that have made them. Yeats shifts away from the Romantic vision of an art that can transcend time toward the vision of a future of cyclical fall and regeneration, new civilizations rising out of the ashes, the "tragic scene" of the old and fallen thanks to what Yeats calls the "gaiety," the creative energies of humankind. Even that bleak vision seems rosy given the future-time that infects our imaginations, a future when Armageddon is no longer the religious expectation of the millennium, the end of time with the coming of the rapture of eternity, but a palpable physical possibility of the end of time—no one left on earth to clock it or remember it or anticipate it.

Corollary to the poetics of time-past and time-future and the tensions between the various orders of fast-time, there remained for many writers and readers in the nineteenth century the possibility of a poetics of time-present, notably in the transcendent ideals of human immortality, of constancy in love, and of chivalric courage and honor in war.

The compounding lament of Tennyson's *In Memoriam,* composed between 1833 and 1850, envisions the possibility of a present tense beyond the reach of time, a triumph for the "living will," which Tennyson defines elsewhere as the moral will of mankind. Given the "diffusive power" of that presence, the Christmas season (the season that carries for Tennyson the most intense personal awareness of the loss of Arthur Hallam, the friend whose death was the occasion for the poem) will be realized as a season of transcendent nativity.

The lovers' kiss in the present tense of marriage becomes the spiritual sign that will unite their twin souls forever and invite the angel of wedded love into the house, as in Coventry Patmore's celebration of married love, *The Angel in the House,* one of the most popular long poems of midcentury.[22]

One death in the now of 1 July 1916 on the Somme could be read as the heroic gesture that wipes out the drudgery of half a life "spent / Toiling at ledgers in a city grey." The hero, "his lance . . . broken . . . lies content" and "goes to join the men of Agincourt," according to Herbert Asquith, the popular poet who happened to be the prime minister's son.[23]

Romance with time present and with an aestheticized Middle Ages brought with it a fascination with the medieval book of hours, secularized into a book of seasons, grounded in well-established metaphors: the round of the day images the round of the week (and the six days of creation in Genesis), day and week image the round of the year, and all image the round of a human life, the round of a civilization. Thoreau experimented with the book-of-hours model in *A Week on the Concord and Merrimack Rivers,*[24] and, as discussed above, adopted it as one of the several structural principles of *Walden.*

He began his residence at Walden Pond "by accident," he says, "on Independence day, or the fourth of July, 1845." In the same ironic vein, he remarks that he will give the account of his stay at the pond "for convenience, putting the experience of two years into one";[25] that is, for the convenience of the book-of-hours metaphor. Chapters 3 through 5 begin to encapsulate that experience descriptively and metaphorically in the round of the day and year. In chapter 3, "Reading," he focuses on Homer or Aeschylus (at the dawn of civilization) and remarks that students might well "consecrate morning hours to their pages." In the following chapter, "Sounds," he moves contemplatively "from sunrise till noon" into "this summer afternoon . . . for the rest of the long afternoon," until at chapter's end it is "late in the evening." Chapter 5, "Solitude," is a compilation and interweaving of night experiences the year round, including "the long winter evenings." The structural rhythm of the book of hours recedes after chapter 5 to reemerge toward the end of chapter 12: "In the fall the loon *(Colymbus glacialis)* came, as usual, to moult and bathe in the pond," and the book then moves seasonally from "Housewarming" (chapter 13) through "Winter Visitors," "Winter Animals," and "The Pond in Winter" to "Spring" (17) and "Conclusion" (18).

And in conclusion comes the crunch. Thoreau's aim was to reawaken himself and to be perpetually awake in a radically expanded time-present; "to be awake," he says, "is to be alive."[26] But in a book of hours, the present tense must also continue its rounds. Day dawns again; the week renews itself after a day of rest; spring renews the year after the sabbath of winter; but the sojourner's life moves inexorably toward its evening and its winter. Once time has escaped from the confines of Browne's small parenthesis, the book of hours seems to develop a fatal metaphoric flaw. It no longer urges the round of the day as devotional preparation for the "transcendent endowment" of the soul in eternity (outside time, outside that small parenthesis). It urges instead a curious stop-time, the round of the day fixed in a perpetual mode of morning wakefulness, spring wakefulness, the wakeful consciousness of eternal youth. The round of day and week and year develops a metaphoric mismatch with that post-

Newtonian linear extension of time, which sharpens the sojourner's sense that he moves not toward perpetual rebirth but
toward inevitable confrontation with his own mortality. The
intensifying stridency of Thoreau's determination to "live
deliberately"[27] cannot prevail against it.

Joyce develops the poetics of time-present in a richly contrasting
way: in the round of a specific Dublin day, 16 June 1904, in
Ulysses; in the watches of a less specific early-twentieth-century
Dublin night in *Finnegans Wake.* The clock-day of *Ulysses*—8
A.M., 16 June, to just before sunrise, 3:33 A.M., 17 June—is expanded to surprise and subvert the reader's expectation of conventional accounts of the times of a day. To read the whole of
Ulysses aloud (as it should be heard in the head) requires forty-
odd hours, more than five eight-hour working days—except that
most of us can't manage much more than three hours of well-
concentrated reading per day. So the fictional day of *Ulysses* will
occupy us for at least two weeks, in contrast to the four-day read
(at three hours per day) that can readily accomplish the year of
Walden.
    But the asymmetrical relations between the clocks within
the novel and the clocks that measure our reading of it are only
part of the time story of *Ulysses.* The novel asserts itself as existing
in dramatic time as Aristotle defined it: the action of the novel,
complete with peripeteia, is confined to one day. *Ulysses* also
exists in epic time,* its action a phase in the life such as, Aristotle
says, the homecoming of Odysseus, his reunion with his ever-
faithful wife, the coming of age of his son, and the restoration of
order on Ithaca. In *Ulysses,* the epic action may include Stephen
Dedalus's coming of age; Leopold and Molly Bloom's resolution

---

*Living epics in contemporary Turkey, where a bardic tradition still lingers, are
usually performed in evening sessions of about two and a half to three hours, a
time that accords fairly well with the novel reader's three-plus hours per sitting.

of an uncertain marriage; Ireland's fumbling approach toward nationhood.

These epic dimensions are folded into 16 June 1904 in such a way that we as readers can cantilever them out to bridge backward into a narrative of the past[28] and forward, not toward a narrative of the future, not toward a predestined this-will-happen, but toward a sense of the possibilities that may be realized in the futures of the three central characters and the surrounding chorus of Dubliners. In that time-future, Stephen may become the literary artist he aspires to be; the Blooms may experience the slow coil of reconciliation; Ireland may, in the words of Thomas Osborne Davis, become "a nation once again"; but none of these futures is certain. In its double time frame, *Ulysses* imitates at once a day in the lives of its central characters and ten years of those lives.

The night of *Finnegans Wake* shares (without the emphasis on indwelling clocks) the one-day dimension of *Ulysses,* but the infolded temporal dimensions of that one night are not confined to ten-plus years of before and after. That one night encompasses the entire round of human history in the *ricorso,* the told-over-and-over rosary of the Viconian cycles. The night of *Finnegans Wake* predates the eighth-century *Book of Kells,* and it predates the night of the wake of Finn MacCool, the semilegendary third-century Irish giant and hero, and it includes among its recurrent falls that of Adam and Eve and of the Tower of Babel. The all-inclusive embrace of that one night resembles in its superepic scale the idealized Easter season* in the course of which Dante's journey through hell, purgatory, and heaven is accomplished in *La Divina Commedia.*

Ulysses and *Finnegans Wake* are both shaped by Joyce's profound skepticism of Romantic time. In both works, the

---

*Dante's journey begins "in a dark wood where the straight way was lost" on the night of Maundy Thursday in 1300 and ends as the sun sets in Jerusalem on the following Thursday.

rhythms of time never escape this small parenthesis or aspire to transcend "the fact of vital growth, through convulsions of metamorphosis, from infancy through maturity to decay." In the indifferent reaches of "the cold of interstellar space," human life is and remains "a parenthesis of infinitesimal brevity."[29] The day of *Ulysses* and the night of *Finnegans Wake* affirm their own limitations as parentheses, even as one day and one night can enfold the entire parenthesis of an individual life and, given a nine-billion-year-old universe, the not appreciably larger parenthesis of human history.

By contrast, Romantic time rests on the coordinated assumptions that past experience can be fully remembered and repeated in the future and that such repetition will at some point be realized as a radically expanded and enriched time-present. In the present tense of our fallen, state, memory has, of course, its limitations; it is not so much recall of the what-was as it is reconstruction and fabrication of the what-must-have-been.[30] Romantic time imagines those limitations as set aside in favor of the idealization of past moments of intensity. Those moments, once poeticized, are projected into the future and anticipated as points of rendezvous, those luminous moments when, it is hoped, time-present will enjoy all the poetic resonance that can be packed into time-past.

The flaw in the poetics of Romantic time is implicit in the time frames of Thoreau's *Walden.* The awakening at Walden Pond didn't take place in the present tense of the life lived there (from July 1845 to September 1847) but in the present tense of the book (1854). The book appears to imitate life at the pond but in actuality creates that life. Thoreau himself became increasingly aware of this flawed relation between present and past and repeatedly complains after 1854 about the inadequacy of the poetics of time-present.

> I would fain make two reports in my Journal, first the incidents and observations of today; and by to-morrow I

review the same and record what was omitted before, which
will often be the most significant and poetic part. I do not
know at first what it is that charms me. The men and things
of today are wont to lie fairer and truer in to-morrow's
memory.[31]

In the opening volume of *Remembrance of Things Past,*
Proust undertakes an exhaustive exploration of the limits of the
present tense of Romantic time and the perpetual miscarriage of
anticipations based on the idealization of memories that don't
enjoy the immediacy of involuntary memory but are the intellectual constructs of what Proust calls "the voluntary memory,"[32]
memory that is summoned by an act of will rather than a memory
that is a spontaneous upwelling of recall. Proust's distinction
implies that something forced and superficial (antipoetic) results
from voluntary (willed) memory, as against the rich exfoliation
of imagery consequent on those rare moments when memory
presents something of "the past itself," as with the much-quoted
crumb of madeleine soaked in tisane.

The paradox involved in the Romantic dream of a time-
present that enfolds and thus transcends both past and future is
focused in another way in Faulkner's *The Sound and the Fury*
through Quentin Compson's desire to realize in time-future a
violation of such enormity—a classical incest and a Wagnerian
love death with his sister—that it will transcend time, just as the
permanent mark of a Greek tragedy transcends time. Instead,
what Quentin achieves in his suicide is, metaphorically, not a big
splash but silent immersion in the backward-flowing stream of
time.

The final irony of the assumptions of Romantic time (assumptions that are still around as common sense to infect our expectations) is that they not only render the future an elsewhere but
also make past and present elsewheres in their turn. We can
photograph and record visual and aural images from the elsewhere of the immediate past and reproduce them in time-present,

but they remain images of an elsewhere we cannot relive, even though we can store seemingly inexhaustible archives of the elsewheres of time-past against the elsewheres of time-future.

There may be reassurance, if not cure, in the metaphors of other traditions. "In the mountains [of the Haute-Savoie]," according to John Berger, "the past is never behind, it's always to the side."[33] And one Amazonian people imagine the future as behind their backs, approaching unseen, while the past is in front of them, where they can at least imagine themselves as seeing clearly.

INTERLUDE. David Jones said that his prose poem *In Parenthesis* was not a war book. At first glance, the parenthesis seems, however, that of the Great War and the poem is apparently "about" experience of the war from the perspectives of a private soldier and his Anglo-Welsh infantry platoon. But the parenthesis of the war expands to include the time necessary for the experience of war to become ingested and known and realized as poetry, a parenthesis that doesn't end until publication of the book in 1937. The parenthesis is also Browne's small parenthesis, that of Jones's life (1896–1974). And, in retrospect, the period between the two world wars acquires status as a parenthesis. In the late 1930s, from the point of view of a reasonably anxious survivor-observer of the first war, the parenthesis that followed the pause of 1918 was all too obviously about to be closed.

Early in the poem, the central character John Ball,* on the eve of his platoon's first tour of duty in the trenches, has a concentrated anticipation of time-future.

*John Ball is the namesake of the English priest (executed 15 July 1381) from Colchester whom Froissart called "the mad priest of Kent" and whose preaching prepared the popular mind for Wat Tyler's rebellion (1381). Ball's favorite sermonological text: "Whan Adam delft and Eve span / Who was then a gentle-manne?"

Moving into the line. It had all the unknownness of something of immense realness, but of which you lack all true
perceptual knowledge. Like Lat. 85° N.—men had returned
and guaranteed you a pretty rum existence. The drifting
unwholesomeness of incinerator smoke hurt his eyes, in
which superficial discomfort the conjectured miseries of the
next day and tomorrow lost themselves.[34]

Latitude 85° north draws a circle with a radius of approximately
350 miles around the North Pole; within that circle is a wasteland
of ice field, less familiar to David Jones in 1937 than it is to us in
the 1980s, now that we know it to be one of those places where
nuclear submarines lurk and play.

That wasteland can in turn remind us of what nuclear weapons themselves, or rather the fact and anxiety of their existence,
have done to time in our time. As Martin Amis has written,

The past and the future equally threatened, equally cheap-
ened, now huddle in the present. The present feels narrower
. . . straitened, discrepant.[35]

Apart from the possibility of nuclear immolation of the Earth
and human time, there are the extraordinary ways in which
industrialized-consumerized humanity has, in its preoccupation
with immediate gratification and immediate profit, hastened the
processes of evolution: expending in days the solar energy that
took millenia to store in the Earth's horde, destroying ecosystems
in weeks that took an ice age to evolve, accelerating the processes
of extinction with use-it-up technology and pollution, speeding
the processes of mutation (and speciation) through radioactive
contamination.

Thus, though we cannot make our sun
Stand still, yet we will make him run.[36]

And dance to a faster, more exciting, more frenetic beat of time.

What then is time? If no one asks me, I know what it is. If I
wish to explain it to him who asks me, I do not know.

Saint Augustine

THE ECONOMICS OF TIME. Turning from the poetics of time to
the proposition that time is money, I am closer to the assumption
that time (whatever it is) is that which is measured by clocks,
closer to the assumption that man is a time-factoring animal and
that calendars and clocks are the basic tools of that factoring. In
Gulliver's Travels, the Lilliputian officers who inventory the con-
tents of Gulliver's pockets come to the conclusion that Gulliver's
pocket watch is

> the god that he worships . . . because he assured us . . . that
> he seldom did anything without consulting it. He called it
> his oracle, and said it pointed out the time for every action
> of his life.

Gulliver's slavish dependence on his watch might have made
sense for the timing of sailors on watch at sea, but it would have
appeared far more eccentric to Swift and his contemporaries than
it does to us. Gulliver ashore would have been moving in a world
where clocks, let alone pocket watches, were notoriously undependable and time anything but fixed or standardized.* But Gulliver, whose mental processes are entirely governed by a bureau of
weights and measures, locates everything in the landscape of his
experience by the measuring rod, the scales, and the clock. He is,
in effect, an early manifestation of utilitarian, industrialized man,
the rhythms and the time of his life governed by mechanisms that
one hopes, he could (but doesn't) resist or control.

By the early nineteenth century, when the transforming
effect of the industrial revolution began to be felt in England, the

---

*Chronometers accurate enough to provide a basis for the determination of
longitude were not developed until the 1760s, by John Harrison (1693–1776).

clock had become the measure of the laborer's time. In an essentially agrarian economy, time and the work it measures tend to be patterned by the biological rhythms of domestic animals and by the seasonal rhythms of crops. Those rhythms can be taskmasters as demanding and unrelenting as any clock, but they also have a natural logic that makes the demand comprehensible. If rain threatens, the cured hay must be brought to the mow; if the cow calves at midnight, she must be attended; if the farm-house clock stops, no matter, it can be reset by referring to the sunrise and sunset times listed in the *Farmers' Almanac* (founded in Dublin, New Hampshire, in 1792 by Robert B. Thomas and published annually ever since). Clock time didn't matter all that much anyway. Gilbert White almost never mentions hours and minutes in the *Naturalist's Journal,* even though the column for entries on temperature was divided into hours. He prefers morn-ing, afternoon, and evening as times of the day. On 20 March 1784, he made an exception, "at 9 in the morning," because it was cold (29 degrees Fahrenheit) that late in the season and so long after sunrise.

In a mercantile economy, however, time is more clock dependent. The clock monitors the schedule of appointments and transactions, but time determined by a town clock with a healthy bell is sufficient for that dependency; the merchant arriving from out of town can readily adjust to local time. The work the mercantile clock measured was somewhat more regular, less subject to seasonal variation than the rhythms of the agrarian world, but trade and commerce still have their seasons. In an industrial community, when the factory clock takes over, the work day is even less subject to seasonal variation, particularly when steam power compensates for or replaces the seasonal irregularities of water power. Time, measured by the factory clock and whistle, relinquishes its bio-logic, and becomes the coinage, money for worker and employer alike, whether the relation is determined by daily or hourly wage or by piecework.

In the 1830s and 1840s, when the railroad and telegraph

suddenly sprang up between the factory towns, time was further transformed, both in the way it was clocked and the way it was experienced. Once established, factory time-as-money invited legislation. Congress limited the work week to fifty-four hours at not less than $4.40 per week after the Bread and Roses Strike of 1912 in Lawrence, Massachusetts. Overtime (for higher wages) was brought under control, and the machine-made concept of time off was invented, on its way to becoming vacation with pay. These concepts were possible in the factory, but not on the farm. Cows don't rest on Sunday.

From their beginning, the railroads required a standardization of time to provide schedules for both travelers and railroad employees. All the station clocks on a given line had to keep the same time, and time checks by telegraph could accomplish that and set the time of the railroad's home or terminal city as the operative time for all the other stations. This worked fairly well within the confined and London-dominated spaces of England, and Greenwich Time evolved quite naturally from the international mariner's standard into the national standard for England. But in North America, confusion was the rule when two or more lines from different terminal cities met in another city or town. Some cities (Cincinnati, for one) wound up trying to tell time by as many as five different clocks, varying by as much as one and a half to two hours. Out of this confusion came the 1882 Prime Meridian Conference in Washington, D.C., and the development of a world system of standard time based on Greenwich Mean Time. The United States and Canada standardized in 1883; the rest of the world had followed suit, piecemeal, by 1904.

The standardization of time encouraged by the needs of the railroads and the communities they brought together was made feasible by the virtually instantaneous electronic communication of the telegraph. Standardization has, in turn, been enormously reinforced by the advent of radio and television, the electronic networks that do so much to determine the time rhythms in which we live. These networks have potentially disorienting arrhythmic effects. The continental United States is divided into four times zones, only one of which is Washington, D.C./New York City prime time. Several hours to the north, I live comfortably, without thinking much about it, in that prime-time zone unless brought up short by concern that my sunrise doesn't match sunrise in Boston or Chicago or that projections of national election winners announced in East Coast prime time might well influence West Coast voters, their polls still open in their pre-prime-time zones. China, to present the exception that proves the rule, has lumped its five geographical hour bands into one national time zone (for the convenience of bureaucracy rather than of television).

Conceivably, no matter what the clock says, we should be able to set and follow the rhythms of our own daily ways, but that's not as easy as it sounds, given our dependencies. We could standardize like China and make what would strike us as fantastic local exceptions, or we could revert and adjust our clocks town by town so that time zones dissolved; wherever we were when the sun was at its zenith, it would be high noon. When it was noon in Washington, D.C., it would be 12:12 P.M. in New York City; 12:24 P.M. in Boston; and 12:15:15 here in Williamstown. Noon in Dublin would be 12:25 P.M. in London, as it was on 16 June 1904. Theoretically, we would be localized, in sync at last with our diurnal rhythms. In practice, we'd wind up with dozens of different clocks cluttering our houses, one for each of the radio and television stations on our dials, one for each of the transportation facilities nearby. And we would be farther than ever from any sense of the electronic marketplace, that placeless, two-dimensional time-screen over which (or behind which) money rolls around the world by satellite to be omnipresent where the money-marketers and their computers are always awake. Or would we be paradoxically nearer than ever to one universal time in which time would be money?

Our time rhythms are constantly being modified, sometimes by things as apparently simple as the recent change in fashion from clock dial to digital display. That change substitutes what sounds like numerical precision, "It's 4:46," for the less precise spatial designation, "It's quarter to five." This new specificity can be brushed off—who wants to know that it's 4:46?—but there may be something more subtle in the shift of metaphors. The appearance of numerical precision and the widely advertised accuracy of timepieces based on quartz crystals seems symptomatic of the false hope that because we are increasingly capable of precise measurements of time, we are increasingly capable of the management of time.

The precision is certainly there in the wonderfully sophisticated technology of ephemeris time (a measure defined by the orbital motion of the planets), which guides Voyager II past Uranus toward Neptune, and in the cesium clocks, which mark the nanoseconds that aid the atomic physicist's exploration of time among the particles. But when that capacity for astronomical and subatomic precision intrudes into the world of our everyday clocks and stopwatches, the result is frequently blur and obfuscation rather than precision and focus. When I read that an Olympic downhill skier has bettered his rival by three-hundredths of a second, I pause. I know that no hand-held stopwatch could reliably measure that split-second interval. And I know that I can't count three-hundredths of a second, that my eye cannot catch more than three or four of the hundredths as they tumble by on my stopwatch each second, just as I couldn't possibly count an ephemeris second (1/31,556,925.9747 of the tropical year for epoch 1900 January 0). I can imagine the interval between the first and second skiers only as a photo finish, a photographic juxtaposition of bodies fixed in a two-dimensional spatial instant at the finish line. But that image won't do because they race against the clock (and quartz time), not against each other in space. It also won't do because the interval I can't see to count is not the interval of victory but of accident—a hiccup produced by a pebble of snow or a puff of crosswind or a misplaced arm at the moment of the electronic eye. This year's random three-hundredth seconds awaits next year's three-thousandth seconds of downhill accident. But what is to become of the synapse that can't count three-hundredth seconds when it is faced with the sea-skimming missile, spotted on radar six seconds from impact, six seconds for the multisecond chain from radar operator to bridge to weapons system to firebreak—or *impact*—the suicide squeeze being urged upon our so-called national defense by the computerized time in which sophisticated weapons systems have their being. And it is in that computerized time that the Iranian airbus is mistaken for a hostile fighter and shot down over the Persian Gulf in July 1988.

This romance with precision in the timing of human events lurks behind that singularly opaque and Newspeak phrase broadcast into the language of current events during the Watergate controversy: *at that point in time* or *at this point in time*, as if there could imaginably be such a thing as a linear geometry of time and thus a point, "a dimensionless geometric object having no property but location."[37] Given the multidimensional nature of mnemonic time, how can there be any such thing as dimensionless? And what could the sole property of location mean but a memory-blank, which in fact is what the phrase in the months of the Watergate principals frequently *indicated.*

As metaphor, point-in-time came to suggest the mechanization of time and memory by film and tape recording. Thus the phrase could mean "in those two or three frames of film" or "in that brief segment of tape," as though events arranged themselves as a linear sequence of freeze-frames, freeze-syllables, instead of being submerged, as in George Eliot's phrase, "heavily in a dim and clogging medium."[38]

But when point-in-time surfaced to permeate NASA's public discussion of the *Challenger* disaster in 1986, the opacity of the phrase became positively sinister. Did *at that point in time* mean *at that moment in the trajectory?* Had the phrase become in-house jargon for what should be the agency's understandable preoccupation with the ballistic precision of the flight paths of its space vehicles? But then we were told that sensing devices on the *Challenger* were transmitting forty thousand bytes of data per second to monitoring devices on the ground: in seventy-two-plus seconds of flight, more than 2,880,000 bytes of data. To seek point-in-time in that welter of data became the search for a single, isolable cause—dimensionless, its sole property location—unattached by the usual mess of ganglia that entangle events in the dim and clogging medium of our experience. Point-in-time suddenly dissolved in that medium of discrete bytes to end again and again in rerun: images of that blur of explosion.

With the jargon and illusion of point-in-time, we have come full circle, with a vengeance, to William James's discussion of "the *specious* present":

> In short, the practically cognized present is no knife-edge, but a saddle-back, with a certain breadth of its own on which we sit perched, and from which we look in two directions into time. The unit of composition of our perception of time is a *duration*, with a bow and a stern, as it were—a rearward- and a forward-looking end. It is only as parts of this *duration-block* that the relation of *succession* of one end to the other is perceived. We do not first feel one end and then feel the other after it, and from the perception of the succession infer an interval of time between, but we seem to feel the interval of time as a whole, with its two ends embedded in it. The experience is from the outset a synthetic datum, not a simple one; and to sensible perception its elements are inseparable, although attention looking back may easily decompose the experience, and distinguish its beginning from its end.[39]

In the present tense of personal time, the seventy-year-old author looks at the photograph of the chubby two-and-a-half-year-old (seated, hands firmly on knees, eyes front) and knows that it is he at two and a half because the handwriting on the back of the photograph says so. The writing also details time and place, but memory calmly refuses anything but a general recognition of the place, refuses utterly the before, during, and after of that point in time—which is not a point at all but a locus clustered around the impact of light on sensitized film for one-thirtieth of a second, a saddle-back that includes in its configuration the time required to place the child's chair in a sunny angle of the house, to set up the pose and peer through the viewfinder, to develop and print the film and compose the inscription. Not a point in time at all but a locus or duration block that includes overlapping phases in the times of several lives—the child's and the photographer's and the anonymous darkroom drudge's who made the print and the mother's who wrote the inscription.

These precisions that claim to measure human gestures in hundredths of a second and to explain complex events as a geometry of points in time are misleading metaphors, misplaced exactitudes. How much more apt is Coleridge's "palimpsest tablet of memory" and those metaphors of mnemonic and experiential time as a stream, all its moments in peristaltic flux, "backward as well as forward sluing"[40]—a time that will accommodate Gertrude Stein's definition of consciousness, "a space of time, filled, always filled with moving."

What has changed so strikingly since 1798 is the interrelationship between time and space. Consider travel through space. In 1798, distance seemed a constant. Travel on land was by walking, horseback, or horse-drawn vehicle—all dependent on the bio-rhythms of organisms (horses, donkeys, camels, human beings) that get tired and have to be rested and fed. A healthy human being can comfortably walk fifteen to twenty miles a day, depending on the terrain and the weight of his or her pack. In 1798, sustained travel on horseback (using a single animal) could accomplish forty or fifty-odd miles in a day, and, given decent roads, much the same distance could be accomplished by chaise (a light horse-drawn vehicle). Travel by post chaise (using a relay of someone else's horses) could be considerably faster—one hundred miles in a day was not uncommon.*

In the early nineteenth century, with frequent changes of horses and over much-improved roads, the London-to-Liverpool mail coach, the pride of the English postal service, made the 205-mile run in twenty-four hours, averaging eight and a half miles per hour. Fine, provided one could stand the coach-sickness, as Gilbert White could not. (No wonder Dickens's male characters consistently seek seats on top, out in the fresh air.) There were, of course, stunts like the Pony Express (1860–61). With relays of riders and horses, the express carried the mail from St. Joseph, Missouri, to Sacramento, California, on an eight-day schedule. Over the nearly fifteen hundred miles, the couriers apparently averaged twelve to fourteen miles per hour. That speed was demanded, or at least paid for, by a people already hooked on a timespace that, east of St. Joseph, had been transformed into near-immediacy by the telegraph and by overnight railroad delivery of the mail. Appropriately, the Pony Express was discontinued in October 1861 when the Pacific Telegraph Company completed its line—which the Plains Indians called the singing wires—to California.

Numbers of this sort are just estimates, subject to all sorts of exceptions and variations. But what was land travel like in 1798? In Williamstown, 1984, we're used to a New York City that is three and a half hours away by private automobile. If we traveled that distance on horseback, the city would be three and a half or four days away (thirty-six times "farther" than it is by car); on foot, ten days away. At first, we might imagine the walk or the

---

*In *Pride and Prejudice,* Elizabeth Bennet and her aunt and uncle Gardiner, spurred by the scandal of her sister's elopement, travel the hundred-plus miles from the vicinity of Chatsworth in Derbyshire to the fictional Longbourn in Hertfordshire in a little over twenty-four hours. They leave between eleven o'clock and noon and, "sleeping one night on the road, reached Longbourn by dinner-time [four or five o'clock] the next day." This was, as Jane Austen's narrator remarks, traveling "as expeditiously as possible."

ride as a marathon of monotony and impatience. But that could hardly have been the case when one was in the midst of it. One must have settled into a rhythm, the mind and eye busy with a passing scene rich in complex detail unavailable to us in our glass and steel cocoons at sixty miles per hour. There must have been time for interior voices and tunes, time for Montaigne's wonderful complaint:

> But I am dissatisfied with my mind in that it usually brings forth its profoundest ideas, as well as its maddest and those I like best, unexpectedly, and when I least look for them, for they will instantly vanish if I have no means at hand for fixing them; on horseback, at table, in bed, but mostly on horseback, where my thoughts wander most widely.[41]

In 1798, the traveler must have assumed that his pace was much the same as that of an "antique Roman"; he must have assumed that "distance was a constant,"[42] now as then. And the rhythms of staying awhile once he reached his destination must have been quite different from ours, somehow coordinated with the pace and rhythms of his travel. While we think nothing of exchanging the seven-hour round-trip drive to New York City for a weekend's stay, the rate of exchange must have been quite different in that other rhythm. In *Pride and Prejudice,* Sir William Lucas, one of the minor characters, visits Mrs. Collins, his recently married daughter, two comfortable post-chaise days away from his home near the Bennets. The narrative voice remarks that "Sir William staid only a week," implying that the visit was short, given its purpose (to see for himself how well his daughter was settled). And Lady Catherine de Bourgh, one of the prideful fools, complains to Elizabeth Bennet, who is also visiting Mrs. Collins, that the six weeks of her visit seem two weeks less than would have been expected—a foolishness and an impertinence but nevertheless a measure of the expectations of time. Later in the novel, when Elizabeth and her aunt and uncle Gardiner are on a tourist ramble, they settle in a Derbyshire village near Chatsworth and, though interrupted, were obviously prepared to spend not a few 1984 hours but five or six days inspecting "all the principal wonders" of the surrounding countryside.

I get a glimpse of what that pace of life, that way of inhabiting timespace must have been like when I think of the Wordsworths (William and his sister Dorothy) in 1797–98 when Wordsworth and Coleridge embarked on the collaboration that resulted in the publication of *Lyrical Ballads*. To be near Coleridge, the Wordsworths moved from Racedown in Dorset to Alfoxden House in the Quantock Hills in Somerset, only four miles to the north over those steep-shouldered hills from Nether Stowey where Coleridge lived. Coleridge and the Wordsworths were together almost every day—an eight-mile round trip for one or the other, and apparently in any sort of weather. Once together, they often continued to walk, rambling the countryside equipped with campstools and notebooks. Not that the neighbors regarded their behavior as entirely normal. They were fond of walking at night as well as by day, and that, together with the notebooks and Dorothy's gypsy tan (white skin was the middle-class fashion) and the Wordsworths' north-country accents (foreign, by George!), was strange enough to arouse the countryside and bring down an undercover agent named Walsh from the Home Office in London to find out if they were French spies gathering intelligence for an invasion.

In spite of the eccentric nature of their behavior, they give me a glimpse of a profoundly different attitude toward the rhythms of life on foot. If I were on foot (and there were no telephone) and my collaborator lived four miles away in South Williamstown, how different the timespace of this town would be. I think of myself as spatially and temporally liberated by the everyday technologies at hand, but my freedom means that the rhythms of my experience are in a different sort of bondage. Of course I can choose to walk, but that is perverse choice rather than unquestioning acceptance of a given. In 1798, I would have been bound to the rhythm of walking but free to observe the intimate textures of the space around me and to inhabit the rhythms of my own thoughts and conversation. Conversely, I am free to overleap the four miles to South Williamstown but bound because I cannot more than glance at what I'm overleaping. When a shrike chases a crow through the boughs of an apple tree as I pass at fifty-five miles per hour, I can't pause to be sure it's a shrike, to witness the action and its denouement, to savor the excitement of that event. And at fifty-five miles per hour, the rhythms of my thoughts cannot be as regular as walking or breathing because driving requires some concentration. I must be alert because the exceptional (and potentially accidental) can happen so quickly.

Thoreau plays with trade-offs of this sort in *Walden.* A neighbor encourages him to take the train from Concord to Fitchburg (twenty-five miles to the west) in order to "see the country." Thoreau reflects that it would take a day's labor to earn the fare to Fitchburg and that he could just as easily walk there in a day. A day's labor would dull the mind; a day's walk would free the mind for observation and contemplation. In sum, "I have learned that the swiftest traveller is he who goes afoot."[43] The economics of speed are of course being measured here in terms of how rapidly one approaches the goal of the life of the mind, consciously sustained. In 1984, I cannot but assume that long hours on foot or horseback would have encouraged one to attend to the rhythms and tunes in one's head—what better to do than compose poems or listen to pre-Walkman music. But it should be said that not all is lost: given the different, mechanical, and irregular rhythms of driving, one can learn the discipline of a sort of set-aside concentration on the driving that leaves the mind free for some of its own tunes and rhythms—provided, of course, that radio or tape deck doesn't usurp the silence. In Faulkner's *Light in August,* the central choric character, Byron Bunch, says of a particularly mindless young man,

> He puts me in mind of one of these cars running along the street with a radio in it. You can't make out what it is saying

and the car aint going anywhere in particular and when you
look at it close you see that there aint even anybody in it.[44]

But there is still something to be said for Edith Wharton's observation that, after the tyranny of the railroad train and the ocean
liner (and the airliner she never knew), "the motor car has
restored the romance of travel."

Travel on water in 1798 would have been by sails or oars or
paddles or poles in boats or canoes, or in canal boats drawn by
draft animals, or on barges or rafts propelled downriver by
currents. There is a muscular rhythm in propelling craft by oars
or paddles or poles akin to that involved in walking or riding
horseback. Drifting downriver on a raft or under sail in open
water, there is still dependency on the seasonal rhythms of the
river or the variations of winds and currents and tides at sea. For
passengers on water (not those who propelled themselves), the
change to continuous mechanical motion might not have been as
striking as it was on land. Once steam became dependable at sea,
the pace of travel could be steady, not subject to as much
interruption by shifts of wind and currents or by being becalmed.
But there is still a similarity between the rhythms imparted by
waves to the sailing ship and the steamship—and a marked
dissimilarity between the irregular motion of the saddle horse or
horse-drawn vehicle on uneven roads and the train's continuous
mechanical motion over well-laid rails, which is in turn similar to
the smoothness of travel by canal boat. An aside: It is interesting
that, for several decades, steamships settled for speeds that were,
by several knots, less spectacular than those achieved and sustained by the clipper ships and their descendents, the Down-
Easters. Apparently, the regular schedules and increased tonnage
that the steamships could promise were preferable to the speed
records that those man-killers, the clippers, could set.

Out of all this technological transformation of the worlds of time
and space rises a complex of unanswerable questions. When and

how did the speed-up occur? Did the impulse to beat time by speeding up the pace of travel and communication predate the speed-up and demand invention of the technologies that made the speed-up possible? Did the technological explosion coincide with and interpenetrate the speed-up in a tangle of reciprocities? Or did the technological change predate the desire for speed and drag the all-too-Western desire to beat time along in its expanding wake? Never mind the Arab proverb that haste is from the Devil.

To look for answers to these questions on the farther shore of the eighteenth century is to discover not so much a desire to increase the speed of travel and communication as a desire to smooth the way, to make travel easier and more comfortable, to make the delivery of letters and messages more regular, more frequent, more dependable.

In Great Britain, in the course of the eighteenth century, both passenger travel and shipping by water increased enormously. Coastal shipping grew at an impressive rate as did shipping on inland waterways. By 1725, the network of improved and therefore navigable rivers in England was so extensive that "few people now lived more than 15 miles from a waterway." Beginning in the late 1750s, "canal fever"[45] accomplished a further and extensive elaboration of inland waterways. Not that most travel by canal was a speed-up; it moved at the pace of the draft animal on the towpath. But it was smooth and comfortable and free of the dust that so troubled travelers on summer roads.* Passengers could move about and stretch their legs, free of the wretched confinement of the coach, and would arrive at their destinations rested and unshaken. Goods could be transported with far less danger of breakage; and, given their eighty-ton capacity, eighteenth-century canal barges made possible the transport of the

---

*Gilbert White wrote to his niece Molly, 9 April 1781, to announce the proposal of a canal from the vicinity of London to Alton, a few miles north of Selborne, and the prospect of comfortable, dust-free travel. Holt-White, *Life and Letters of Gilbert White*, 2: 69.

heavy loads of coal and ore and bricks and machines that fueled the industrial revolution.

During the same decades in Great Britain, and well before the advent of the steam locomotive, the railroad was being developed, primarily for heavy transport in and around industrial and mining centers. On iron rails "a horse could pull a load three times heavier than on an ordinary road."[46] By 1816, there were approximately 228 miles of railroad track in and around Newcastle, and there were similar systems around the ports of Cardiff and Swansea in Wales and around Edinburgh and Glasgow in Scotland.[47]

In the course of the eighteenth century, there was also a road- and bridge-building revolution in Great Britain and Western Europe. Improvements in design and in building materials (though macadamizing wasn't introduced until 1815) and in maintenance produced "new roads capable of taking 'carriages at full gallop.' "[48] Roads were opened into and through areas previously accessible only on foot or horseback and by pack animals. For example, the Brenner Pass, connecting Austria and Italy over the main spine of the Alps, was opened to carriage traffic in the summer of 1772. Better roads were matched in turn by improvements in carriage design—lighter carriages with much better suspension thanks to Henry Mill's carriage spring (1706) and subsequent developments. As roads and carriages improved, the number of staging posts increased, toward a post every twenty miles on well-traveled roads. The quality of the posts and their horses and drivers improved, and during the closing decades of the century, the great age of the highwaymen (the criminal elite of the time) began to wane.

Horse breeding also made a difference. The eighteenth century witnessed the commercialization of the sport of horse racing and a rapid rise in the demand for fast young horses. But speed-horses were for luxury and sport, less important for travel than horses with the stamina to maintain a good steady pace for the average twenty miles between staging posts. It was a breeding competition in which the Cleveland Bay won top honors. The end result was that "the period 1700–1840 was the true age of the horse."[49]

All these improvements transformed travel on land. They "had cut sometimes by half the time taken to travel across France between 1765 and 1780."[50] Much the same transformation took place in England. In 1715, the average trip by coach from London to Gloucester (105 miles) took five days.

> By 1800 all towns south of the Trent and east of the Severn were within a comfortable day's journey from London, whereas in 1700 it had taken three days to reach the city from Southampton [seventy-nine miles].[51]

The road-building revolution was achieved with extraordinary speed, capped by inauguration of the great age of the English mail coach (Bristol-Bath-London, 1784; the London-to-Liverpool coach, a scheduled 205 miles in twenty-four hours, by 1800).

Paul Valéry's dictum that Napoleon moved no faster than Caesar needs to be qualified. Napoleon did move faster than Caesar, not because Western European roads in 1798 were better than Roman roads, but because there were so many more of them, improved roads and bridges in a well-maintained network. Moreover, Napoleon was adept at dividing his army into travel units dispatched to live off the land along a number of different routes and timed to arrive simultaneously at a concentration point chosen to embarrass the enemy with the magic of an army that seemed to move with incredible speed, if not to materialize out of thin air. Among other things, it was this magic with roads that deserted Napoleon in the 1812 invasion of Russia. The road- and bridge-building revolution hadn't reached the great spaces east of the Niemen, so Napoleon's advance was slowed to Caesar's pace: one road, one vulnerable line of communication. In October, when his bid to retreat south and west from Moscow along the Kalúga Road toward Kiev was frustrated by the drawn battle of

Málo-Yaroslávets, his only line of retreat lay along the devastated Smolensk-Moscow road by which he had come. Napoleon had left the early nineteenth-century landscape of Western Europe to invade what was in effect the early seventeenth-century landscape of Russia. That landscape, with considerable help from the Russian armies, the weather, and the indiscipline of the French and their allies on the march, spelled disaster.

Historically, the considerable (and what hindsight might see as premonitory) improvements in travel in the eighteenth century did little to prepare the Western world for the advent of travel by continuous mechanical motion. The change from the old bio-rhythms, when it came, seemed not only unprecedented and sudden, but a fever, noisy and inescapable, troubling and exciting. In 1833, Wordsworth celebrated the beginning of the transformation in the sonnet "Steamboats, Viaducts, and Railways." He acknowledges that these new presences may "mar / The loveliness of Nature" and be "at war / With old poetic feeling." Nevertheless, as poet (laureate ten years later), he feels called upon to affirm the "prophetic sense of future change."

In 1837, the diarist Charles Greville recorded his first experience of railroad travel, which covered the ninety-four miles from Birmingham to Liverpool.

> Nothing can be more comfortable than the vehicle in which I was put . . . and there is nothing disagreeable about it but the occasional whiffs of stinking air which it is impossible to exclude altogether. The first sensation is a slight degree of nervousness and a feeling of being run away with, but a sense of security soon supervenes, and the velocity is de-lightful. Town after town, one park and *château* after another are left behind with the rapid variety of a moving panorama . . . very entertaining.[52]

After the return journey, he adds praises for the railroad's "exact punctuality which is rendered easy by the great reserved power of acceleration" and reports the trains capable of forty-five miles per hour, though they traveled at a moderate twenty to twenty-five miles per hour.

Upon the occasion of the completion of the first transcontinental railroad (and the Suez Canal, both 1869), Whitman could be even more celebratory of the world transformed by the triumphs of time over space.

> *Singing the great achievements of the present,*
> *Singing the strong light works of engineers,*
> *Our modern wonders, (the antique ponderous Seven*
> *   outvied,)*
> *In the Old World the east the Suez canal,*
> *The New by its mighty railroad spann'd,*
> *The seas inlaid with eloquent gentle wires.*[53]

Not everyone, of course, greeted the change with utilitarian or poetic delight. In England, John Ruskin lamented the cost of the world thus transformed, the mechanization of the human spirit. William Morris sought to escape his vision of the English Midlands ("six counties overhung with smoke") in poetry and organic, antimechanical design. There were doubters in America as well, Thoreau and Henry Adams among them; even Whitman in *Democratic Vistas* laments what he sees in the American republic as the spiritual shortfall of the new materialism. But whether the response to this world-transformation was enthusiasm, ambivalence, or loathing, the pace of it must have been simply staggering. In America, the railroads grew from twenty-three miles of line in 1830 to 30,600 miles in 1860; in the much more confined spaces of England, Scotland, and Wales, they grew from fifty-seven miles to 10,500 miles in the same decades.

Time's triumph over travel, beginning in the 1830s, was almost immediately topped by time's triumph over communications, the space that once limited the sending and receiving of messages largely to the pace of human travel, to messages hand-carried, to line-of-sight signals. At midcentury, in a print commemorating fifty years of progress, Currier and Ives feature the steam-driven printing press (1814), the railroad, and the electromagnetic telegraph. The combination of the high-speed printing press and high-speed distribution via the railways made possible the new communications networks of the big national monthly magazines, which began in both America and Great Britain in the 1840s. As for the telegraph, skilled operators could send and receive messages at speeds of up to twenty-five words per minute (which increased to forty after the invention and development of the typewriter in the 1870s and 1880s). The telegraph made it possible for the railways to establish and maintain their schedules, but far more importantly, it was to transform the timetables of domestic and international business and commerce, as it would transform the time it took to transmit the news. As a result, and somewhat more gradually, it changed the nature of the news itself.

The news involves not only the content of what one comes to know, but also how and how quickly one comes to know it. For example, Sir Robert Clive's victory at Plassey in Hindustan on 23 June 1757 was the virtual founding of the British Indian Empire. This news of extraordinary importance to the British economy and international power reached England (via the Cape of Good Hope) in February 1758. Closer to home, in 1773 Parliament and the Crown were groping toward a tighter and more authoritarian control of the American colonies. The result in the Massachusetts Bay Colony was a marked increase of general unrest, muttering and, climactically, the Boston Tea Party, 16 December 1773. News of that protest reached London over a month later, precluding any reaction specific to the event other than to take note of the protest and understand, or refuse, its significance. The before, during, and after of the occasion had been completed; the principals had long since retired peaceably to their homes and beds. In any case, the packet boat that brought the news from Boston would have been held up until after the occasion so that the report could be complete; in such a news transaction, a day or two hardly matters.

Conversely, the instant news to which our electronic timing has accustomed us frequently scores anticlimax. Imagine, for example, that an American journalist held as a spy (or simply as a hostage) in Moscow is released. That would constitute a major news story for that day, even if the story were still in its during phase, even if no one knew the conditions of the negotiated release or what sort of deal had been cut. The evening news would feature much discussion, most of it unfounded speculation, all of which might be rendered meaningless tomorrow or a week from tomorrow when the conditions of the deal were revealed. The joy of the during might sour in the balancing of accounts that constitutes the after, but the news of the day would have been served. Contrast this with the timetable of the Islamic fundamentalists who hold their hostages in the Beirut of the 1980s. Their skill at manipulating television news is not inconsiderable, but their clocks are those of the medieval Hashishin,* their forebears; the bargaining could go on for generations, as it did during the Crusades. The timetable of our attention is the twenty-four-hour span from evening news to evening news. Captured plus twenty-four hours equals off-screen, out of mind.

Trapped, General Burgoyne surrendered to Colonial forces at Saratoga on 17 October 1777. The news of that notable defeat (or success) reached London on 2 December, and it reached . Benjamin Franklin in Paris (where the news was to make a considerable difference) two days later. In the 1870s, the message would have been across the Atlantic in a matter of seconds. The

---

*The Hashishin (from whom our word assassins) were the fanatic hit men of the Isma'ilites, a branch of the Shi'ite sect. The Isma'ilites implemented their political policies by kidnapping and assassination and terrorized Asia Minor and Persia from the end of the eleventh to the middle of the thirteenth century. The Hashishin were given their orders (and the hashish after which they were named) by clerical students who answered to the Isma'ilite mullahs. Eventually, the counterterror of massacre put an end to the Isma'ilites and their Hashishin.

electronic news wouldn't have come as a thunderclap after long
silence; it would have been preceded by daily, hourly, even
minute-by-minute accounts of the two agonizing months that
Burgoyne and his forces spent in that cul-de-sac on the Hudson
River before the surrender.

But there are further complications. While that news was en
route to England, several members of Parliament were urging
with some success a moderate plan that would have conceded a
considerable measure of independence to the Colonies. An intelligent and well-intentioned plan, it came to nought, but it surely
would have been dismissed as treasonable compromise if daily
bulletins of Burgoyne's worsening situation had punctuated the
compromise proposals and the campaign in their support. And
would France, slowly responding to Franklin's charm and diplomacy, have been triggered into support by instant, dramatic news
of the surrender (after two months of the to and fro of daily
bulletins detailing Burgoyne's foundering), or was the slow coil
of event and news of event to the advantage of Franklin's diplomacy and the ultimate interest of the Colonies?

I wonder, for example, if a constitution for the United States
could have been achieved at the Constitutional Convention in
Philadelphia (1787) if each of the delegates from twelve of the
thirteen ex-Colonies had, at the least sign of disadvantage to the
interests of his state, been able to pop out into the hall and
telephone his home state for instructions? As it was, requests for
instructions were infrequent and took days to arrive by courier
or packet boat. Meanwhile, the discussions at the convention
proceeded both in heat and at leisure. One could argue that the
Constitution was achieved precisely because the delegates were
and remained discussants, partially incommunicado, not the
pawns of immediate instructions from the home office, not pulled
up short if a bright compromise occurred to them during a walk
in the woods.

That successful failure of communication has its converse. In
his *History of the United States during the Administration of*

Thomas Jefferson, Henry Adams remarks that many visitors to the new nation at the beginning of the nineteenth century formed "sober if not sad" impressions of the governability of the country. Even Jefferson, puzzling over the immense areas of sparsely populated interior, came to wonder whether "one government could comprehend the whole."[54] To compound that doubt, he negotiated the addition of the vast and unexplored expanse of the Louisiana Purchase in 1803. But this growth of territory and the westward drift of population were, in little more than three decades, to coincide with the revolution in timespace that would (in spite of the convulsions of sectional strife and civil war) make it possible for that one government, neither militant nor authoritarian,* to comprehend the whole.

In *Walden,* Thoreau was characteristically skeptical and witty about the revolutionary improvements promised by the telegraph.

> We are in great haste to construct a magnetic telegraph from Maine to Texas; but Maine and Texas, it may be, have nothing important to communicate.[55]

The wit resides in the way means (telegraph) and ends (communicating something important) jostle each another. That jostling continues into our own time. When the topic is communication, it is never easy to know whether the real topic is how to say something important and have it understood or yet another elaboration of technologies and facilities and jargons—courtesy of communications officers and departments and courses, communications rooms, communications centers with their organiza-

---

*The comparison to the vast (ungovernable?) spaces of czarist Russia was both frequent and popular, particularly after 1812.

tion charts and flowcharts and computers and scramblers and satellites and feedback loops and hundreds of millions of bytes of information.

When I try to imagine the impact of the opening phase of the triumph of time over space, the seismic heave of technological change between 1830 and 1860, I pause to wonder whether assimilation of and acculturation to that first phase was anything like complete or comfortable to live with while it was going on. For that matter, has it ever been complete or comfortable to live with any time since? It's fashionable nowadays to dismiss Thoreau as a neurotic and irresponsible malcontent. But each time I return to him, I become more sharply aware of his implicit feeling that something vast and unassimilable was passing, had passed, that the world was being, as David Jones put it, "metamorphosed by a technocracy the full ramification of which [he could not] and we cannot guess."[56]

In the years 1861–65, did anyone—with the possible exception of U. S. Grant—guess the full ramification of what the combination of railroad, steamship, and telegraph would do to upset Napoleonic assumptions about the nature and conduct of war? Did anyone realize that the concentrations of men and supplies achieved by the Union toward the end of the Civil War made it possible to abandon the concept of battle as a one- or two-day set piece in favor of continuous contact (the Wilderness campaign and after) that was perpetual battle, on its way toward the stalemate and carnage of World War I? Not until after World War I did military historians and students at European military academies begin to be curious about the Civil War and the generalship of Grant and Sherman and Lee—but by then it was too late to learn from that fall from innocence, and it was about to be too late to learn much from the parenthesis 1914–18, as the fall of the Maginot line in 1940 was to demonstrate.

It seems to me that we can still surprise in ourselves that

exciting and uncomfortable sense of assimilation still going on, acculturation by no means complete, especially when we are stationary people in an enclosed place such as this Williamstown or Gilbert White's Selborne or Thoreau's Walden Pond and Concord Village. Even if these changes had suddenly ceased in 1884, allowing us a century in which to take them all in, would our habituation to the altered timespace now be comfortable and complete? I doubt it, though nostalgia for the farther shore of 1884 and what we imagine to have been the agrarian simplicities of that remote time is easy to awaken.

A further question: How far is it in time from 1884 to 1984? The change in timespace between 1798 and 1884 was a change in kind, from biorhythms to mechanorhythms in travel, from some order of personal contact to quasi-instant electromagnetic communication. But it is also a long way from railroad trains at thirty or forty miles per hour on a confined track to the private automobile with all its speed and all the freedom of the paved highways (which, as Buckminster Fuller liked to point out, were the other half of the invention), from that to air travel by jet, by Concorde, by the Space Shuttle. It is much, much farther from the dots and dashes of Morse telegraphy to telephone, telex, radio, television, and fax. And it is an equally long way from the 1884 slow-time of memory and scholarship and calculation to the computerized fast-time of 1984. Feats of memory, of compilation and sorting and retrieval of data unimaginable in the great universities of 1884 are within reach of the schoolchild's keyboard in 1984; mathematical calculations that once would have taken weeks or months are available in seconds. So long are these ways from the slow of 1884 to the superfast of 1984, so great are the quantities involved, that the change in timespace may once again be not so much in degree as in kind, just as was the change between 1798 and 1884, another change so quantitatively great that it is qualitatively as hard to assimilate as the initial change was 150 years ago. For 150 years we have been and continue to be foreigners, aliens in a timespace continually accelerating in what seems a self-compounding technocracy of speed.

One way to focus this accelerating change in timespace is to consider what has happened to the present tense, that saddle-back on which people intuit themselves and their affairs and occasions to be taking place. Since the 1860s and the birth of modern journalism, time-present has been expanding. At first, that expansion was the result of the gradual realization that the news was being reported as bits of event in the now of yesterday or today rather than a summary of a whole pattern of event that had taken place in the elsewhere of last week or last month. As the present expanded, the elsewhere of the past began to seem farther off—in Joyce's mocking phrase, "Sufficient for the day is the newspaper thereof."[57] But for all its radical expansion of the present tense, the newspaper was still time-present through the indirection of hearsay. Radio offered the possibility of ear-witness, a further expansion of time-present; motion-picture newsreels added eye-witness (though after the fact) to the ear-witness. Television has topped them both with its illusion of immediacy.

The expansion of the present tense has gradually altered our sense of what constitutes an event (an occurrence of signifi-cance), and crisis has been redefined in our imaginations as something today-sudden, described at the White House as a firestorm, subject to immediate and "hopefully" one-day measures called damage control. The military imagery, itself unsettling, also implies explosive immediacy, as though an international crisis were to be comprehended only within the flight time of a barrage of nuclear missiles instead of through the complex web of na-tional interests at odds and the slow coil of information, misinfor-mation, opinion, and diplomacy.

In the realms where news is made, there are events that are considered unnewsworthy, in effect censored because they coil so slowly, because they happen not as action-news in the TV-present but as osmosis-news in what Gertrude Stein called the "continuous present" of individual or community consciousness.

Events are judged newsworthy if they fit, or can be crafted to fit, the TV-present and are often hard to distinguish from media events, those facts laced with fiction staged for and in the TV-present. Media events, cherished as they are by television, are hardly a television invention. They have a healthy legacy that includes one of the longest-running media events of our recent history: William F. "Buffalo Bill" Cody's Wild West Show. Organized in 1883, it continued until his death in 1917; its offspring (all claiming to be the original) survived as epilogues in the traveling circuses of the 1920s and 1930s. Buffalo Bill's show, itself a circus, was billed as "a representation of actual life on the plains," including trick riding, trick shooting, unbroken broncos, a herd of buffalo, and the excitement of hostilities: Indian villages and cavalry raids and appropriate Indian response, complete for a time with Sitting Bull himself as entertainer. All this began seven years after Custer's last stand on the Little Bighorn and seven years before the atrocity of Wounded Knee; a circus of fiction, dead center in a time of profoundly discomfiting, not to say nationally humiliating, historical fact.

In media events, the present tense as moral dimension (a space of time filled with rights and wrongs always moving) is flawed by the ambiguous relation between the event as staged and the event as history happening. In 1885, Buffalo Bill posed for a photographic portrait with Sitting Bull—the enemies reconciled for the purposes of show business—except that Sitting Bull was to disappear back into the turmoil of Indian unrest, white betrayal, the "Messiah" movement, and his death while "resisting arrest" at the hands of "forty-three Indian police—backed up by a detachment of one hundred soldiers and one or possibly two Hotchkiss guns [a light, single-barreled, rapid-fire field gun]."[58]

As more and more events crowd into the charmed circle of media events, the past recedes. The duration-block of present time expands, and the bow and stern of William James's metaphor fade into the mist. The pretelevision past becomes a bore of tell-

items. The United States becomes a nation without history inhabited by a history-blind people. The present as moral-duration is reserved for those who, in the continuing media coup of the 1980s, are dismissed as wimps by those who stand tall in the saddle-back of the historyless present.

These patterns seem to me to derive from a profound change in our sense of what constitutes an event and the timespace in which it occurs; thus a profound change in our perception of that succession called time; and thus a profound change in what was once assumed to be a sequential web of cause and effect in human affairs.

As the elsewhere of the past recedes beyond the far horizon, public events appear to be causeless, or so complexly deployed in the present as to be causeless, and we become vulnerable to simplistic comic-book assertions of timeless cause, inerrant truth in the Bible, original intention in the Constitution, the theological and moral infallibility of the teachings of the church; evil empires there, the golden age of faith here; "Up Rambo and at them!" In the arts, where the nowness we so need and admire is shaped out of the stuff of everything we know and can know as nature and the past, the overstated present tense encourages media stunts that are exclusively and all too mortally *now.*

The past, the time that houses those things we call and prize as antiques, has been accelerating toward and into the present. Once upon a time antiquities were relics or objects of ancient (Greco-Roman) art. That was true for Gilbert White who, when he was at work on *The Antiquities of Selborne,* thought he was stretching the definition by including things from the late Middle Ages. *The American Heritage Dictionary* (1970) updates that definition. An antique is "an object having special value because of its age; especially a work of art or handicraft that is over 100 years old." The United States Customs Service is inclined to agree; jewelry over one hundred years old is antique and therefore duty-free.

In the 1940s and early 1950s, antiques were things fashionably pre-Victorian. Suddenly things Victorian became fashionable; then things Edwardian; things post-Edwardian; and so into Andy Warhol and Ralph Lauren time where all our yesterdays house collectibles. As the past overtakes us on the saddle-back of the present, it is as though we were being crowded into life in the future (postmodern), beyond the present tense, outside the dimension of time.

And yet we are so preoccupied with measuring and keeping time that we read timetables into every nook and cranny of human history. Time-factoring (to keep time and thus to beat it) must, we speculate, account for the orientation of the pyramids at Giza and for the lithic patterns of Stonehenge. It must somehow account for those enigmatic armies of standing stones at Carnac in Brittany and for the engraved bone plaques of prehistoric man found in Zaire and in the Dordogne. They must, in their crude ways, have aspired to calendars and clocks like ours. Apparently, our perceptions are so saturated with timekeeping that we have trouble imagining the roots of civilization* as being anywhere other than in the mystery and science of time-factoring man. It is as though being outside the biorhythms of our earth and our lives we cannot imagine—without a great heave of effort—what being on the inside would be like.

Once the self-opening doors of the supermarket have welcomed us to that windowless, air-conditioned space, all sense of seasons and the seasonal has been left outside. In that timeless present, it is always all seasons, spring lamb and Thanksgiving turkey year-round. What was once the annual surprise of oranges for Christmas is forgotten in favor of an orange every day, with the result that most of us don't know what once were (and presumably still

---

*In *The Roots of Civilization* (New York, 1972), Alexander Marshack speculates that in time-factoring is to be found "the cognitive beginnings of man's first art, symbol and notation" (his subtitle).

are) the seasons of the fruits and vegetables and meats and fish that seem always available. Lost on us is the cruelty of that cruelest month, April, when what one had stored of last year's harvest would be running out, while nature greened with promise but couldn't be expected to deliver until its due season. The supermarket has brought to a sort of breathtaking perfection (Open Twenty-four Hours) the art of beating time.

4.
Quantity and Scale and the Confetti of Numbers
· · · · · · · · · · · · · · · · · ·

The more I explore provinces such as eye and ear, time and space, the more they seem to overlap and merge into one another. One moment I think I've detected discontinuity; the next I perceive interpenetration toward continuum (repetition with variations). So it goes with the province I want to explore in this essay: quantity and scale.

In the previous essays, the 1850s have seemed pivotal to the search for ways of imagining the distance to the farther shore of that arbitrary date, 1798, the year of *Lyrical Ballads* and of Thomas Malthus's *Essay on the Principle of Population.* One event that took place in the 1850s, that time between times, offers a concentrated metaphor for that distance: the Crystal Palace exhibition, held in London's Hyde Park from May through October 1851. Billed officially as "The Great Exhibition of the Works of Art and Industry of All Nations," it was intended as a celebration of the new all-encompassing cult emerging from the union of science, industry, and the arts, primarily the so-called practical arts. The success of the exhibition was a fitting tribute to the enterprise and vision of Queen Victoria's prince consort, Albert of Saxe-Coburg-Gotha.

During the planning phase, there occurred what can only be called a crisis of numbers. The expectation of overwhelming crowds of spectators gave rise to incredible and fanciful public anxieties. The exhibition would, some said, breed civil disorder, even irreversible revolution. Hyde Park would become "a bivouac of all the vagabonds of London." Others predicted that these vagabonds would be the riffraff from all of Europe, all of the empire. Some, whom Prince Albert ironically called mathematicians and political economists "prophesied a scarcity of food in London owing to the vast concourse of people"; those whom the Prince labeled doctors imagined that "owing to so many races coming into contact with each other, the Black Death of the Middle Ages would make its appearance as it did after the Crusades."[1]

This specter of the faceless hordes was by no means new. It was nurtured on the well-advertised excesses of the French Revolution and rekindled by the failed European revolutions of 1848. The fear that the floodgates would open and the hordes pour through to overwhelm social order was pandemic during the fifty-year debate over parliamentary reform that climaxed in passage of the Great Reform Bill of 1832. The bill temporarily suspended the debate by cautiously broadening the franchise to include men of the educated classes. Even after the predictions of the doomsayers of 1832 and the doctors and political economists of 1851 failed to be realized, there was another striking outburst of hysteria—Thomas Carlyle at the forefront—when the Reform Bill of 1867 extended the electorate from 1.36 million to 2.46 million men, an extension that resulted in almost no redistribution of seats in Parliament. The floodgates had opened to accommodate a trickle of change.

In part, this hysteria reflected the fear that authority, and the class structure necessary to its maintenance, would be eroded; in Wordsworth's anxious phrase, "Hourly the democratic torrent swells."[2] (Matthew Arnold dismissed this with scorn as "the religion of inequality.") But in greater part, the hysteria was a function of the new population concentrations and the modes of transport and communication that could sustain those concentrations with supplies and increase them with new recruits. In effect, by the middle of the nineteenth century, the democratic torrent had become visible and physically, palpably present in the new urban-industrial landscapes created by the industrial revolution. In *Bleak House* (1853), Dickens lampoons this rather class-bound anxiety as "the Wat Tyler direction,"[3] worked into a refrain linking James Watt and the steam engines that drove the industrial revolution with Wat Tyler's peasant revolt of 1381. That, in turn, is linked to the bit-part presence in the novel of Watt Rouncewell, the ironmaster's son.

This fear of the hordes in their new numbers wasn't matched in America until the end of the century, when the rise of New York and Chicago created population densities comparable to those of the mining and industrial centers of England, Scotland, and Wales. Americans also had coasted past any anxiety about the revolutionary propensities of the urban poor on the strength of the comforting assumption that America had already had its revolution.

But in 1851, so great was the public agitation in the weeks before the opening of the Crystal Palace exhibition that many of the royal families of Europe prudently excused themselves from attending the opening. To ward off the democratic torrent, the sponsoring Royal Society of Arts set the entry fee at the steep price of five shillings, something on the order of forty or fifty dollars in the currency of the 1980s. When the rampaging vandals failed to materialize, the society lowered the entrance fee to one shilling for the first four days of the week. The exhibition played to over 6 million well-behaved spectators in the course of the summer.*

One result of the exhibition's popular success was a signifi-

---

*The population of London in 1851 was just short of two and a half million.

cant rise in museum fever, which accomplished something of a democratic revolution from the eighteenth-century assumption that museums should be reserved for the research uses of the educated and privileged few to the new assumption that museums should be for the entertainment and education of the many. The tide of the democratic torrent had turned. Henceforth, museums were to be regarded as "instruments of social amelioration," a "new, acceptable and wholesome excitement" for the working classes.[4] The profits from the Crystal Palace exhibition were accordingly spun off into the South Kensington Musuem, now the Victoria and Albert. This museum was destined to raise its upscale architectural replica of the royal crown over the whole complex of museums, colleges, and institutions that have come to dominate Kensington.

From the point of view of Canon Stanley of Saint Paul's Cathedral, the exhibition's celebration of the grand alliance of science, industry, and the practical arts consecrated the Crystal Palace as a temple. He likened the royal procession that opened the exhibition to "the entrance of the Pope into Saint Peter's on Easter Sunday."[5] From the beginning, Prince Albert had planned the exhibition as a vast school of instruction, and his ten-year-old son Albert Edward, Prince of Wales, was for several weeks sent with his tutor to study the exhibits as though they were illustrations in a textbook. The democratic torrent joined in that study and helped Prince Albert turn the tables on the prophets of social doom; after 1851, such exhibitions were regarded not as occasions liable to excite the masses to riot but as occasions that calmed through the beneficence of their educational presence.

The Crystal Palace provides a concentrated image of the ways in which the perception of population pressures and of the public's interests and preferences was being altered in and by the new urban-industrial concentrations. And the exhibition exemplifies other shifts in the perception of quantity and scale. Victorians didn't regard the Crystal Palace as architecture but as a triumph of engineering. Designed by Sir Joseph Paxton, it was a giant greenhouse supported by a frame of mass-produced cast-iron columns and beams so that it could be dismantled as easily as it was erected. One of the conditions imposed on the exhibition by the Commissioners of Woods and Forests, who were responsible for Hyde Park, was that the building had to be temporary. Paxton's solution was a vast glass tent that was disassembled and rebuilt on a smaller scale in 1854 in a park in Sydenham south of the Thames. It initially housed a permanent fair before its decline from use and destruction by fire in 1936.

The scale of the original structure fascinated the Victorians, and there was endless interest in the numbers involved. The structure housed over twenty-one acres of floor space and covered a land area of over nineteen acres, "four times the size of Saint Peter's in Rome, and six times the size of Saint Paul's," as the catalog of the history of the Great Exhibition announces.[6] The building required 3,500 tons of cast iron; 550 tons of wrought iron; 900,000 square feet of glass; 600,000 square feet of wood; 30 miles of gutters; 202 miles of wooden sash bars. The public curiosity about quantification of the structure's engineering wonders seems to have been insatiable. The Royal Society of Arts selected a mind-boggling quantity and variety of exhibits from the hundred thousand plus items submitted from almost fourteen thousand would-be exhibitors. There were giant steam engines and printing presses and machine tools, a fantastic array of artworks and decorative crafts, curios and gadgets such as a fountain of eau de cologne, a full-sized armchair carved out of a single block of coal, a silent-alarm bedstead that tilted to deposit the unwary sleeper in a bath of cold water, and a sportsman's jackknife with eighty blades, which was still on display in a Bond Street shop window in 1984.

The variety of exhibits was so impressive, their sheer quantity so overwhelming, that even the most studious mind couldn't hope to take it all in. By a sublime law of paradox, this rich variety disappears off one end of the spectrum and reappears as an elaborately homogenized sameness at the other. The Crystal

Palace ushered in the vision of sameness in variety that our grandparents faced in the Sears, Roebuck Catalog and that we face daily in supermarkets and shopping malls and on the television set and in the flood of mail-order catalogs, the wish books that clutter the daily mail. In this world of homogenized variety, tourism becomes an endless shopping trip, the quest for the grail of something completely different. The national boutique-super-market-mall dissolves its boundaries to include overseas and urges on us the paradox of that democratic torrent of mass-produced variety and uniqueness that adds up to more than we can comprehend of the homogenized one-and-the-same.

Dr. Johnson, commenting in 1750 on the apparent uniqueness of human individuals, was impressed not by the uniqueness but by the "uniformity in the state of man, considered apart from adventitious and separable decorations and disguises."[7] As those decorations and disguises were multiplied and variegated in the nineteenth century, the perception of uniformity beneath the disguising surfaces was virtually reversed. The surfaces became so overanimated that the disguises began to lose their variety, and apparent uniqueness began to give way as sameness took command. As the industrial world urbanized the individual and increased his dependency on the infrastructure of transportation and communication and on the social fabric that supplies the goods and services he "needs," there came into being what Germaine Brée has called "that nineteenth-century invention par excellence—the free-standing individual," an ideal companion for the Crystal Palace paradox. As human beings became more uniform in their urban dependencies and conformities, they more stridently attempted to characterize and perceive themselves as personally unique, freestanding individuals.

Tocqueville observed a similar paradox in the fabric of American society circa 1835 in the way the popular assertion of radical individualism coexisted with a social and political conformity that threatened to become slavish and, from his point of view, dangerous to American democracy. It's both strange and not strange that the widely asserted tradition of rugged individualism, so familiar to our legend of ourselves, has been assumed to have risen out of frontier experience. In fact, the frontier demanded a very high order of neighborly cooperation and communal enterprise: united, they survived; divided, they perished. In the second half of the twentieth century, American cults of nonconformity—whether hippy, dropout, counterculture, or punk—have seen what Johnson called their "adventitious and separable decorations and disguises" co-opted almost overnight by commercial interests, mass-produced and mass-marketed for the young who were discovered, in the late 1950s, to wield the greatest sum of uncommitted—that is, free—money. The end result is that counterculture itself has come to reinforce uniformity in the state of man.

In other words, the metaphoric corollary to the mind-boggling sameness in quantified diversity of the Crystal Palace is the khaki uniform. These uniforms were first worn in 1848 by the Guide Corps, a regiment of British and Indian frontier troops. By the time of the Indian Mutiny in 1857–58, the use of khaki had spread to several regiments of British regulars, and by the end of the century, being much more difficult to spot in the battlescape than a red coat crisscrossed with white webbing, it was the field-service uniform of almost all British and native troops in the empire. In America, the colorful marching-society uniforms of the opening months of the Civil War soon gave way to the drab anonymity of the blue and the gray. In the new warfare, as Melville saw it, "War [had] laid aside / His Orient pomp" and "a singe" had run "through lace and feather."[8] In the closing years of the Civil War, the general of the Union armies himself relinquished gold braid and lace and feather in favor of a private's tunic.

The anonymity of the mass-produced khaki uniform was to achieve one of its masterworks in World War I, when the tiny British regular army in France was brought up to something like continental strength by the hastily recruited and minimally trained civilians of the Kitchener battalions—just in time for the slaughter-yard of the Somme. All too appropriate, then, is the derivation of the Urdu word *kbākī*, meaning dusty or dust-colored, from the Persian *kbāk*, dust—"for dust thou art, and unto dust shalt thou return," as God says to Adam and Eve in Genesis 3:19. And yet by the law of oscillating contraries that operates in the natural history of perception, nothing can sharpen one's sense of personal uniqueness the way the anonymous disguise of khaki can. In the "solid dark" of a December night in 1915, a platoon of Royal Welch Fusiliers moves forward toward its first tour of duty in the trenches,

> feet plodding in each other's unseen tread. They said no word but to direct their immediate next coming, so close behind to blunder, toe by heel tripping, filemates; blind on-following, moving with a singular identity.
>
> Half-minds, far away, divergent, own-thought thinking, tucked away unknown thoughts; feet following file friends, each his own thought-maze alone treading; intricate, twist about, own thoughts, all unknown thoughts, to the next so close following on.[9]

Historically, the habit of treating human beings and their societies as measurable quantities, composed exclusively of measurable physical characteristics, was sufficiently vigorous and irritating by the time of Jonathan Swift to invite the savage indignation of his satire. Swift's traveler, Lemuel Gulliver, with his pocket watch as God, is an acme of that weights-and-measures mode of perception. As Gulliver perceives them, all the intelligent and intelligible creatures he encounters are to be judged on the basis of their physical characteristics and the conventional assumptions that those characteristics excite. Gulliver tends to patronize the six-inch-tall Lilliputians as cute and, because they're so small and obviously puny, he is much preoccupied with his own physical size and prowess, with how superhuman he must appear to them to be. What Gulliver fails to see is just how human—or rather,

how English and Western European—these tiny men and women
are in their preoccupations and vanities, in the disparities between their stated principles and their actual behavior, in the
pettiness of their quarrels about politics and religion and customs
such as which end of the boiled egg one cracks or the fashionable
height of the heels on one's shoes.

On his second voyage, marooned among the sixty-foot giants
of Brobdingnag, Gulliver is still preoccupied with his own physical prowess, but with the equation reversed. Now he's the puny
six-inch creature, coping with wasps the size of partridges and
swaggering around brandishing his sword to impress (or look
cute for) his massive hosts. The king of Brobdingnag proves
himself much shrewder about Gulliver's version of mankind than
Gulliver was about the Lilliputian. The king overcomes the isn't-
he-cute prejudice and treats his guest seriously. While Gulliver
doesn't perceive it, we recognize in the king a much more
benevolent ruler than any prince known to Gulliver's history or
our own. The king is aghast when Gulliver avidly describes the
role of gunpowder in European affairs and refuses Gulliver's offer
of the formula as a gift. Gulliver assumes that the king must be
dull witted, as popular wisdom knows all giants to be. Any
responsible ruler would immediately recognize and desire the
advantage of the physical force and capacity for coercion that
gunpowder (or nuclear weapons, or x-ray lasers) would afford his
government.

On his fourth voyage, Gulliver is faced with a different test
of his weights-and-measures mode of perception. In Lilliput and
Brobdingnag, Gulliver's myopia is induced by differences in scale
(or degree), which baffle him as differences in kind. In
Houyhnhnm-land, the bafflement is induced by confusions of
physical form and the psychological nature that physical form
conventionally suggests. Horses in physical form, the
Houyhnhnms behave, as Gulliver perceives them, as rational
creatures. But what we see over his shoulder are minimally
rational creatures with computerized brains and a language that

resembles, in Hugh Kenner's phrase, "an early form of Fortran."[10] It never strikes Gulliver as strange that the horses make no effort to understand his language (as computers make no effort to understand ours). Instead, he thinks these horses the wisest of creatures; what the reader perceives as pallid and mechanical intellect is belied, from his point of view, by the horseness of the Houyhnhnms' physical form. Conversely, the Yahoos, the humanoid creatures of Houyhnhnm-land, are physically repulsive and psychologically more bestial than any beast of our world. Gulliver's Houyhnhnm master, his eye informed by the physicality of the Yahoos, also suffers from Gulliveritis: he consistently misperceives Gulliver because Gulliver looks like a Yahoo, and Gulliver keeps pace with his master by identifying with the Yahoos in paroxysms of self-loathing.

The confusion that derives from judgments made on the basis of physical characteristics is compounded in the choreography of Swift's satire. A talking (and superficially rational) Yahoo, Gulliver, is as opaque to the Houyhnhnms as talking (and superficially rational) horses are to him. Climactically, the Houyhnhnms, despite Gulliver's protestations about their extraordinary benevolence, contemplate with rational equanimity genocide as the "final solution" to the "Yahoo question." And in their mechanized benevolence, they solve the "Gulliver question" by ordering him to swim back whence he came. This order—sanitized in their version of Newspeak as an "exhortation"—is modified to allow Gulliver to construct and sail away in "a sort of *Indian* canoe."* But for the escape-art of fiction, Gulliver would sail to his death

---

*The irony here is that satire anticipates anthropology. While Swift in all probability couldn't have known it, some Polynesian peoples (including the Maori of New Zealand) did practice a sort of execution by suicide, with the malefactor voluntarily putting to sea in a canoe and drifting to his death. As far as I can determine, knowledge of that custom wouldn't have been available in England until three or four decades after 1726.

in an unseaworthy vessel. Presumably, that death would satisfy the conditions of Houyhnhnm benevolence by dint of being offstage, at sea where Houyhnhnms never venture and cannot conceive of venturing, because they are utterly without imagination.

At the end of the eighteenth century, Blake was even more vehement than Swift in his sustained protest in favor of "Vision" and against what he called "Newton's Sleep," the reduction of all perception to the evidence of the senses, to the dimensions of the physical and measurable.

> *How do you know but ev'ry Bird that cuts the airy way*
> *Is an immense world of delight, clos'd by your senses*
> *five?*[11]

But Blake was, as he himself recognized, howling in the wilderness. The sensory closure of perception, confining it to empirically measurable quantities, was a powerful presence by the early decades of the nineteenth century, reinforced by achievements in the natural sciences and by the success of classical mechanics as it evolved into industrial engineering. The metaphor of that success was far too powerful to resist, and sensory closure, together with quantification, emerged to dominate thinking about man and society in the utilitarianism of Jeremy Bentham. Fundamental to this doctrine was the social principle of "the greatest good for the greatest number," in which "the good" was defined as the measurable, quantifiable presence of pleasure or the absence of pain. Bentham's hedonic calculus ruled out any concern with a qualitative hierarchy of values; as he put it, "the quality of pleasure being equal, pushpin [a child's game on the level of tiddlywinks] is as good as poetry." That's quite possibly sardonic overstatement on Bentham's part but perhaps not when one recalls his fully dressed skeleton with wax image of his head seated in its glass case in the entry hall of University College, London, and the instructions that deliver the case, figure and all, to meetings of the college's governing body.

John Stuart Mill, a second generation utilitarian, did attempt to modify Bentham's overstatement by the reaffirmation of poetry and other such pushpin concerns as human enterprise of significance and value.[12] But Bentham's rigor—and his insistence that poetry was "misrepresentation"—handily survived such attempts to meliorate and soften his radical reduction of all qualitative concerns to the measurable and quantifiable. Thomas Gradgrind, that "man of realities," introduces himself as the caricature Benthamite in Dickens's novel *Hard Times.*

> With a rule and a pair of scales, and the multiplication table always in his pocket, sir, ready to weigh and measure any parcel of human nature, and tell you exactly what it comes to. It is a mere question of figures, a case of simple arithmetic.[13]

But Bentham's calculus survived Dickens's sustained satirical and melodramatic assault as handily as it survived Mill's attempts to alleviate it with poetry. Indeed it is alive and well in the entertainment and consumer worlds of 1984. How, for example, can we contest the television producer's flat assertion, "If it gets the most numbers, it's the best"? To question what "the best" means is to invite again the quibble over pushpin and poetry, irrelevant to the numbers that really do the talking and that translate so readily into cash. And in the coast-to-coast shopping mall, our standard of living is not judged by awkward, elitist questions about the quality of the lives being lived but by the safely demonstrable measurements of comparative purchasing power. Pushpin or poetry, a rise in purchasing power equals a rise in the standard of living and is, therefore, good.

The habits of mind of which Houyhnhnm rationalism and Benthamite utilitarianism are symptomatic have had the effect of driving imagination and intuition into the corner of negative definition, so that we tend to define them not as the positive human faculties that, well nurtured, they are, but in terms of what they are not. Intuition is "essentially, arriving at decisions or conclusions without explicit or conscious processes of reasoned thinking."* Imagination is, from a utilitarian point of view, the opposite of realistic perception, seeing things that are not. The Houyhnhnms have no word for *to lie* except the circumlocution *to say the thing that is not*; consequently, they have no capacity to imagine anything beyond what is immediately present to their passionless senses and no capacity whatsoever for metaphor, which by definition must be unrealistic, a misrepresentation, a lie. Utilitarianism shares these negations, although a well-disposed utilitarian can, without being cynical, justify lying, particularly white lying or disinformation, if it enhances the greatest good of the greatest number.

Even those Victorians who, like Tennyson, wanted to believe in faith tended to give away the store by accepting the assumption that quantitative empiricism is the only firm basis for human knowledge. As Tennyson puts it in the prologue to *In Memoriam* (1850),

We have but faith: we cannot know,
For knowledge is of things we see.

---

*The passage in *The Oxford Companion to the Mind* continues, "The term is used in philosophy to denote the alleged power of the mind to perceive or 'see' certain self-evident truths (Latin *intueor*, to see). The status of intuition has, however, declined over the last century, perhaps with the increasing emphasis on formal logic and explicit data and assumptions of science." Richard L. Gregory, ed. (Oxford, 1987), 389. The safety net provided by those words *alleged* and *perhaps* suggests a certain anxiety about including a definition of intuition at all, and the *Companion* provides no entry under *Imagination* (though there are several references listed under *Imagination* in the index).

In the parenthesis of 1798–1984, counterutilitarianism has become and remains one of the mainstreams of our cultural heritage. However, to mix the metaphor, it has been consistently and overwhelmingly outvoted since midparenthesis. And now, in the 1980s, when computers have turned every day into an election day, the outvoting is constantly urged on us by polls taken "scientifically" in the name of public opinion, political power, and financial gain.

In the course of the nineteenth century, the utilitarian perspective developed some rather awkward corollaries, among them the conviction that quantitative measurements are absolute, demonstrably based on and derived from sensory evidence, and the further belief that ultimately those absolutes would, as Zola said, demonstrate that "a new law governs the stones of the roadway and the brains of men."[14] Meanwhile, and until their sensory and quantitative basis can be demonstrated, qualitative measurements are relative. If you prefer faith in a realm unseen to doubt of that realm's existence, that's your business, provided it doesn't threaten the pleasure of others. If you prefer the pleasures of pushpin to the pleasures of poetry, it may bring pain to poets and those of us who profess poetry, but they and we are hardly the greatest number, so there the case can be allowed rest.

The proposition, the greatest good for the greatest number, could also be adopted into evolving concepts of democracy as the basis for a majoritarian ethic in which value judgments were not to be made on the a priori basis of previously established ethical principles such as the law of the prophets: "therefore all things whatsoever ye would that men should do to you, do ye even so to them" (Matthew 7:12). Ethical judgments were to be based instead on the quantitative estimates of pleasure maximized and pain minimized throughout the affected population.* The majori-

---

*This would seem to promise an ideal fit with Thomas Jefferson's assertion that one of the "inalienable rights" was "the pursuit of happiness," except that Jefferson

tarian ethic involves an implicit conflict with bill-of-rights democracy because it can so easily be translated into a doctrine of
majority-rights, which overrides and dismisses minority rights as
unsettling to the pleasurable calm of majority rule. From that
perspective, even a minority's right to articulate painful truths
should be curtailed in favor of the greatest good for the greatest
number, the good in that case being the pleasure of anesthesia.

In industrial applications, the utilitarian perspective makes it
possible to regard and treat individual human beings as inter-
changeable parts, tools to be kept free of rust and in good working
order, not to be upset and rendered inefficient by qualitative
concerns such as faith or poetry or domestic disorder or social
protest. Factory workers in the Dickensian refrain from *Hard
Times* become "the Hands"—troublesome because their "ultimate object in life . . . is to be fed on turtle soup and venison with
a golden spoon." But, if properly handled, they will return to and
accept their places as the hands in the appropriate "tabular
statements."[15]

Early in the nineteenth century, considerable force and energy were added to utilitarian perspectives by what Emerson
called "the new science of Statistics."[16] The word *statistics* was
introduced into English from German in the 1780s, just in time
for Thomas Malthus to take it up in his *Essay on the Principle of
Population as It Affects the Future Improvement of Society*. The
mathematics for the statistical study of human populations and
their behavior was in place before the end of the seventeenth
century. In the 1660s, Captain John Graunt and Sir William Petty
examined—with what they called "Political Arithmetic"—the re-

---

was using *happiness* not in the utilitarian sense of *pleasure* but as the common
(and unfortunately rather lame) translation of the Greek *eudaimonia*. "To the
Greeks, *eudaimonia* means something like 'living a good life for a human being';
or, as a recent writer, John Cooper, has suggested, 'human flourishing.' Aristotle
tells us that it is equivalent, in ordinary discourse, to 'living well and doing well.' "
Martha C. Nussbaum, *The Fragility of Goodness: Luck and Ethics in Greek Tragedy
and Philosophy* (Cambridge, England, 1986), 6n.

lation between birth rates and mortality rates in London and Dublin in the 1660s. But population samples large enough and record keeping centralized enough to constitute statistics were not readily available before the advent of the urban concentrations and improved communications that accompanied the industrial revolution in the Western world.

Gilbert White was well aware that only long-term and broad-based measurements of natural phenomena such as rainfall will provide a valid statistical base for ascertaining the mean quantity of rainfall at Selborne, and he is apparently content to settle for the limitations of his data. "I am not qualified," he will say, or "I only know that . . ."[17]

One hundred years later, however, such skeptical hesitancy no longer seemed necessary—the term of measurement was readily accepted as long enough, the base broad enough. Symptomatic of the rise of statistics as a new and compelling way of thinking about human beings and their affairs was the emergence of public delight in statistics (accompanied by a sustained countercurrent of protest). There was what Lynn Barber calls

> the usual Victorian enchantment with statistics: if all the offspring of a single pair of herring were allowed to multiply unmolested for twenty years, they would 'exhibit a bulk ten times the size of the earth,' and if all the eggs in a single cod's roe were to hatch and attain adulthood they would weigh 26,123 tons and fetch £195,000 in the market.[18]

The same enchantment is evident in the fascination with the quantification of the material necessary to build the Crystal Palace. And Thoreau notes in a journal entry for 17 April 1854, "It is remarkable how the American mind runs to statistics," in this case meteorological statistics and records of migratory birds.

In the realm of protest, statistics gets it early and often in Dickens's *Hard Times* as a mistaken and destructive way of thinking. In one climactic misapplication, Thomas Gradgrind urges his twenty-year-old daughter Louisa toward her loveless and doomed marriage with the fifty-year-old Bounderby.

> In considering this question, it is not unimportant to take into account the statistics of marriage, so far as they have yet been obtained, in England and Wales. I find, on reference to the figures, that a large proportion of these marriages are contracted between parties of very unequal ages, and that the elder of these contracting parties is, in rather more than three-fourths of these instances, the bridegroom.[19]

In *The Ring and the Book*, Browning's Pope, speaking obviously with Browning's approval, complains of

> *the sagacious Swede*
> *Who finds by figures how the chances prove,*
> *Why one comes rather than another thing,*
> *As, say, such dots turn up by throw of dice.*[20]

The identity of this Swede is problematic, but Browning's attitude is not. The Pope goes on to suggest that statistical approaches to understanding and judging individual human behavior are about as sound as judgments based on superstitions such as *sortes Virgilianae*, the Virgilian dip—opening Virgil, or the Bible or Shakespeare, at blindfold random and accepting as relevant wisdom the passage one's finger falls upon.

In Marx's *Capital: A Critique of Political Economy* (1869), much of his indignation at what he calls "the spirit of capital" results from the way the laborer and his circumstances are reduced to the status of anonymous things, interesting only as summaries in columns of figures, those "tabular statements" Dickens consistently lampoons.

The new science of statistics was to do wonders for the natural sciences between 1798 and 1984, but it also was to enjoy a hand-in-glove fit with the preoccupations of the utilitarians and their clients in the emerging industrial nations. Political economists in the nineteenth century were fascinated by the possibilities for social engineering that they saw in the statistical concept called the law of large numbers, the assumption that the causes of social phenomena could be divided into two categories: individual, accidental, or disturbing causes on the one hand; "essential or primary causes" on the other. Causes of the first sort "have no constant tendency to act in one direction rather than another and, accordingly, no tendency to move the group as a whole in any one direction."[21] The law of large numbers simply asserts that if the statistical sample is large enough, the individual, accidental, and disturbing causes cancel one another out, and the essential or primary causes stand clear. This achieves a comfortable fit with the utilitarian assumption that qualitative measurements (individual, accidental, or disturbing) are relative, that quantitative measurements (essential or primary) are absolute. Then as now, the social sciences were and are in a bind: many of the important things don't lend themselves to measurement and quantification; therefore things that do lend themselves tend to be invested with an importance that is frequently out of proportion.

Another result of the nineteenth century's enchantment with statistics was a reification of numbers, which encouraged the uninitiated to accept as absolutes statistical statements that anyone trained to think about numbers would regard as only one or another order of probability. This mistaken faith is very much with us in 1984 in the way, for example, that weather forecasters can predict a sixty-percent chance of showers one afternoon without any clear indication of whether that means showers over sixty percent of the geographical area covered by the forecast or a sixty-percent probability in the immediate time frame of the afternoon. But if it rains, sixty percent suddenly equals one hundred percent; if it doesn't, that doesn't mean forty percent but zero. And what sort of miscarriage of numbers takes place when the same language of prediction by percentages is used to predict the behavior of a suicidal patient in a hospital ward?

Consider a reification so many of us have learned to accept

without complaint: the assertion that a poll taken from a "scientifically chosen" sample of fourteen hundred of our 220 million fellow countrymen can be said to tell us how the nation thinks and feels about its president, the budget deficit, the nation's foreign policy and military preparedness. Translated, further reified by the policy and political choices of those who govern, these measurements of the national mood are treated as though they reflected the will of the majority and should, therefore, rule. The tangle of assumptions involved is impressive. In the first place, the choice of sample takes place in contexts devoid of any close or widely understood definition of what it means to think and to feel. Then there is the assumption that the pollster and his questions could explore those thoughts and feelings plus the assumption that representative democracy means government by public opinion, an assumption that Jefferson and the framers of the Constitution found abhorrent, threatening as it did a "tyranny of the majority." But the assumption is all around us that our representatives should represent public opinion, "what people," in Hugh Kenner's phrase, "think other people think." As though our representatives should be vote-tabulating machines, putting the statistically determined preferences and opinions of the political power centers among their constituents into legislative and executive action. In the 1980s, a politician has to be courageous, if not foolhardy, to abide by Edmund Burke's eighteenth-century dictum:

> Your representative owes you not only his industry but his judgment, and he betrays instead of serving you if he sacrifices it [his judgment] to your opinion.

In the middle of the last century, Thoreau explored the dilemma of majoritarian democracy in "Resistance to Civil Government," now usually called "Civil Disobedience." Gandhi, Martin Luther King, Jr., and others have regarded this essay as "a grammar for action," but Thoreau's discussion seems considerably

more inconclusive—a grammar of questions—and far less pro-
grammatic than the history of civil disobedience has led us to
assume.

What happens, Thoreau asks, if the government and the
majority that presumably supports it are just plain morally and
ethically wrong? as in the general case of the institution of slavery
in the United States and the specific case of the Mexican War,
which Thoreau and many of his New England contemporaries
regarded as an unprincipled land grab, an attempt to extend the
slaveholding territories and thus the political power of the South.
But when Thoreau first gave the lecture, the Mexican War was
over and the land had been grabbed; the war was not an immediate issue but an example of what, a few months before, had been
a case in point.

Isn't majority rule a form of tyranny, he asks, another form of
might makes right? In principle, isn't the person who is against
slavery in general and against this unjust war in particular morally
and ethically right, and shouldn't his principle therefore constitute a "majority of one" and govern by right? What of the
conventional wisdom that says if you disagree in principle with a
government that undertakes an unjust war and perpetuates the
institution of slavery, you should campaign against that government and vote the rascals out of office? That sort of action, from
Thoreau's point of view, is unethical—not asserting and acting on
what is right in principle, but gambling on the principle being
declared right by the might of the majority in the lottery of the
next election. What if principle loses that election? Since you
gambled on might making right and lost, no further course of
action is available except the individual's act of seceding from the
state, refusing the state his support, which should have been the
honest citizen's action in the first place. Nor could Thoreau argue
that those who refused support should band together and march
on city hall or on the Pentagon in a show of strength because that,
too, would come dangerously close to using might rather than
principle to make right.

Many assume that Thoreau's civil disobedience was the symbolic act of refusing to pay his poll tax, which resulted in the symbolic act of going to jail. But Thoreau's refusal began in 1842 and his night in jail wasn't until 1846. Neither became symbolic until the real act of civil disobedience, two lectures given at the Concord Lyceum early in 1848, eighteen months after the night in jail and after seven years of flouting the poll tax. The next year he published the essay distilled from those lectures. From his point of view, publication was the primary means for urging the public mind to turn from might toward right. When he first delivered the lectures, and when the essay was published, Thoreau was in complete control. His words and gestures were not at the mercy of reportorial and editorial modification, the media distortion we accept as the norm in news coverage of acts of civil disobedience.

I shudder to think what Thoreau would say if he could see the elected representatives of the 1980s, surrounded by their staffs of experts and advisers and pollsters, more and more prepared for elaborately computerized attempts at statistical accommodation of their varied constituencies. The art of getting and staying elected now approaches the art of the racing form, and the gamble isn't on the chance of establishing a principle but on the chance of winning. Thoreau offered no answers to the dilemmas involved in the perception of democracy by the numbers, and the numbers have multiplied in mind-boggling fashion since the 1840s, to the point where demographic analysis is universally substituted for, and accepted as, political thought.

Freedom and Equality is one of the frequently heard battle cries of this democratic republic. One state sports the motto Live Free or Die, of which Thoreau would have approved. No state, however, suggests that we live equal or die, perhaps because while there is little freedom in the demographic nation-state, there is even less equality when the numbers take over. The demographic state, with its capacity for instant computer analysis of what it defines as public response and opinion, tends in practice to be static, homogenized, bureaucratically evasive. It tends, in short, toward passive authoritarianism, toward the subversion—if not the outright suppression—of freedom and equality. At best, those twin ideals suggest a marriage of incompatibles in what must nevertheless be a no-divorce state if intelligent and intelligible democracy is to survive.

The numbers are obviously useful for predicting and tabulating voter behavior and for encouraging the flow of campaign monies, but numbers are also infiltrating and restructuring the legislative and executive processes themselves. The Executive Office staff of the White House circa 1984 includes 1,247 advisers, not counting additional personnel on advisory loan from other departments in the executive bureaucracy. The U.S. Secretary of State flies to Moscow to lay the groundwork for a summit meeting. He is accompanied by two plane loads of advisers. By 1987, congressional staff totaled 18,659. Those staff members, together with the hundred senators and 435 representatives they advise, constitute two deliberative bodies with the input of over nineteen thousand voices.

These numbers are justified by the unquestioned assumption that several researcher-advisers can combine the detailed complexity of their information into an overall grasp of a subject or an issue, that quantity of advice assures quality of understanding, and thus that quantity will ultimately assure quality of decision. That is, if the president hears a number of well-developed and conflicting opinions on a given issue, he will be better prepared to make a wise decision, because all these aides and advisers are experts in their various fields. Unfortunately, an expert in 1984 tends to be not just an informed and knowledgeable discussant but someone who establishes exclusive turf and defends it against all comers. The rules of the game of expertise encourage a politics of competition and confrontation. The rewards go not to the experts who come close to getting it right but to those whose opinions prevail within and through the politics of the hierarchy from the outer circles of junior advisers up the ladder toward and through the senior advisers.

When these assumptions about numbers and expertise are challenged, the usual answer is that the world is infinitely more complex than it used to be. Never mind that halfway to that farther, infinitely simpler, shore, Abraham Lincoln ran the Civil War with a White House staff of two secretaries—and with some success, in spite of the obstruction of incompetent, political generals and a frequently obstreperous Cabinet. Never mind that no generation in the history of history has ever considered its world simpler than the preceding generation's, though a generation ago, John Randall, a professor at Columbia, used to take delight in assuring his students that there had been one period of thirty years in twelfth-century Europe when absolutely nothing happened and life was, for once, truly simple. Otherwise, at our backs we always hear the myth of the Edenic simplicity of the lives of our forebears.

This chorus of expert voices at the executive and legislative centers of our nation is of course augmented by voices from innumerable think tanks and consultants and lobbyists. From the point of view of a stationary man in the enclosed place of this Williamstown, the effect is an electronic Tower of Babel: a cacophony of mostly anonymous voices, each protesting its expertise or its influence as insider but agreeing to speak only on condition that its identity be withheld. Out of this cacophony rise the slogans (Read my lips, no new taxes) of over-simplification and confrontation, the sort of politics that Burke condemned as a "barbarous philosophy . . . the offspring of cold hearts and muddy understandings." It remains a mystery how the fifty-five delegates to the Constitutional Convention managed to sustain their discussions through the summer of 1787, meeting and arguing and compromising as often as five or six times a week.

*   *   *

Quote of the century: Speaking to the American Statistical Association in 1914, S. N. D. North, head of the Bureau of the Census, divided all modern history

> into two periods, the non-statistical and the statistical; one the period of superstition, the other the period of ascertained facts expressed in numerical terms.[22]

With this grand division of history, he unwittingly proclaimed "out with the old superstition, in with the new."

In 1812, the French astronomer and mathematician Pierre Simon, Marquis de Laplace* announced the advent of "probability man" in his *Théorie analytique des probabilités;*[23] in 1835, the Belgian astronomer and statistician Lambert Adolphe Jacques Quetelet published what amounted to the invention of the average man.[24] These two concepts have fed two contrary and yet strongly complementary modes of perception that we have come to welcome as commonsensical wisdom about both ourselves as individuals and our collective experience.

On the one hand, there is Quetelet's assertion, following in the wake of Laplace's analysis, that "the greater the number of individuals, the more does the influence of the individual will disappear."[25] This version of the law of large numbers Emerson called "the terrible tabulation of the French statists,"[26] and he enshrined it as one aspect of fate in the essay of that name.

> One more fagot of these adamantine bandages is the new science of Statistics. It is a rule that the most casual and extraordinary events, if the basis of population is broad enough, become matter of fixed calculation.[27]

---

*Napoleon appointed Laplace minister of the interior only to sack him after six months. "He carried the spirit of the infinitesimals into his administration."

Under that rule, the individual knows from fixed calculation what will become of him as probability man if he smokes cigarettes or drives without buckling up or exercises too little and ingests too much cholesterol.

On the other hand, the average man is precisely he who is not me. He is the frame of reference against which I measure my uniqueness: I am taller/shorter, faster/slower, richer/poorer, smarter/dumber than the average. The big numbers of the average man tell me how different I am until the realization strikes that uniqueness is a common property of all living things. The bell curve clamps down; the khaki uniforms are issued; and we pause. If we get married or divorced or die, we don't influence the terrible tabulation—we disappear into it. That pause marks one of the more unsettling distortions of perspective in our world—the awe-inspiring asymmetry, the distance between the little numbers that represent us as individuals and the big, inclusive numbers that spell out the adamantine bandages of our vulnerabilities and limitations and indeed our mortality.

This asymmetry reminds me of the Cheyenne fable that explains the white man's cultural dyslexia as a function of having lost his human eyes and substituted two borrowed eyes: a buffalo's eye in one socket, a mouse's in the other.[28] We can restore some of our perspective by reminding ourselves that the numbers that describe us as individuals are whole and indivisible; each of us is One. The numbers that describe us collectively are divisible, partial, fragmentary; as individuals we belong in the quantified categories and are exceptions at the same time. All too frequently, even the authority of the big numbers is cloaked in anonymity. The numbers themselves aren't quoted, only the probabilities they suggest. Too much cholesterol combined with too little exercise results in heart disease, but there is no definition of too much or too little, no citation of the statistical studies on which those definitions and probabilities are based, just the passive authoritative voice. The big numbers say that over forty thousand reliable studies link smoking to lung cancer and heart disease. But all too frequently, the big numbers sound like a joke. As a result of the Reagan administration's generous tax cut, the average taxpayer will have $120 more per year to spend as he sees fit, ten dollars a month, hooray! Because of the now-defunct fifty-five-mile-per-hour speed limit, the average American spent seven hours more per year on the highway than he would have spent had he been allowed a sixty-five-mile-per-hour pace! How can I locate my preferences and habits when the big numbers say that the per-capita consumption of soft drinks in the United States soared from 13.6 gallons per person in 1960 to 37.8 gallons per person in 1981. Does our only hope lie in that formula of absolution, not statistically relevant?

But even the jokes proclaim the asymmetry more than they alleviate it, and the asymmetry is nowhere more striking than in how we perceive our relation to what is now called the economy, a relation that frequently seems to intend a grim irony at the expense of the individual and his experience. How does the person below the poverty line feel when reassured by the statistical assertion that the average person's income rose by seven percent in the last calendar year? How does the unemployed person feel after another month of fruitless job-hunting when reassured that the Department of Labor's latest statistics show a decline in the rate of joblessness? We need two sets of eyes: one for the big picture and one for the close-ups. A circuitry of comfortable discontinuities between them wouldn't be a disadvantage.

Thoreau began his natural history of *Walden* with a chapter entitled "Economy." To Thoreau and his contemporaries, the word meant the support and management of a household—how one acquired and used food, clothing, and fuel and how one built or acquired and maintained one's shelter. Ostensibly, that's what Thoreau's introductory chapter is about—to answer, he says with tongue in cheek,

> very particular inquiries . . . made by my townsmen concern-
> ing my mode of life, which some would call impertinent,

though they do not appear to me at all impertinent, but, considering the circumstances, very natural and pertinent.[29]

Metaphorically, as the wordplay of pertinent and impertinent suggests, Thoreau's chapter is about a much larger question of economy: how many hours of mind-dulling drudgery have to be invested in the physical economy of housekeeping in order to earn the freedom to live one's own mind? What we call the economy, Thoreau and his contemporaries would have called *political economy*—the consideration of the production, distribution, and consumption of the wealth of nations. The distinction between the political economy of nations and the economy of the individual household suggests a useful way of calling attention to the asymmetry that besets us, but the distinction was blurred and lost toward the end of the nineteenth century as political economists—proponents of what Carlyle called "the dismal science"—were increasingly discredited by the repeated failures of their scientific theories in that practical arena called the marketplace (and, I suspect, as the theories and practices of political economy were increasingly distorted by the confetti of numbers). Our heritage is thus one of asymmetrical discomfort, which isn't improved by the fact that the elaborate statistical language that enables us to see the big picture of the wealth of nations has no counterpart in the lenses we use for the close-ups of our own homes.

The average man and his sidekick the probability man provide us with another version of the Crystal Palace paradox. They subsume our uniqueness in homogenized anonymity and highlight that uniqueness at the same time. They are the individual human beings we can't see because all cats are gray in the statistical dark. Each, in his way, is the other who is not one of us. Both average man and probability man stand in striking contrast to the presence of everyman in our literary heritage, where everyman is consistently the odd man out. At the beginning of the medieval morality play *Everyman* (c. 1485), the protagonist is approached by Death and Everyman's fair-weather friends (Fellowship, Kindred, Cousin, and Worldly Goods) immediately desert him. Good Deeds, Knowledge, Discretion, Strength, Five-Wits, and Beauty promise to stick by him, but one by one they drop away until only Good Deeds is left to accompany Everyman into his grave. The equation we expect—Everyman is every-us and every one of us is him—is subverted. Everyman is the other of total aloneness; his fate is upsetting not because we will all come to share that aloneness, but because as long as we can contemplate it, it won't be ours.

After the invention of average man and probability man, the idea of everyman takes on a new resonance as we expect him to be average and to participate in the probabilities of everyday life. He proves, however, to be out of step. In *Walden,* Thoreau is marching to the beat of "a different drummer."[30] The village eccentric with the gadfly persona, he is attempting to be that odd man out who is, in fact, everyman.

> I do not propose to write an ode to dejection, but to brag as lustily as chanticleer in the morning, standing on his roost, if only to wake my neighbors up.[31]

In "Dejection: An Ode," Coleridge lamented the loss of his "shaping spirit of Imagination." Chaucer's Chanticleer in "The Nun's Priest's Tale" struts toward his almost-downfall in foolish pride of flesh and intellect. Thoreau is announcing that he won't lament the loss of psychic vitality in his world but will make a fool of himself in the name of that vitality. His chanticleer persona strikes many modern readers as so noisy and abrasive that he can be dismissed as more odd than every, but to speak as and for everyman was Thoreau's aspiration.

The greatest everyman in twentieth-century literature upsets in a much more quiet way those comfortable expectations of the average and probable. The improbable but epic hero of Joyce's *Ulysses,* Leopold Bloom, is "Everyman or Noman,"[32] noman be-

cause that is the name Odysseus assumes in *The Odyssey* when
he's trapped in the cave of the Cyclops and because that is what
Bloom as a character in a novel must be: no man, but the imitation
of one. And as everyman, Bloom is utterly improbable. In Irish
Catholic Dublin, he is Jew/Protestant/Catholic/Freemason/agnos-
tic/atheist. In Nationalist Dublin, where the citizenry is unanimous
in its conviction that only revolutionary violence will make
Ireland "a nation once again," he stands alone in his fumbling
way.

> —But it's no use, says he. Force, hatred, history, all that.
> That's not life for men and women, insult and hatred. And
> everybody knows that it's the very opposite of that that is
> really life.
> —What? says Alf.
> —Love, says Bloom. I mean the opposite of hatred.[33]

In sports-loving Dublin, he is all thumbs and has two left feet. In
Dublin's pub culture, where manhood is measured by the pint, by
competitive put-down, swagger, and curse, Bloom refuses the free
drinks ("God almighty couldn't make him drunk")[34] and charita-
bly refrains from aggressive self-assertion, except for one outburst
that worries him for the rest of the day ("Mistake to hit back," he
thinks).[35]

Bloom's function as everyman is not to be average man or
probability man. He is not there to represent every-us but to be
the catalyst, to precipitate a crisis of revelation for his fellow
citizens in the mythical city of Dublin and for us in what David
Jones calls our "placeless cosmopolis."[36] We touch ourselves in
and through Bloom not because he subsumes us in the bell curve
of his averages and not because he reassures our comfortable
sense of ourselves as exceptions, but because, like him, we fail
both to be unique and to be the same. In that failure and in our
recognition that Bloom is the only man of unself-conscious *cari-
tas* (Christian charity) and *pietas* (loyalty and devotion to family

and country) in braggart-Christian, Nationalist Dublin, we find the possibility of exploring and clarifying the everydayness of our lives. Molly Bloom is present in the novel as odd woman out to round off that day in the life because her womanly vitality (including the adulterous vitality that, pending for years, is finally asserted on 16 June 1904) precipitates a crisis that reveals her Dublin contemporaries for the anemic "lot of sparrowfarts"[37] they are. The Blooms' odd marriage out functions in its flawed way to show up the failed sacrament that is marriage Dublin style, not by being average or ideal, but by evoking the presence of both while denying the possibility of either.

The asymmetrical disparities multiply as we oscillate between the big picture and the close-ups of our individual lives. Average man jostles probability man; mass-market sameness and mass-market uniqueness compound each other and confuse our attempts to locate ourselves in the "placeless cosmopolis" of our world. But these disparities are a function not only of numbers but also of scale. In the middle of the nineteenth century, John Stuart Mill gave an elegant opinion about population growth in his *Principles of Political Economy.*

> There is room in the world, no doubt, and even in the old countries for a great increase in population, supposing the arts of life to go on improving and capital to increase. But even if innocuous, I confess I see very little reason for desiring it. . . . It is not good for a man to be kept perforce at all times in the presence of his species. A world from which solitude is extirpated, is a very poor ideal. Solitude, in the sense of being often alone, is essential to any depth of meditation or of character: and solitude in the presence of natural beauty and grandeur, is the cradle of thoughts and aspirations which are not only good for the individual, but which society could ill do without.[38]

But Mill was thinking of human beings still human in scale, closer to those on the farther shore of 1798 than to us.

Population has, of course, grown exponentially since Mill's time, but something more than just population density has happened to our perceptions of how we crowd one another, how our solitude is oppressed. The scale of our actions and habitations has been radically transformed during the same period. Technology has enormously extended the reach of the human musculoskeletal system. As individuals, we are much larger and much more powerful than the sixty-foot creatures Gulliver encountered in the Land of Brobdingnag. Those creatures were eighteenth-century giants without gunpowder (not to mention nuclear power), without the internal combustion engine to overleap local space and to transform axes into chainsaws, without jet and rocket engines to swing past time and put man on the moon, without electricity to light and heat living spaces and to power the thirty-odd electric motors that ease the workload in the average American household, without the fabulous networks of electronic technology that put our eyes and ears in touch worldwide and bring worldwide crowding into our workplaces and homes and that make the superspaces and superdensities of our skyscraper cities habitable.

The change in scale is staggering. For example, the infantry soldier in 1798 was armed with a musket and bayonet. The musket could deliver fire that would be felt—that is, it could wound or kill—at one hundred yards and that could be more or less aimed and regarded as decisive at forty to fifty yards; well trained, the infantryman could reload his single-shot musket in twenty to thirty seconds and thus could deliver two to three shots per minute. In 1914, the well-trained infantryman's bolt-action magazine rifle could fire, roughly every two and a half seconds, shots that would be felt at twenty-five hundred yards, aimed at a thousand, decisive at five hundred, and annihilating at three hundred. The quantum extension of the reach of an infantryman's arm between 1798 and 1914 is all too obvious.

The power gap between the reach of 1914 and the reach of 1984 approaches science fiction, given the fantastic technologies that have taken over the business of annihilation in the middle distances of the battlescape. The 1984 infantryman's automatic assault rifle is terrifyingly aggressive, in sharp contrast to the relative passivity of the 1914 bolt-action rifle. The 1984 weapon fires a continuous stream of smaller caliber bullets at velocities so great that the steel-jacketed bullets behave like the dumdum bullets that were outlawed at the Hague Peace Conference of 1899 because they caused such bone-shattering wounds. As its name makes clear, the assault rifle is ideal for bursts of annihilation in close combat—not to mention in acts of terrorism—and requires no more skill than, as John Keegan says, the use of an aerosol can of household insect spray.[39] In short, when we consider twentieth-century firepower, it is unimaginably farther from 1914 to 1984 than it was from 1798 to 1914.

The extension of the reach and power of our hands has been more than matched by the extension of the range of our nervous systems. The physical metaphor of the Brobdingnagians is useful for suggesting the ways in which those giants are dwarfed by our physical size as enhanced by our technology, but it is useless when it comes to comparisons with our extended capacity to see and hear, not to mention the capacities of our memories and the speeds at which, thanks to the computer, we can index and cross-reference and calculate.

The augmentation of our neuromusculoskeletal system is frequently useful and exhilarating, but as we all know, it has its drawbacks. We are superdependent on the goods and services that enable us to inhabit our altered scale. All too often, we're not up to our scale: one small error, a misplaced finger, a moment of impatience, or an averted glance can be devastatingly magnified by a power saw, automobile, assault rifle, or the nuclear button. As a result of our hyperscale, we are more vulnerable to and invasive of one another. Solitude, in Mill's benign sense of the word, is at a new premium. The telephone, the automobile, the portable tape player—the teeming and still-multiplying products of our technology—have raised the interest rates.

*   *   *

Another of the legacies of paradox from the Crystal Palace world of the nineteenth century is what I call the Rosetta Stone syndrome. That slab of black basalt, dating back to 195 B.C., was found in the Nile Delta in 1799 and eventually deciphered (circa 1822) by Jean François Champollion and others. The hieroglyphic languages of ancient Egypt were suddenly open to translation and study, and that instance can stand as a metaphor for what nineteenth-century research and scholarship were to achieve in the study and translation of the vast compendia of the world's languages and literatures. In effect, the great age of Western imperialism was matched by a cultural fever to possess, to establish a cultural imperium that gathered an extraordinary range of literary works into the libraries of the Western world and published those works for the rapidly growing audience of the literate. The British Museum Library began in 1753 with the modest nest egg of Sir Hans Sloane's collection of fifty thousand volumes; by 1900, the collection had grown to over 2 million volumes, not counting the fifty-five-thousand-plus volumes of manuscripts and the hundreds of thousands of maps and other documents. In 1900, the Bibliothèque nationale in Paris, which traces its lineage to the libraries of Louis XII and beyond to Charlemagne, topped the British Museum Library with 2.6 million printed volumes and 102,000 volumes of manuscripts.

These numbers describe the explosion of eclectic opportunity in the nineteenth century. Omnivorous readers of the eighteenth and early nineteenth centuries—Dr. Johnson and Coleridge, for example—rarely complain that the range of their reading is dwarfed and humiliated by the vast number of books available. By the early twentieth century, that complaint is pandemic to the point of plague and is attended by a chronic sense of the world of the mind as disoriented, cut loose from its traditions, its center lost and irrecoverable. T. S. Eliot's lament for the fragmentation of what he calls the "Tradition" and Ezra

Pound's wonderfully ravenous response to the range of opportunity opened by the eclectic explosion are contrasting cases in point. For Dr. Johnson and Coleridge, realizing the ambition to be generally well read was within reach, and a community of the educated who shared that distinction was at least imagined to be a given among educated men and women.* In 1984, the idea of being well read and of belonging to such a community is a joke we have politely learned not to mention except with a shrug of self-deprecation.

In 1984, the English-speaking commercial and university presses of the world published over fifty thousand books, of which only a small fraction is reviewed or brought to public notice.** If half that number were dismissed as trash and if teams of reviewers prepared one-page single-spaced summaries of the worthwhile half, the aspirant to an overview would have to spend over fifty eight-hour days surveying these summaries as his overview dissolved. And these big national numbers leave out of account the thousands upon thousands of books in languages other than English, the thirty to fifty thousand scientific journals published each year in the Western world, and the quasi-infinite production of paper that the computer has made possible.

---

*In his letters, Gilbert White obviously assumes that his correspondents share his acquaintance with those we would think of as the important writers and works of his day: Dryden, Pope, Swift, Addison, Steele, Thomson, Gray, Johnson, Hume, Gibbon, Sterne, Priestly, Adam Smith, John Gay, Boswell; in the background, the Bible, Homer, Virgil, whom White calls "that notorious poacher," Horace, the Koran, *Piers Plowman,* Chaucer, Shakespeare, Milton. This was the communal literacy of the well read.

**The *New York Times Book Review* covers over a thousand titles a year and the daily newspaper between 350 and four hundred, but with many overlaps. *The New York Review of Books* manages roughly 550 titles a year, and the *Times Literary Supplement* another fifteen hundred, but again with many overlaps. Thus the assiduous reader of reviews would notice only something like three to four percent of the books published each year.

As daunting as these numbers are, do they constitute a fair reflection of poetic, critical, scholarly, and scientific enterprise in our world? Over a twenty-seven-year period from the 1950s through the 1970s, the Viking Press is said to have received 134,999 unsolicited manuscripts and accepted exactly one for publication. (Surely not all of the other 134,998 were as off the wall as the one I once evaluated for the press: a book-length poem in heroic couplets that sought to resolve the dilemma of the nuclear age.) How much larger is the actual scale of creative enterprise than the already intimidating scale of what is published and noticed?

In the United States alone, and not included among the fifty thousand books, there are more than thirty-six hundred little magazines and private presses that publish relatively unknown literary writers for small audiences, presumably of their friends and neighbors. A competent critic couldn't possibly sift through that in a year, and to undertake to do it in three would be a nightmarish chore.* Even those vague numbers—thirty-six hundred ventures that publish thousands upon thousands of writers per year—may provide a poor measure of the actual number of closet writers, or, if we take the word *writers* as figurative, of unknown or unrecognized creative talents of all kinds in our midst. For example, ninety-six thousand people in New York City identify themselves for the census takers as visual artists. On average, there are fifty to sixty gallery or museum shows of living artists each month in the city, and by no means all of the six-hundred-odd artists who do get shown each year will be selected from the resident ninety-six thousand. Even if they were, we would only be looking at a city-wide representation of six-tenths of one percent of those who aspire to be counted as visual artists.

Figures of this sort suggest yet another mind-boggling dispar-

---

*The magazine *Poetry* receives approximately seventy-five thousand unsolicited poems in the mail each year. An editor who spent two minutes on each of those poems—eight hours a day, five days a week—would be at it for more than a year.

ity between the scale of our enterprise as individuals and the big numbers associated with publication and national recognition. This disparity in turn tempts us to politicize creative and scholarly enterprise. Little wonder that we find ourselves seeking and cultivating agents and contacts in order to achieve publication, banding into schools, wangling appearances on talk shows, behaving in flamboyant and outrageous ways, and performing stunts in order to excite and attract notice. Consider how hard it is to follow René Dubos's advice to think globally and act locally when, thanks to the reach of our hands and the range of our amplified voices, thanks to our superhuman scale as individuals, we are constantly tempted and frequently half-convinced that we can enter and act in the big picture.

These disparities suggest to me that there is a greater chance at present than ever before in our history that a major talent—a major poet, for example—could be and remain lost among us. One of the great miracles of American literary history is that Emily Dickinson didn't get lost. Only seven of her poems appeared in print during her lifetime, all of them anonymously, apparently none of them at her urging. After her death, the 1,775 short lyrics that survived were closer to the fire than it's comfortable to think; and we now regard her as one of the major poets in English in her century. Melville and Thoreau also had their troubles in the lost-and-found department of that century. But the numbers and the noise that advertised and obscured in the nineteenth century were as nothing compared to the numbers and noise of 1984.

These questions of the quantity and scale of individual creative enterprise in our timespace continue to trouble my perception. The city-state of golden-age Athens had a stable population of about twenty-five thousand. What did the inhabitants of that city see as they moved about in a century or so dominated by Aeschylus, Sophocles, Herodotus, Euripides, Thucydides, Socrates, Aristophanes, Plato, and Aristotle among them? What of High Renaissance Florence, population one hundred thousand, with

Dante, Cavalcanti, Giotto, Masaccio, Donatello, Leonardo da Vinci, Michelangelo, Galileo, and Alfieri in its midst? Why has Ireland, with a stable population of 4.5 million since the late nineteenth century, had and does it continue to enjoy such an extraordinarily rich literary renaissance? Is there hope for the 4.7 million of us in Massachusetts?

Proverbial wisdom says that two can keep a secret if one of them is dead. In the 1980s, we now have this national hue and cry about security and secrecy. A secret is presumably information of importance known to a few and not to be shared with others, particularly not with others who are opponents or enemies. But that commonsensical notion dissolves once we encounter the numbers. In 1984, the U.S. government classified over 19.6 million documents, sorting them into four categories: sensitive compartmented information, the most secret; top secret; secret; and confidential, the least secret. In that same year, there were more than one hundred thousand people cleared for the first category; six hundred thousand cleared for the second; and 3.5 million with lesser orders of clearance. To define secrecy in the context of such numbers defies the imagination as well as the lexicographer. So overwhelming is the quantity of secrets that no individual could hope to achieve an overview; presidents, beginning with Eisenhower in 1956, have found the President's Foreign Intelligence Advisory Board (PFIAB) a continuing necessity. But even that board can no longer guarantee an overview because, thanks to their anonymity, those who share secrets in the service of national security can create secret secrets on their own. Criminals require a cloak of secrecy to protect their enterprises. Conversely, when the security-state provides its operatives with an official cloak of secrecy, those operatives are free to behave in criminal ways, and the security-state is free to disclaim responsibility for those criminal ways as in that tangled web called the Iran-Contra affair.

Once upon a time, a secret was something qualitative, valuable to keep, and presumably coveted to one degree or another by those from whom it should be kept. A secret was a two- or three-person deal like the plan to surrender West Point to the British that Benedict Arnold shared with Major André (until André was accidentally captured between the lines and the plot was revealed). But these 1984 numbers of secrets and secret-keepers suggest that secrets are no longer personal; that they are quantities to be processed, sorted into categories, stored, and circulated; and that to be a spy is not to learn a secret from a careless or inept or corrupt secret-keeper but to gain access to the realm of process where the classified documents flow. This is accomplished through electronic eavesdropping, through computer manipulation, and, increasingly, through individuals—not those who reveal secrets for old-fashioned reasons such as animosity toward superiors or hidden loyalty to an enemy, but individuals who sell their security clearance, their access to the classified flow. For once the jargonmongers have gotten it right: these salespeople are called access agents. When they are caught and indicted, the number of documents they have conveyed to the purchasing agents of the other side is measured not by the page but by the cubic foot—360 cubic feet in one outstanding case.

When those of us on the outside of this supermarket of secrecy condemn such behavior as amoral, we have missed the point by thinking of secrecy and loyalty in terms of the moral imagination of the individual. The bureaucratic mind that presides over the security process opts instead for quantification; it quantifies the secrets and their keepers into categories and calculates the risk of loss at each level. In this realm, honesty and loyalty are no longer individual modes of behavior vulnerable to the cynical axiom that every man has his price. Honesty and loyalty become probabilities to be appraised in much the same way that manufacturers and merchandizers appraise the brand loyalty of their customers: loyalty by Nielsen rating. As for the amorality of those who sell secrets, the quantification of secrets has had the effect of turning secrets into a currency. They flow like money and are therefore for buying and selling, and that is why these supposedly amoral spies sell for what sound to the outsider like very modest if not low prices—thirty-odd thousand dollars a year over a period of ten years for photocopies of naval-intelligence documents, no big deal.

When the White House undertakes "a sweeping, secret overhaul of U.S. defenses against spying," the enterprise is described in terms that announce a further bureaucratic quantification of secrecy.

> The changes were culled from 400 recommendations suggested in studies begun by the NSC [National Security Council] staff in 1981, and in consultation with affected agencies and Congress.

The secret report "outlines 40 new proposals and improvements in more than 60 other areas."[40] Once upon a time, we settled for Duke Ellington: "A slip of the lip / Will sink a ship."

An interim solution would be to assemble copies of all the classified documents of the last ten years, scramble them, and then crate and ship the lot to those we perceive as our enemies. If each classified document amounted to ten typewritten pages (and such brevity is very doubtful indeed), the assembled material would add up to nearly two billion pages, enough to fill my house solid with paper from cellar to garret almost sixteen times. That mountain of paper would, I submit, fulfill for years to come the splendid toast "Confusion to our enemies."

At the heart of Judeo-Christian tradition lies the axiom "For God's Justice, he who kills one man destroys the world."[41]

Just as the quantification of secrecy undermines the moral imagination, so also, and in ways that are much more disturbing, the quantification of outrage and tragedy undermines our sense of justice.

At the beginning of the thirteenth century, Genghis Khan and his Mongol armies conquered their way from Peking to the Dnieper. Conquered cities that had been courageous or foolhardy enough to resist heard the cryptic command "The hay is cut, feed your horses," the exhortation and permission for the Mongol horsemen to pillage and massacre. In 1221 at Nishapur, the chroniclers say, it took the conquering Mongols twelve days to pile the skulls in pyramids and count the dead, all 1.75 million of them. A few years later, Nishapur was "a vast barley field," and the Mongol armies were elsewhere. From the perspective of 1984, Nishapur seems remote, fixed in a fictional space created by chroniclers known for their gross exaggerations (those numbers) and macabre inventiveness (those pyramids of skulls), a fictional space stylized by Persian prints. Nishapur seems more immediate to us as the native city of Omar Khayyám, the Persian astronomer, mathematician, and poet who died a hundred years before the massacre. The peaceful, sensual presence of *The Rubáiyát* seems to screen us from the massacre, though legend has it that one of Omar's boyhood friends grew up to found the Hashishin, the dreaded assassins whose heirs stalk the modern world as the so-called terrorists of Shi'a Islam.

The dilemma we face is how to live with the pity and the terror of massacre in this century of massacre without relegating it to a quasi-fictional past or dismissing it into the oblivion of numbers so large that they are incomprehensible or translating it into something transhuman and therefore sacramental. How are we to keep alive our moral outrage at the human injustice without suffering from what the jargoneers call compassion burnout. How are we to avoid Wilfred Owen's curse:

> *But cursed are dullards whom no cannon stuns,*
> *That they should be as stones;*
> *Wretched are they, and mean*
> *With paucity that never was simplicity.*
> *By choice they made themselves immune*

To pity and whatever moans in man
Before the last sea and the hapless stars;
Whatever mourns when many leave these shores;
Whatever shares
The eternal reciprocity of tears.[42]

World War I, 8.5 million dead; 7.25 million missing, most presumed dead; 21.25 million wounded. For the popular imagination there was, of course, the anesthetic of high rhetoric, of Arthurian chivalry and the defense of Camelot, of the Angels of Mons, of the honor and nobility of "the great sacrifice," of "the war to make the world safe for democracy," and "there shall dawn a radiant peace." Meanwhile, there were relatively large numbers of day-to-day casualties, dismissed by Field Marshal Sir Douglas Haig and his staff as "the natural wastage" of trench warfare to be endured until the dream of a breakthrough and victory could be achieved. The general staffs on both sides assumed that the preparatory assaults for breakthrough would be statistically costly. But the casualties at Verdun and during the Battle of the Somme in 1916 surprised even those expectations; at the same time, the numbers somehow sanitized the carnage until the strategy of breakthrough could be rephrased as the strategy of attrition. Casualty figures became a currency of exchange for the measurement of success, and the weekly body-count reports of progress in Vietnam were reckoned in similar coin.

Deprived of these anesthetics by a first-hand view of the wasteland called the Western Front, the anonymous participants in khaki, "the foot mob," came to know the moral bankruptcy of the sentimental heroics and idealisms of "Civvie Street" and of what appeared to be the high command's mindless insensitivity to the appalling waste of trench warfare. The general headquarters of the British armies in France was at Montreuil, a village with a well-appointed château, a comfortable seventy miles from the front. For the Battle of the Somme, an advanced headquarters was established at Beauquesne, fifteen miles from the front and well outside the five-mile-deep killing zone of the German artillery (airplane bombing had yet to realize its promise).

But a vision of the vast quantity and scale of the outrage wasn't available to the trench soldier either. He was locked within the narrow horizons of his bit of trench, his few square yards of wasteland. The fine print of the casualty lists in the newspapers might have given him some hint, but the normal response was not to gain an overview but to scan in search of friends and acquaintances. The trench soldier translated the casualty lists back into the immediate context of his experience of the battle zone, following the fate of his battalion from the distance of his hospital bed as Robert Graves recalls having done in *Good-bye to All That.*

Writing to his family from Paris in July 1815, not quite three weeks after the Battle of Waterloo, Edward Nevil Macready, ensign of the Thirtieth Regiment, sums up his experience.

> But I am endeavouring to do an impossibility to describe a battle, so little did we know of it next morning as we fought till dark that I assure you I expected to see the enemy on the heights opposite.[43]

The killing zone of that ten-hour battle was approximately half a mile deep and three miles wide. Ensign Macready's regiment was deployed on the forward side of a gentle slope in the front of the British line, about 450 yards to the right of center. What he did see was his battalion in square repulsing repeated French cavalry charges with evident good humor; he records the behavior, living and dying, of the men immediately around him. What he didn't see—thanks to the confines of stress, the limitations of the terrain, the dense clouds of black powder smoke, and the eventual fall of darkness—were what the historians describe as the five phases of a battle, which, while "a damned, close-run thing," according to the Duke of Wellington, was to result in a crushing defeat for the French army, which, during the night of 18–19 June 1815, virtually ceased to exist.

Ensign Macready was above ground on a battlefield that could have been surveyed from the slope where he stood. A hundred years later at the four-and-a-half-month Battle of the Somme, the killing zone was five miles deep and over twenty miles wide and so lethal that most of the eyewitness's life was spent underground except for brief spurts of assault, a few nightmare minutes out in the open. From my desk-chair perspective, I can enter the sharply confined horizon of the individual soldier-poet on the Somme. I can share his sense of outraged pity and terror at the despoliation and massacre on his few square yards of front, but when I raise my eyes to attempt the big picture, I draw a blank. The outrage is there, magnified, if that's possible, but invested with a stubborn disbelief that infuriates and numbs at the same time.

In his prose poem *In Parenthesis*, David Jones seeks a metaphoric bridge between the confining particularity of the individual's field of vision and a larger sense of the incredible waste of that war. He establishes a frame of reference that calls on the heritage of Anglo-Celtic poetry of warfare and disaster and focuses through a center of consciousness that, while close to Private John Ball's, expands toward choric inclusion of other voices and consciousnesses in Ball's platoon, Seventh Platoon, B Company, in an unspecified battalion of the Royal Welch Fusiliers. The result of this choric consciousness (with Ball as lead soloist) is that when the platoon is wiped out in an assault reminiscent of the assault on Mametz Wood in an early phase of the Battle of the Somme, the massacre becomes communal, a collective death.

But, no matter how effectively the locus of metaphor and the range of allusion urge a communal catharsis in poetry, the vision is frustrated when the magnitudes are quantified and published as numbers. At eyewitness time, the physical limits of the trench world and the blinders imposed by stress deny all possibility of overview. After the fact, sanity resists recall, let alone multiplication. In Robertson Davies's novel *Fifth Business,* the protagonist

Dunstan Ramsay briefly describes the battlefield at Passchendaele where he was wounded in 1917 and adds,

> I write of this now as briefly as I may, for the terror of it was so great that I would not for anything arouse it again.[44]

When he returns to the now "neat and trim" scene in 1924 in search of "the tiny area I knew about," he cannot find it, nor can he locate a sense of the whole.

> Even the vast cemeteries woke no feeling in me; because they were so big, I lost all sense that they contained men who, had they lived, would have been about my age.[45]

Much later, he approaches from a different angle the awesome disparity between the personal experience of being wounded and alone at night in the mud at Passchendaele and the big picture of the carnage (such experiences multiplied literally millions of times) in that 485-mile strip of wasteland from the North Sea to Switzerland,

> I am sure there has been worse wretchedness, fright, and despair in the world's history, but I set up a personal record that I have never since approached.[46]

If the eyewitness in fiction as well as in fact has to struggle to comprehend the scale of things beyond the limits of personal disaster, small wonder that we, only a few decades removed in historical time, find the full-scale carnage and horror of it so hard to grasp. The decades since 1918 have been crowded with outrage and massacre: in 1918–19, twenty-five million dead in the influenza epidemic that swept the world (taking its origin, the superstitious said, in the charnel house of unburied dead that was the Western Front); in the 1930s, millions of deaths in the U.S.S.R. (estimates vary from 20–40 million) consequent on Stalin's campaigns to collectivize agriculture, to suppress Ukrainian nationalism, to settle the Soviet nomads of central Asia in fixed abodes, and to purge the Communist party bureaucracy and the military; late in the 1930s, the Japanese massacre at Nanking and further carnage during the invasion of China; World War II and its depredations, including the fire-bombing of Dresden and Tokyo and the nuclear annihilation of Hiroshima and Nagasaki; twenty million dead in Hitler's Lebensraum invasion of Russia; and climaxing with the Nazi concentration camps, slave-labor camps, and death camps. The death-dealing has gone on, in Korea, Vietnam, Cambodia, in Central America and Afghanistan, in Ethiopia and the Sudan, in the Iran-Iraq war, and on the other killing fields, and in the torture chambers of the world.

Aspiring to know the agony of these disasters through their magnitude and finding it unknowable has its paradoxical flip side: disbelief that ranges from the perversity of outright denial (of the historical fact of the Nazi death camps, for example), through the forgetfulness born of not wanting to know (refusal to share historical guilt), to the shrug of indifference.

The corollary of this failure of the historical and moral imagination is that not being able to imagine the past, we cannot imagine the future. The immediate and future possibility of nuclear war and the annihilation of time is refused or shrugged off in callous disbelief. Large segments of our population continue to believe nuclear war survivable, even winnable. The big numbers that so clearly say otherwise defeat only themselves. The attempt to quantify outrage and tragedy subverts and denies tragedy, which cannot be intensified by quantity, as in Yeats's lines,

> *Though Hamlet rambles and Lear rages*
> *And all the drop-scenes drop at once*
> *Upon a hundred thousand stages,*
> *It [tragedy] cannot grow by an inch or an ounce.*[47]

The big numbers baffle us. What does a billion dollars mean? If I had been given a billion dollars on 1 January in the first year A.D., had collected no interest, and had spent one thousand dollars a day since, I would still have enough in January 1984 to go on spending for another 754 years, until 2738 A.D. Even as I write that, it strikes me as wrong, and I run to check with my pocket calculator. What can it conceivably mean to say that the nations of the world collectively devote nearly 900 billion dollars a year to military expenditures? That translates into 1.7 million dollars per minute, and that attempt to make the scale and folly of the waste understandable dissolves in a dance of meaningless numbers.

On the other hand, the big numbers perform miracles for the scientist intent on the atoms or the stars. Those realms are fabulously remote from the midrealm of our habitations, and as a consequence, the elegant approximations that describe those remote, and therefore conjoining, realms have the force of fable to fascinate and stimulate our wonder. But when sheer quantity is substituted for the scientific success of visionary approximations such as quarks* and black holes, when the numbers are reified and stand areferentially alone, then there is trouble—as in the spring of 1985 when the voyage of the *Challenger* was advertised as a success because it brought back 250 billion bits of computer data, enough, NASA said, to fill fifty thousand books of two hundred pages each (a year's worth of publishing). What conceivable relation does this blizzard of factlets have to the elegant approximations that are the scientific facts of the fabulous realms? And when we attempt to focus this midrealm of ours through the lens of the big numbers, the approximations should trouble us even more because they leave so much that matters out of account, because they seem so much more fragmentary than elegant.

Jane Goodall has spent over twenty years studying chimpanzees

---

*"Three quarks for Muster Mark! / Sure he hasn't got much of a bark / And sure any he has it's all beside the mark." Joyce, *Finnegans Wake,* 383.

in the wild and has immeasurably enriched our knowledge of those animals, of their intelligence and emotional complexity. And yet an interviewer with evident good will asked her recently if she could make a truly definitive statement about the nature of chimpanzees on the basis of the seventy-odd individuals she has studied. Goodall answered, "Of course not," just as she should—the obligatory answer to a profoundly mistaken question. The question assumes that only the big numbers qualify as definitive, but chimpanzees are, in the jargon, nonuniform events, so complexly so that no study of them could be regarded as definitive until the last individual chimpanzee had been counted and was dead. Meanwhile, Jane Goodall has vastly informed our intuitive expectations of chimpanzees and of ourselves. She belongs in that select company of natural historians fathered by Gilbert White whose fascination with the "manners . . . the life and conversation" of plants and animals commits them to a lifetime of observing and recording nonuniform events. Their virtue is the elegant patience that can accept the facts of nonuniform events as valuable in themselves.

So many aspects of our midrealm experience defy or subvert quantification. Dream researchers find that subjects start out reporting vivid and animated dreams, but that after a few sessions the dreams go dull, as though the alter ego or subego stage-managing the dreams had become reticent and decided to draw a veil. Thus the researcher's attempt to build toward a significant if not definitive, accumulation of data drifts toward ambiguity. The dreams or the dreamer have asked him to avert his gaze, to look elsewhere.

And there are even more elusive subjects, such as extrasensory perception. When we consider how much we as individuals can anticipate and perceive and understand on the basis of minuscule amounts of data in our everyday contacts in this midrealm (in the leaping and glancing shorthand of conversation between intimates, for instance), it is at least as though we had some form of ESP. But the researcher in the 1930s who undertook to explore this aspect of our mentation created a deck of fifty cards composed of ten identical five-card suits and asked the subjects of the experiment to extrasensorily perceive the individual cards as the researcher at a distance concentrated on them one by one. Subsequent research has asked similar questions with more elaborate controls. Most subjects in these ESP experiments score, as we would expect, close to the level of probability. A few subjects begin as adepts but gradually fade away toward the gray of the probabilities. And why not? Why would any intelligent creature want to trivialize such an unconscious, preconscious, consciousness-elusive capacity (if it exists) in a guessing game with five contentless, meaningless symbols. Why wouldn't most of us reserve the capacity for ESP for enterprise of significance? These sterile experiments with humans are like those we devise to test the intelligence of dolphins and orcas, as though Hula-Hoop games complete with rewards of fish are any measure. The real measure of intelligence is the orca who, trained to cooperative proficiency in all the games, quit one day and quite for good, intelligent enough, apparently, to recognize the trivial and dignified enough to reject it.

I come again to the fundamental disparities between the big picture and the close-up and find that another version of the Crystal Palace paradox awaits me. The distance between the close-up of Williamstown and the big picture on the national and global periphery is constantly challenged by the web of communication that keeps us so closely in touch with those peripheries, and those contacts are compounded by the challenge of the nuclear weaponry that threatens not just this or that target but the whole globe. Suddenly the far-periphery flips, and we perceive a world so shrunken in size that each of us lives at its center.

5.
Personal Worth and Self-Esteem

· ·

The various transformations of our modes of perception, and of the world we perceive, have so skewed things that we frequently and understandably don't know how to gauge personal worth or know whether our self-esteem is coming or going.

This essay began as "Celebrity and Personal Worth," but the bipolarity of that working title pitted the statistical anonymity of probability man and average man against the glitter and anomie of celebrity. An easy equation, it neglected and threatened to negate the third point of the triangle where the self, or perhaps more appropriately, the soul, the vital core and its worth, is to be found—in that geography of self-esteem mapped by David Hume when he suggested that, as individual human beings, we should be able to take a realistic pride in our talents and in their appropriate application.

The word *subjectivity* entered English usage in the 1820s, just in time to lend itself to the rapidly advancing process of the internalization of the individual self and a corresponding redefinition of self-knowledge, of what it would mean to fulfill the Apollonian urgency to know thyself. For Dr. Johnson in 1750, human individuality, "apart from adventitious and separable decorations and disguises,"[1] could be affirmed as that "uniformity in the state of man" basic to *consensus gentium,* basic to the tribal psyche shared by all well-disposed and reasonably educated men and women, the ability to reach accord and live in agreement. That tribal self was assumed to perceive and define itself in public, communal terms, in terms of its outward behavior, its conversation, and its disposition toward moral cooperation with others. Humanity was an estate held in common by educated men and women.

Within half a century, Wordsworth had pioneered a new sort of self-exploration, summoning up and contemplating "the picture of the mind,"[2] by which he meant the emotional and intellectual history of his own evolving mind—personal to him as the "Fair seed-time" of his soul[3]—and at the same time a metaphysical microcosm of "the Mind of Man / My haunt, and the main region of my song."[4] Wordsworth's "musing in solitude" involved transposing memories of subjective experience, "that which was before [earlier] the subject of contemplation,"[5] into a presence in the mind "kindred to" the recollected experience and at the same time not merely a subjective state but an objective presence that could be contemplated as though it were outside the mind.

The principal fruit of this radically new self-exploration was the so-called poem to Coleridge, Miltonic in its scale and sonorities, complete as early as 1805, published posthumously as *The Prelude* in 1850. When he first heard the complete poem read aloud over several evenings during the Christmas season of 1806, Coleridge found the poem immensely stimulating, "More than historic, that prophetic lay"; "An Orphic song."[6] But there was also a dark side to Wordsworth's self-exploration. In 1799, Coleridge was already apprehensive about his friend's "self-involution," concerned as he wrote to a mutual friend, "dear Wordsworth appears to me to have hurtfully segregated and isolated his being."[7] Sixteen years later, Coleridge traces to this hurtful segregation Wordsworth's unfortunate tendency to proclaim as great personal and introspective discoveries

> truths, which the generality of persons have either taken for granted from their Infancy, or at least adopted early in life.[8]

Wordsworth had his own apprehensions about this self-involution. He perceived it as a risky undertaking, treading on "shadowy ground," capable of breeding more "fear and awe" than the contemplation of Erebus or Chaos, and he gave as one reason for withholding *The Prelude* from publication his conviction that it was "unprecedented in literary history that a man should talk so much about himself." When it was finally published after forty-five years of intermittent revision, *The Prelude* disappeared into the Victorian pond with hardly a ripple. Only since the 1940s has it come to be regarded as the centerpiece of Wordsworth's *oeuvre,* as Coleridge had maintained it should.

Had *The Prelude* been published in 1806, its unprecedented self-consciousness would have joined Jean Jacques Rousseau's *Confessions* (1781) in the real-life wing of the new pantheon of literary heroes. The fictional wing of that pantheon was to include those grand *"Isolatoes,"** those *angengers* (Anglo-Saxon for "alone-goers"): Goethe's Faust, Shelley's Prometheus, Byron's Childe Harold and Manfred and all their lonely siblings, including Milton's Satan, recycled in the early nineteenth century as the Romantic rebel warring against abstract and impersonal authority. The *angengers* of Anglo-Saxon poetry—"The Wanderer," "The Seafarer," and even Grendel—stand in interesting contrast to this new breed of alone-goers. The Anglo-Saxons lament their aloneness, their lack of a lord as focus for their allegiance, and their

---

*"*Isolatoes* too, I call such, not acknowledging the common continent of men, but each *Isolato* living on a separate continent of his own." Herman Melville, *Moby-Dick.*

need of a troop of fellows with whom to share the warmth of the mead hall. The Romantic hero, on the other hand, affirms himself alone—as "the wandering outlaw of his own dark mind"[9] who revels in that darkness, outside the realm of rational conformity and the distraction of society—because the quest for forbidden knowledge (Faust), for a picture of the deep withinness of the mind (Wordsworth), for "a being more intense" (Byron)[10] becomes a quest for a higher level not of self-assertion but of self-being. This quest must by definition be outside the probable and ordinary course of social and conscious experience. So urgent was the desire to conceive the self as internal that the blank of Shakespeare's personal life became a positive embarrassment. A life had to be invented or found for him (Bacon? Oxford? Southampton? Rutland?) so that his inner life could be said to have given rise to his art, so that he could stand revealed as the "thought-tormented" Hamlet in disguise.

By the middle of the nineteenth century, this self-involution, this focus on the individual psyche, had expanded to include the exhilarating (and threatening) possibilities of psychological relativity, which were explored by Melville in the mythopoeic enterprise of *Moby-Dick* and in the tormented shadow world of *Pierre: or, the Ambiguities.*

> Say what some poets will, Nature is not so much her own ever-sweet interpreter, as the mere supplier of that cunning alphabet, whereby selecting and combining as he pleases, each man reads his own peculiar lesson according to his own peculiar mind and mood.[11]

Melville's masterpieces went unread and disappeared into oblivion—largely, I suspect, because their vision was too dark and forbidding, the psychology, particularly of *Pierre,* too harrowing. It was far easier to shoot the messenger than to read the message.

Not so with Browning's *The Ring and the Book,* a poem that explores the same tangled web of psychological relativity. But

Browning—even though he had been accepted by 1869, along with Tennyson, as one of the two official great Victorian poets—was widely regarded as "difficult of comprehension, hard of assimilation,"[12] and his determination to baffle the British public's "sentence absolute for shine or shade"[13] could be sidestepped along with the difficulty of comprehension in favor of the poem's "transcendent spiritual teaching" and "the immortal features . . . [the] insufferable beauty" of the poem's martyr-heroine, Pompilia.[14] She in turn could be sentimentally fused in the public mind with the dedicatee of Browning's poem, Elizabeth Barrett Browning, dead seven years when the poem began to appear.

At the end of this century of anticipation, there was Freud and the theory and practice of psychoanalysis—a Calvinism for the twentieth century—to urge guilty exploration of the repressed sexual energies in the unconscious dark of the isolated self.* Wordsworth and Coleridge had assumed that the deep withinness of the mind, while scary, is ultimately and essentially benign; not so the Melville of *Moby-Dick* and *Pierre* at midcentury, and certainly not Freud at the century's end. But our modes of perception haven't been so much darkened by the somber expectations of Freudian theory and practice as they have been modified to expect the self to reach toward self-definition by deep introspection and, if necessary, with the aid of an analytic confessor.

What was avant-garde in the opening decades of this century has become so commonplace, if not commonsensical, that even

---

*And a strange corollary: by the 1920s, Freud was fashionably (and eventually popularly) supposed to have argued for radical personal liberation from that repressive sexual morality widely caricatured as Victorian. That mistaken application of Freud was assumed to assure psychic health via sexual permissiveness. The poor Victorians were blamed for a morality that had been firmly in middle-class place in plenty of time to trip up Byron, and much earlier to comfort Richardson's heroine in *Pamela, or Virtue Rewarded* (1740). That morality was vigorous enough one hundred years before Victoria to survive Fielding's burlesque response in *Shamela* (1741) and *Joseph Andrews* (1742).

the most superficial preferences and prejudices ("I love peanut butter and hate umbrellas") are confessed on television's talk shows as though they had deep psychic roots in the "dark backward and abysm" of personal history ("I feel so good about myself since my divorce and thanks to this wonderful new therapy and diet and my exercise program"). I turn from such talk with the impatient conviction that our narcissistic definition of self needs a countervailing emphasis on the self as seen from the outside, not in mirrors but as defined with the help of the refracting, reflecting presence of others and the Other. I don't mean more of that relentless emphasis on socializing with which we oppress the young and through which we promise rewards not to those who inhabit themselves but to those who turn themselves inside out.

Impatience with Romantic self-involution is hardly new. Goethe anticipates that impatience in his reaction to the Werther-cult that developed among sentimentalists who overlooked the controlling ironies of *The Sorrows of Young Werther* (1774). Indeed, he added a blunt tag to subsequent editions of the novel: "Be a man, nor seek to follow me!" Byron appears to indulge romantic self-contemplation—and what Bertrand Russell miscalled "Titanic cosmic self-assertion"—in *Childe Harold's Pilgrimage* and in *Manfred,* but Byron undercuts the Romantic self as "quicksilver clay" in *Don Juan* (1819–24), a splendid orchestration of ironic reversals. In that comic epic, there are numerous indications of Byron's turn away from self-involution, including his repeatedly expressed desire to overleap the subjectivism of Wordsworth and Coleridge's aesthetic and to rejoin Fielding, Pope, and Dryden in an artistry that reasserts the aesthetic distance of satire and restores the self to its social face, outside out instead of in.

These contraries, the vigorous tradition of self-definition by self-involution as against the frayed tradition of the self defined in social and communal terms, suggest the possibility of a self-esteem realized through coordination of an understated personal dimension with reinvigorated public dimensions. Given the past two centuries of overemphasis on self-involution, it would seem that playing down the personal dimension should give us the most trouble in seeking a coordinated sense of self; we can well imagine self-involution to have been so deeply ingrained in us as to be virtually impossible to shake. The paradox is that the public dimensions may very well prove much the more troublesome to recover. As George W. S. Trow has argued, "the middle distance" has fallen away and only two grids remain to us, "the grid of two hundred million and the grid of intimacy."[15] For some sense of a reasonably scaled public worth, most of us would have to depend on communities of response that have disappeared into the void of the lost middle distance. Without them, we are deprived of the refracting, reflecting presence of the Other. We are left with the affirmation of the immediate few with whom we are intimate and with the responsiveness, if we are fortunate, of the relatively small circles of our domestic and working acquaintance. Beyond these localities, the public worth of the self becomes a matter not of presence but of politics, the politics of national reputation, the politics of celebrity, the politics of managing to be wanted for appearances on television talk shows and for snapshots in *People* magazine, for the intimate close-ups promised by *Vanity Fair* in a promotional letter ("Jerry Hall with no clothes, Ron and Nancy with no inhibitions, Raquel Welch with no holds barred") as though any intimacy would remain after such publication.

On the face of it, media attention seems to offer to touch us, to let us know that we exist, but that knowledge turns out to be illusion. José Torres, former New York State athletic commissioner, fingers this illusionism when he denounces the popularity of professional wrestling:

> In America, it's the era of the fake. "Miami Vice" is a fake. Rambo is a fake, and even President Reagan is a fake. When we idolize what is not real, it frees us from responsibility.[16]

It also closes the circuit of illusion. The managing editor of *People* was refreshingly candid with G. W. S. Trow and made the symbiotic relation between the magazine and its celebrities all too clear. To sell itself, he said, the magazine needs "certain celebrities." To this end, the magazine cooperates with the "movie studios and networks" that have an interest in those same celebrities.[17] In turn, the celebrities and studios and networks need the magazine to celebrate and sell themselves. From *People*'s perspective, there are three classes of people: "certain people we want," the staple celebrities; "marginal people,"[18] people in for a day or two by lottery or accident; and, unstated, the nonpeople, a class that includes all the rest of us in what Henry James called "the horrible numerousity of society."

Ishmael locates himself and us as the third-class people in the headlines he imagines at the beginning of *Moby-Dick*:

> *"Grand Contested Election for the Presidency*
> *of the United States*
> "Whaling Voyage by One Ishmael.
> "BLOODY BATTLE IN AFFGHANISTAN"*

Most of us, like Ishmael, have only bit parts in history. Fair enough. But our awareness that we are only spear-carriers is rubbed in daily by the media's celebration of people whom we correctly perceive as not much more knowledgeable or skilled or brilliant or cogent than many of us or our neighbors or fellow workers in the small towns where we sojourners are, for the moment, stationary.

Once more, a version of the Crystal Palace paradox: we find ourselves caught in the torque of asymmetry between the human scale of our daily lives and neighborhoods and the big pictures that we cannot enter without a near-fabulous combination of

---

*The "Grand Contested Election," though in doubt, is probably William Henry Harrison's 1840 defeat of President Martin Van Buren's bid for a second term. The "Bloody Battle" was the massacre in 1842 of the British army of occupation as it retreated from Kabul.

personal endowment and luck and intense personal ambition and political effort. We also cannot enter without the risk of lives preempted by the media and the audiences the media have imagined or conjured into existence; we cannot enter without the risk of lives invaded by celebrity-seekers and inhabited by a committee of agents, lawyers, CPAs, ghostwriters, personal secretaries, make-up artists, coaches, handlers, hangers-on, and bodyguards.

The media do their annual December-January duty. The old year is passed in review, summed up in an index of twenty-odd names of people well known, apparently in some in-world remote from our neighborhood. Only a few of the names are known to us, but we assume the others are similarly known to others. The names turn to face the new year and utter wise predictions about the year 2000. Gradually we become alert: little as we know these talking names and heads, we know them as the sources of their utterances far better than we know the truth of their predictions.

Until late in the nineteenth century, the word *celebrity* suggested something a good deal more solemn than its present connotations. It carried the solemnity we associate, for example, with celebration of the Mass or, its secular equivalent, the opening line of Whitman's "Song of Myself," "I CELEBRATE myself, and sing myself" (1881). In the 1913 edition, *Webster's New International Dictionary* offers this definition of celebrity:

> 1. Celebration; solemnization. *Obs.*
> 2. State of being celebrated; fame; renown; as, the *celebrity* of Milton. "An event of great *celebrity.*"
> 3. A celebrated person. *Colloq.*

By 1970, what was colloquial in 1913 has become sober and primary:

> 1. A famous person.
> 2. Notoriety or renown; fame.[19]

Or, in Ellen Goodman's colloquial version, "people who are known for being known."[20] In a strange way, the word in 1984 seems to be seeking its Indo-European root (*"kel,* to drive, set in swift motion")[21] in order to remind us that nowadays celebrity is life in the fast lane, where the newest in-word is *celebrityhood.* It may also just possibly be trying to remind us of Milton's ringing conviction:

> Fame *is the spur that the clear spirit doth raise*
> *(That last infirmity of noble mind)*
> *To scorn delights, and live laborious days.*[22]

What Milton had in mind was not so much the infirmity induced by the ambition to be famous but the Renaissance faith that the aspiration to fame would spur the individual to virtue—in Milton's case, the virtue of the poet-prophet. This fame wouldn't be judged by human or worldly praise but by the "perfect witness of all-judging *Jove.*"

A century after Milton, in the secular terms of 1798, fame was still thought to spur the individual to manifest deeds of political virtue, to be judged, as Burke and Washington and Jefferson and their peers thought, not by popularity or public acclaim but by one's peers and at the bar of history. Fame in itself was to be regarded as sufficient, society's highest reward for public virtue.

In 1984, the desire for fame doesn't spur us as much toward virtue as toward money and power; it has become not a reward in itself but a means via which we can seek other, more tangible rewards. Thus celebrity exists in a shadow zone, somewhere between fame and notoriety. The memoirs and lecture tours of celebrity journalists and of Watergate criminals alike command sizable fees, much more sizable than those doled out to my neighbors in this village, many of whom read and write and lecture for a living.

*   *   *

In 1798, at the age of ten, George Gordon became the sixth Lord Byron of Newstead. Overnight, he was released from a childhood dominated by his mother's genteel, grinding poverty and was on his way through Harrow and Trinity College, Cambridge, toward a combination of fame and notoriety that we would call celebrity—but with a difference. His celebrity was still human in scale. As a peer of the realm, Byron was a person of note, to be noticed, not by the masses (except from a deferential distance), but by the aristocracy and the upper-middle and the so-called educated classes, less than one and a half percent of the families of Great Britain and Ireland, a small-scale grid in no way comparable to a media audience in the 1980s. To be known in that class-dominated world was to be known by word of mouth, and, even for a poet like Byron, by gossip as much as by print. Byron's rise to fame began socially when in 1811, at the age of twenty-three, he returned from two years of an unusually daring and romantic grand tour that included Albania, Greece, and the Levant. Political fame was added to his romantic rake's progress in 1812 when he made his maiden speech in the House of Lords, defending the Nottingham frame-breakers* and opposing a bill to make them capital offenders, to be punished on the frame of the gallows. His position was radical enough to cause alarm in the drawing rooms of the upper classes, and he was widely regarded, as he half-feared he might be, as "too lenient towards these men, & *half a framebreaker*" himself.[23] On 10 March 1812, the morning after publication of the first two cantos of *Childe Harold's Pilgrimage,* Byron "awoke," as he said, "to find myself famous," and not only as a poet. By a process of alchemical combination of the poet, his flamboyant personal life, and his hero, Byron-cum-Childe-Harold

---

*The frame-breakers were textile workers who sabotaged new frames, or looms, because they enabled one worker to do work that had previously required five or six. The frame-breakers were protesting technological unemployment. Byron added that the new looms produced shoddy goods that were fit only for export (and for the mill-owners' greed).

became a Werther figure for his generation; famous as a fashion-plate, a role model for the daring, gay, melancholy, disillusioned, world-weary Byronic hero; a heroic figure with a commanding hold on the imagination of his time. His image later in the century was to pass into popular culture,* but it's hard to assess the scale of Byron's fame at its inception. When biographers say that Byron was subsequently lionized by Whig society, they can only be talking about fewer than a hundred families (hardly a Nielsen rating). And when, in 1814, Byron's publisher sold ten thousand copies of *The Corsair* on the day of publication, what was the scale of that literary riot among the 1.5 million inhabitants of greater London, where less than ten percent of the adults were literate? When the notoriety attendant on the highly visible disintegration of his marriage to Annabella Milbanke and the scandal of his incestuous liaison with his half-sister Augusta Leigh drove him into permanent exile in 1816, the scale of that scandal and ostracism could hardly have been much larger than the small circle of his class. And though annoyed by the stares of English travelers on the Continent, he didn't face anything like the number we associate with package tours in these days of easy and frequent travel.

In effect, Byron's celebrity was intimate in scale and largely personal to him, eventually available to him for use in creating an extraordinarily effective satiric persona. In the midst of canto 3 of *Childe Harold's Pilgrimage,* he shifts from a third-person narration that treats Harold as the other, the he of the poem, to first person—as Byron, with tongue in cheek, explains in the dedicatory epistle of canto 4.

The fact is, that I had become weary of drawing a line which every one seemed determined not to perceive . . . it was in

*Molly Bloom recalls that when Bloom was courting her in 1888, he was "trying to look like Lord Byron." Joyce, *Ulysses,* 18.209.

vain that I asserted, and imagined that I had drawn, a distinction between the author and the pilgrim; and the very anxiety to preserve this difference, and disappointment at finding it unavailing, so far crushed my efforts in the composition that I determined to abandon it altogether—and have done so.

When he set to work on his masterpiece *Don Juan* in 1818, he was firmly in control of the public mask, the caricature-persona of Lord Byron. From the public's point of view, the ostensible hero of the poem, Don Juan, the legendary Spanish libertine, was just the immoral sort that the womanizing Byron (driven out of England, and good riddance, by God) would choose. The actual hero of the poem is the narrator, who improvises effortlessly, his tones and moods as constantly shifting as quicksilver clay, his satiric thrusts demolishing the pretension and humbuggery of the established institutions and cherished values of Western society. The voice is close to that of Byron the conversationalist—he was, by reputation, second only to Coleridge in his time—and close to the Byron of the wonderfully spirited letters to those he trusted. Thus Byron turned the tables on the public expectations excited by his celebrity and revealed his true worth in the process—a satiric epic that was readily despised by his enemies, a poem about which most of his friends and well-wishers had their doubts, but about which Shelley was to remark, "Every word of it is pregnant with immortality!"

The figure of Byron as the ultimate romantic poet-hero was formed by a sort of collusion, a complex collaboration between Byron's poetic imagination, the various personae performed by him or attributed to him, and the literary audience, which included many who wanted to identify with the amalgam Childe-Harold-Byron, Manfred-Byron, Byron-the-Corsair. The popular appeal of the Byronic hero kept the satiric Byron of *Don Juan* in eclipse throughout the nineteenth and well into the twentieth century. The Byronic figure offered its audience the possibility of a vicarious life, romance and adventure by proxy and at minimal risk. But in the course of the nineteenth century, the source of those offerings of vicarious lives was to shift from the daydream scenarios stimulated by public and published figures—a Byron or a Shelley or a Beau Brummel or an Elizabeth Barrett or a Robert Browning—to the new diet provided by the dime novel and popular fiction, nourished in the coincidence of a radically broadened franchise of literacy* and the commercial success of the new mass-market publishing houses and that "d——d mob of scribbling women"[24] that was the bane of Hawthorne's existence. The split, so familiar to us now, between commercialized popular culture and whatever the allegedly elitist alternative is called was relatively new but already vigorous in America by the 1840s.

The new literacy, with its broadened franchise, had its ironies. It had the effect not so much of liberating the previously illiterate but of destroying "spoken proverbial traditions" (the rich oral memory bank of songs, ballads, stories, jokes, sayings, proverbs) without admitting the newly literate to "a written cultural heritage."[25] While the written heritage had always been more or less conversant with the spoken traditions, those traditions were gradually lost to both popular culture and to its literate alternative, to the point where the late-twentieth-century teacher of Chaucer, Shakespeare, Dickens, Joyce, Hawthorne, Melville, and even Henry James must be prepared to alleviate his students' ignorance of not one but two foreign languages: that of the written cultural heritage and that of the spoken proverbial tradition.

In 1846, with more apparent than real confidence, Poe could aspire to poems and fictions "that should suit at once the popular and the critical taste."[26] But a year and a half earlier, Hawthorne

---

*From early in the nineteenth century in America and after the educational reforms of the 1830s and particularly that of the 1870s in Great Britain.

had suggested, with rueful and whimsical self-pity, that any such attempt at achieving the middle ground was doomed.[27] So it would seem to have been. Maria Susanna Cummins's bestseller *The Lamplighter* (1854) sold more copies in its first year than all of Hawthorne's novels and collections of short stories sold in the whole decade of the 1850s.

Democratic idealism in this country (and the possibility of making a living through the commercial sale of one's writings) dictated that serious writers aspire to Poe's middle ground, where the popular and the critical taste could conceivably overlap. But the overlap became increasingly rare after the 1850s, and the lens of retrospect offers some suggestions as to why. Hawthorne and Melville (neither of whom could support themselves through their writing, though Melville did enjoy an initial moment of tantalizing success) are readable today, whereas Maria Cummins, Horatio Alger, and their fellow scribblers (who could support themselves) are not. Hawthorne and Melville's best fictions have roots in both the written cultural heritage and in spoken proverbial traditions. As fictions, they keep their aesthetic distance and challenge us to imaginative response. They shift and continue to reward as we probe and reread.

Cummins and Alger's fictions repeat, with pale variations, the same formulas over and over. They are dated, the thin stuff sufficient unto the daydreams of their time. Many commentators suggest that these popular fictions express the prevailing ethos of an age, but Cummins and Alger don't tell us as much about the prevailing ethos as they tell us about how people wanted their daydreams packaged. When we read those novels, we don't encounter substance that invites response. We find instead a tissue of reflective surfaces on which we can read images of the audience's desires: the desire to be reassured that this amusement, however titillating, is morally instructive; the desire to believe that if they were good and unselfish and hardworking, Providence would intercede and provide. The provisions would include, among other rewards, a social pedigree (suspensefully hidden from the orphan heroes and heroines until the last chapter). Both Cummins and Alger were particularly big on social class. Few of Alger's one-hundred-plus heroes are born to rags, though a fall from privilege into rags, or at least into socioeconomic difficulty, is central to their rites of passage. In *Rags to Riches,* where the hero really does start at the bottom, he makes it up the ladder only as far as respectable middle-class servitude. Money, the Alger emblem of success, would also be provided, conferred by deus ex machina rather than accomplished by toil in the world's machine.

Clyde Griffiths, the protagonist of Dreiser's *An American Tragedy* (1925), has an imagination thoroughly infected by the Alger virus. He's always dreaming of, hoping for the miraculous intervention that will vault him from lower class to upper class, that will rid him of the impediment of his working-class girl-friend's pregnancy, and finally, that will save him from the electric chair. The tragedy is that Clyde's Alger-nourished, malformed imagination of the American Dream is precisely what dooms him to be ground to bits in the world's machine.

These popular Cummins-Alger scenarios are widely supposed to be the opiate that alleviated the drab dailyness of the urban-industrial world. But in practice, the commercialization of the daydream seems to have provided a starvation diet that makes the dailyness even more drab and sharpens rather than satisfies the appetite for romance and adventure. How else does one explain the extraordinary outburst of popular and chivalric enthusiasm in England during the summer and fall of 1914 for what promised to be the great adventure of World War I—and in this country in 1917, after the hopelessly achivalric nature of that adventure could and should have been known?

Even in World War II—when the disillusion modern war can produce had become almost a cliché—a few of my contemporaries in the American Field Service in North Africa in 1942 arrived anticipating adventure-at-last. When I was drafted into the Army of the United States in April 1944, most of my fellow draftees were "from the bottom of the barrel," older men with families who until then had held war-industry jobs. On the train to Fort Dix, there was a riotous sense of release, out of the drab dailyness into the army and adventure-for-real. But, after three days at the fort, dawn had begun for the adventurers, revealing a dailyness drab enough to transform their urban-industrial home towns into the dream-province of Camelot.[28]

The daydreaming reader of popular fiction is vicariously one-on-one with the romances and adventures of the faceless heroes and heroines in the hand-held book and with the villainies that beset them. Aesthetic distance gives way to over-generalized emotion; comedy blurs into sentimentality, tragedy into melodrama. But Hollywood added a new dimension to this commercialization of daydream by creating the star system. In that crossover network, the faceless and disembodied heroes and heroines of popular fiction acquired real-life faces that could kiss and bodies that could touch one another on screen, and they could carry that semblance of flesh off-screen into the endless orgies of the gossip columns and movie magazines. The viewer no longer had to endow his daydreams through his imagination. The stars crossed over from the realm of print and were really there, flesh and blood. Hollywood heroes and heroines were being portrayed by the practitioners of a new art, the art of the star, in which a personality not readily distinguishable from the personality of the actor became the primary part the actor was to play. The part assigned by the script became secondary, valuable not as an end in itself but for what it could contribute to the enhancement of the star-personality. The stage door, once symbolic of the discontinuity between the private lives of the actors and the public roles they were to play onstage, was replaced by the revolving door of commercial continuity, the publicized lives created by the star system dissolved into the actors as the actors dissolved into celluloid imagery. Elizabeth Taylor and Richard Burton step straight from the bejeweled extravaganza of their celebrated lives into the celebrated roles of Antony and Cleopatra without a moment's hesitation between the fictionalized fact of their lives and the factualized fiction of Shakespeare on film. Clark Gable doesn't act the part of Rhett Butler in the traditional sense. He acts a personality that has been evolved by and for Clark Gable in clothes and with lines and gestures appropriate to his role in *Gone with the Wind.* The crossover is epitomized in an exchange between John Wayne and Kirk Douglas. Wayne asked Douglas why he was acting the part of a weak, sniveling guy like van Gogh instead of "strong, tough characters." Douglas says that he replied "Hey, John, I'm an actor. . . . It's all make-believe, John. It isn't real. You're not really John Wayne, you know."[29]

The star system, an integral part of the Hollywood crossover network, has been radically expanded by and subsumed into the celebrity industry since the beginning of the TV age. On the assembly lines of that industry, the celebrity finds that the permeable membrane between private self and public image becomes uncertain, subject to rupture and dissolution, to the point where it is more often than not hard to survive celebrity unscathed. Norman Mailer, himself a writer-celebrity, is probing the danger of that dissolution when he speculates at one point in *Marilyn* that Marilyn Monroe had "no psychic skin" and at another that she had "no social skin."[30] The implication is that she had no sense either from inside or outside of where the permeable membrane was that individuated her. Conversely, we as consumers make that membrane uncertain by fawning on celebrities, by imposing our own daydreams on them, even to the mad point of killing to cannibalize them and make their celebrity ours. The membrane we help both to create and fracture deceives us into assuming that beneath the glitter of that celebrity skin there must be realities much more congenial and satisfying than any of the realities that hedge our days.

To date, the ultimate masterpiece of the crossover network

is the triumph of Ronald Reagan, the actor-president who qualified for the role of president not through distinguished political thought and action but by being "a man whose entire career had been based on the assertion of an agreeable personality" and who has behaved as "the genial host [of] the great American talk show."[31] The electorate has become audience. Those who govern do so by right of celebrity. The governed become celebrity consumers who daydream that beneath the surface of the host's genial, aw-shucks manner there must be profundities well-nigh unimaginable. We the audience filled in the vacuum behind the tinseled surface of that agreeable personality by reading ideological prejudice as firmness, resolve, and leadership; by accepting shallow optimism as a renewed sense of national purpose. We forgave his fabulous preference for fiction over historical fact and resented those who quibbled over details as inconsequential as factual accuracy. We applauded the morality plays he substituted for determination of policy. We cheered the photo opportunity of a "nation poised for greatness" without stopping to ask what the word *greatness* on those cue cards meant, so sure were we "that beneath the illusion is some superior reality, and we would all be better off if that reality had been served."[32] What we have overlooked in this consolidation of a society of celebrity consumers governed by celebrity politicians is that the hype promoting the politicians is frequently scornful of us.

Behind the facade of celebrity politics, the bureaucratic state is notoriously impervious to political efforts to change it, to restore it to something vaguely human in scale, something the individual citizen could address with confidence that he might be heard. Now, reinforced by computers, the bureaucracies are evolving into that superimpervious entity, the demographic state. In this new nation-state, political thought is reduced to a numbers game, and the electorate-audience is screened from the implications and consequences of its government's actions by the president as talk-show host and squads of public-relations experts and image manipulators who can portray diplomatic disasters in the Middle East and Central America as the promise of peace at last, who can call moral and economic losses long-term gains, who can fire White House zealots like Oliver North and describe them as national heroes. When, in November 1986, Reagan strayed into the clueless labyrinth of not-knowings and misrememberings called the Iran-Contra affair, the audience was assured day after day, month after month, that one more press conference, one more legal explanation would "put the mess behind him." The first of those press conferences turned out to be Reagan's first difficult one as president—that is, the questions were informed and real—and he left the podium with the bewildered air of a man who has forgotten the way to the men's room in his favorite restaurant.

Government by celebrity means foreign policy by pageantry and display instead of diplomacy in the service of clearly articulated national and international goals. It means domestic policy not formulated through discussion, debate, and compromise but designed instead to produce a series of symbolic occasions that will assure the demographic applause of the public-opinion polls.

The combination of faceless, unresponsive bureaucrats, professional politicians, and celebrity leadership presents the citizens of the megastate with a cruel dilemma. How can we achieve the personal worth of being heard and of expecting a response without either recourse to the game of manipulating numbers and citing opinion polls or recourse to civil disobedience doomed to be lost in media distortion, silence, and apathy. Public-opinion polls don't formulate policy but confuse it, pro or con, with the irrelevance of numbers. Civil disobedience, if it is heard and published as heard, could possibly affect policy. But how rarely the practitioner gets to control his gesture and its publication as Thoreau had the good fortune to do, and yet what he had to say went unnoticed for over half a century. When his questions were finally heard by Gandhi and Martin Luther King, Jr., they were translated into a grammar not of personal independence but of collective action. The success of those movements in India and in the American South depended on unique combinations of inspired and charismatic leadership and latent public energies ready to be sparked. In this age of celebrity and demographics, it is tempting, and probably mistaken, to think that such combinations are there for the making. The Thoreauvian questions about the ambiguous relation between public majorities and the individual majority of one remain unanswered.

The average urban dweller in the United States is exposed to five thousand advertisements per day; few of us, even in small towns, could qualify as other than urban. So great is the quantitative exposure to advertising that inattention has become the rule of the day. Once, in 1940, I stood on a busy street corner in Boston and read all the signs and slogans I could see to a blind friend. We were there—and astonished—for over half an hour. But that seems simplicity itself when I compare it to the flood of sound and image on radio and TV and in the newspapers and in the supermarkets and malls and boutiques and in the clutter of catalogs—nine pounds per week—in our mail box. What remains, the subliminal end product of all this animation, is undifferentiated appetite interfolded with the desire for instant gratification.

As variety overwhelms us with its quantity and promise of uniqueness, all choice other than the arbitrary ("Blue is my favorite color") blurs toward the continuum of gray. The only choice that remains seems the choice of appetite itself. The other imperative is instant gratification, to crave the hit that is now and to reject the bore that is all of the past and the bore of delay, which is, after all, only the future. Together, the twin imperatives of appetite (active) and gratification (passive) urge the abolition of any aesthetic distance that would rebuke appetite and practice the delay of an actively discriminating receptivity.

The flood tide of advertising thus joins the celebrity crowd to eliminate the middle distance, to promise us all a universal intimacy and, as a consequence, to isolate us in the unrelieved littleness of our everyday lives.

In 1940, e. e. cummings focused the two propositions that he regarded as the golden rules of advertising in his poem, "anyone lived in a pretty how town." The hero, anyone, and noone, his lover and wife, are those rare and anonymous beings, natural and virtuous people in tune with the seasonal rhythms of their lives. They are contrasted with the someones and everyones whose time is out of joint in mass conformity.

> *children guessed (but only a few*
> *and down they forgot as up they grew*
> *autumn winter spring summer)*
> *that noone loved him more by more*
>
> *when by now and tree by leaf*
> *she laughed his joy she cried his grief*
> *bird by snow and stir by still*
> *anyone's any was all to her*
>
> *someones married their everyones*
> *laughed their cryings and did their dance*
> *(sleep wake hope and then) they*
> *said their nevers and slept their dream*

The golden rules of advertising are:

(1) Anyone (any nonentity) can wear, eat, drive, own, enjoy an X; if you want to be someone (distinguished, outstanding, celebrated), you should wear, eat, drive, own, enjoy a Y.

(2) Everyone (in-the-know, distinguished, outstanding, celebrated) is wearing, eating, driving, owning, enjoying a Y; only a noone (a nonentity) is wearing, eating, driving, owning, enjoying an X.

In the logic of advertising, the individuals Anyone and Noone share the denegrated middle term X and are both out of it and therefore share an elective affinity. The collectives everyone and someone share the celebrated and coveted middle term Y and are made for the dislocated rhythms of their lives. They are those whom cummings delighted in calling "mostpeople," those who seek at once to be lost in the crowd and to stand out from the crowd. That double seeking defines the undifferentiated appetite urged by advertising and culminates in a self-canceling conformity to the Crystal Palace paradox, celebrity in the demographic state. cummings' everyones and someones live in the grid of the millions; his anyone and noone inhabit the grid of their anonymous privacy and intimacy. Advertising and its handmaiden, celebrity, have swept away the grids in between, the neighborhoods and communities and city-states, where the anonymous we would otherwise seek the echoes and reflections that would enable us to identify our exoskeletal selves.

What about the fashionable and commercially successful cult of youth and its corollary, the cult of fitness and health? Where does the commerce of fitness (the clothes and shoes, the machines and health clubs) leave off and the sense of a healthy body and its mind begin? In the midst of this heightened self-consciousness ("I jog every day and watch my weight and avoid red meat"), who can escape when even reaction against the cult and denial of its claims circle back to feed the self-consciousness, the doubts of the body, its proper condition and strength, its tone, its vitality and sexuality?

Gilbert White and his contemporaries were well aware of the need for exercise, though the assumption was that it would come about in the normal course of the day, through riding and walking, gardening and doing the chores. The emphasis was not on appearance but on staying well coordinated and agile, able to move about and function. When White complains of one of his neighbors who doesn't get much exercise, it is to suggest that soon she won't be able to move about at all.

The advocacy of gymnastics and the corollary emphasis on physical exercise in modern culture dates from the middle of the nineteenth century. It began in Berlin with the strident reformer Fredreich Ludwig Jahn, the *Turnvater* (father of gymnastic exercise). From the outset, his *Turnvereinen* (gymnastics clubs) were closely linked to the intensities and excesses of German nationalism. The rise and institutionalization of gymnastics elsewhere in the industrialized world was summed up in 1904 as

> a product or result of modern life and conditions. The increasing number of densely populated cities, the stress of industrial conditions requiring a correspondingly complex and exacting mental or technical preparatory education, as well as a lifetime spent under conditions frequently injurious to good physical health or development, have all contributed to render the practice of gymnastics an absolute necessity to the individual, and a subject of serious importance to the nation at large.[33]

But in the nineteenth century, exercise was primarily for men and had two distinct purposes: first, to prepare athletes for field sports and games; second, to develop and maintain the physical and mental health of the individual (from Marx's point of view, to improve the work efficiency of the working classes; for those European countries with compulsory military service, to keep the trained reserves fit for active duty). One direction suggests specialization; the other, exercise for the sake of exercise or for the good of the state. The success of specialized exercise can in part be measured by the athlete's or the team's performance. The success of exercise for its own sake is in large part subjective for the individual, statistical for the state, and much more difficult to evaluate. It leads the individual into a tangle of acute self-consciousness, urged by the frequently misleading role-models promoted by fashion, celebrity, and advertising and lures the state into statistical generalities about national health and fitness.

From the beginnings of the commercialization of exercise in

the nineteenth century, the entrepreneurs of exercise have been troubled by the difficulties of evaluation, of how to prove product reliability. One popular solution is to measure success by increase in muscle size. The English strong-man Eugene Sandow made a fortune promoting that solution in person and in *Physical Strength and How to Obtain It* (1897); that book included blank charts in which the reader could record his measurements, measuring his progress en route to the glistening, bulging biceps sported by Sandow himself. And now, a century later, the obsession with health and fitness has become a designer activity that aspires to self-parody, and the loneliness (or rather the narcissism) of the long-distance runner threatens to become hallucinatory. To no avail did nineteenth-century socialists and other critics condemn exercise for the sake of exercise as a middle-class self-indulgence, a waste of what could otherwise be useful productive energy. To no avail then as it would be to no avail today.

The professionalization of sport, particularly since the advent of television, has had the effect of radically intensifying the specialized training of athletes. The traditional distinctions between amateur (low-keyed, relaxed) and professional (keyed to hypertension) are being dissolved, not just in the Olympics and in the frequently scandalous realms of big-time college football and basketball but through the full spectrum of college and precollege sports, major and minor. In the past three decades, training regimens have become superdemanding, even in the most minor-league amateur competitions. Weight training means more or less standardized year-round training for what used to be seasonal sports. Steroids and other drugs are an ever-present temptation. The psychological satisfaction of the game well played, the race well run, even if lost, has given way to new "professional" standards: "Winning isn't everything, it's the only thing." Something of that same spirit has crept in to transform and speed the commercialization of exercise for its own sake.

The cult of youth enshrines a health and fitness measured by looking and acting young—beginning with exercise, diet, and cosmetics, advancing to include psychotherapy, medication, and surgery. The equation of Oscar Wilde's novel is twisted toward reverse. In *The Picture of Dorian Gray* (1891), the portrait of Gray mysteriously changes, depicting the process of aging accelerated by the eternally youthful Gray's dissipations. In 1984, the hidden portrait is the ideally unwrinkled face of eternal youth, the goal in the conditional present of our fitness regimens. Meanwhile, in the everyday dimensions of the unconditional future, undissipated but inexorably, we begin to wrinkle and creak with age.

Has the sexual revolution so widely advertised in recent decades really been so revolutionary? Or do we still peeceive ourselves much as we were before: the public scene changed without significantly altering the drumbeat of self-doubt to which the privately sexual self continues to march? Language and depiction have certainly changed, but whether that change has significantly altered our perception of our own sexual identities and those of others around us remains open to question.

Focused in retrospect through the lens of F. Scott Fitzgerald and others, the 1920s became known as the Jazz Age. But those short skirts and flat breasts, that cynicism and glitter and dishonesty were for the very few dodging in and out of Paris and speakeasies and the rotogravure sections of the Sunday newspapers. Meanwhile, the sober majority of us continued in lives subject to more or less Victorian confines. Ezra Pound, bidding farewell to an England caught in the aftermath of World War I, saw a generation with

> *Daring as never before, wastage as never before.*
> *Young blood and high blood,*
> *fair cheeks, and fine bodies;*
>
> *fortitude as never before*

frankness as never before,
disillusions as never told in the old days,
hysterias, trench confessions,
laughter out of dead bellies[34]

But twentieth-century caricatures of Victorian morality may have led us to overstate the advent of Freud and the coming of the Jazz Age as revolution. A sharp sense of sexual identity and vitality survived the over-quoted repressive severity of Mrs. Grundy and the nineteenth century. Indeed, that severity may well have honed that sharp (and precarious) sense even as it remained disguised and encoded. When Hawthorne's *The Scarlet Letter* appeared in 1850, one guardian of public morality condemned it as "such a dirty story," and another asked, "Is the French era actually begun in our literature?" They were not responding to chimeras but to the explicitly encoded emphasis on the heroine's sexual vitality. When, in the novel's opening scene, Hester Prynne emerges from prison with the emblem of her sin (a healthy three-month-old child) in her arms, the moral form book of Victorian convention says that, burdened by her sin, she should have pined and faded away during her confinement. But Hawthorne openly subverts that moral expectation by describing her dark, "Oriental" (sexually supercharged) beauty as enhanced rather than muted. And when much later she waylays her minister-lover in the "primeval forest" and lets down her hair, the reader alert to the conventions of popular fiction would perceive that gesture as an overt assertion of her sexuality, prelude to a reenactmant of the original seduction that had occurred a year before the opening scene of the novel.

> Her sex, her youth, and the whole richness of her beauty, came back from what men call the irrevocable past, and clustered themselves . . . within the magic circle of this hour.[35]

The Scarlet Letter was, from Melville's point of view, Hawthorne saying "No in Thunder." Melville tried a similar, more strident no two years later in *Pierre,* compounding the novelistic conventions of the fair (pure) beauty and the dark (sexual-sinister) beauty with a lush, romantic incest fascination. But his no was too loud and unequivocal; it all but terminated his faltering literary career. Readers in 1852 knew enough of the dark ways of sexual fantasy to know what they were reading, and according to my father, *Pierre* survived into his generation at the end of the century to be passed tattered from hand to hand as a forbidden book.

Ulysses we know to be post-Victorian, sexually explicit; my students had no difficulty recognizing that, but they did have trouble with Hawthorne and Melville and with the earlier, more conventional Joyce. When, in *A Portrait of the Artist as a Young Man,* Stephen encounters the young woman in the tidal pool, "her thighs . . . bared almost to the hips,"[36] he reads the moment as one of extraordinary poetic transport. But in a world where a glimpse of ankle was a sexually charged event, the moment begs to be read as an intensely sexual encounter as well as an occasion for Pateresque poetry. But for my students, the sexuality of that encounter was a casualty of the new freedoms of the so-called sexual revolution.

That revolution had, of course, its precursors. Declarations of sexual independence were popular among the New Pagans on the eve of World War I. After the war, Freud seemed to many to be advocating such a declaration, and many in my own generation announced themselves as determined to be liberated, to be rid of all inhibitions as though such ridding wouldn't in the final analysis rid one also of the sense of boundaries and limits that are so necessary to our precarious sense of sexual identity. George Lyman Kittredge, one of the great Harvard professors of this century, was fond of saying (when he was accused of being peremptory), "Nothing strengthens the mind like a few healthy prejudices." In paraphrase: "Nothing strengthens sexual identity like a few healthy inhibitions."

*   *   *

Historically, the internalization and subjectivization of the self that has occurred since Gilbert White's time was aided by the development of those traditions of personal privacy that we take so much for granted that we assume personal privacy to have been the desideratum, if not the norm, throughout human history. Not so. Privacy, Witold Rybczynski argues, was one* of "the two great discoveries of the Bourgeois Age," appearing in the Netherlands in the seventeenth century and spreading through England and northern Europe in the eighteenth. One corollary to the development of privacy was an increasing regard for the physical and psychological inviolability of the individual. Torture, for example, so widely used in religious and judicial inquisitions from the thirteenth century through the Renaissance was gradually abolished—in England after 1640; in France, 1798; in Russia, 1801; in the German states, 1806–31. Torture lingered on in various institutional forms of "cruel and unusual punishments," but those also declined, to the point where flogging was abolished in the U.S. Navy in the 1850s and in the British army and navy in 1881.

The institutional abolition of torture didn't, of course, eliminate those casual forms of cruelty we deplore as police brutality, but by the beginning of this century encyclopedic discussions of torture[38] are aglow with cultural self-congratulation: the good guys among moral philosophers from Cicero and Saint Augustine to Voltaire and Bentham have been against torture all along and have at last prevailed; in the enlightened world of Europe and North America, torture is no more. The era of self-congratulation proved short lived, as we too regrettably know. Torture was revived by Mussolini's street-corner thugs who administered massive doses of castor oil to terrify their political opponents with severe intestinal cramps. But that informal violence soon gave way to professional torture in Hitler's Germany and Stalin's Russia.

*The other great discovery was domesticity.[37]

Historically, torture has been rationalized as either punishment for a crime or a means of eliciting confessions and information about others from heretics, dissenters, and criminals. As a means of extracting confessions, torture has always been seriously flawed (and has been known to be). Vulnerability to torture varies widely among individuals: some are mysteriously immune to pain; many are so highly vulnerable that they readily subscribe to false confessions and attest to and even invent falsehoods about others. Indeed, in the gradual elimination of institutional torture, these practical flaws weighed almost as heavily as the concern for personal integrity and privacy. But these humanitarian and practical scruples were swept aside by totalitarian ideologies in the twentieth-century revival of torture, and refined twists on the thumbscrew were added. For example, the quantification of torture in concentration, labor, and death camps and the torture of individuals, ostensibly traditional, shifted toward a more sinister aim, "to coerce the personality of the individual into submission, to destroy self-worth."[39] Subtly and widely advertised, the inclusive purpose of torture and the concentration camps in Hitler's Third Reich was

> not only to punish enemies of the regime but by their very existence to terrorize the people and deter them from even contemplating any resistance to Nazi rule.[40]

The purpose of state terrorism was (and remains) to undermine the personal worth and self-esteem of entire populations. The techniques of that sort of mass dehumanization were incredibly refined by the Nazis. As Primo Levi has pointed out, the death camps were designed as great machines "to reduce us to beasts"[41] and "the SS Command showed itself in such choices [of camp guards and other cadre] to possess satanic knowledge of human beings."[42] At the heart of this method was what Levi calls "useless violence" because "before dying the victim must be degraded so that the murderer will be less burdened by guilt."[43] Indeed, there is also reason to believe that the baroque elaborations of those cruelties were designed precisely to discredit as mad fantasies the stories of any who escaped and tried to tell us. So at the end of World War II, we were all unprepared when the worst of the rumors and reports that had circulated during the war years were confirmed in the discovery and documentation of the camps. We not only absorbed the shock of how unimaginably awful that "inhumanity to man" had been, we also sighed with renewed innocence. "Well, that's over! That's why we fought this war! Never again!"

But since that resolve, variations on the themes of mass detention, disappearances, and torture have spread throughout the world in what has turned into a century of state and local terrorism and massacre. Techniques of torture have been further refined by the development of neuroleptic drugs and the computerization of terror. Even our own Central Intelligence Agency prepared what can only be described as a training manual and terrorists' field guide for the so-called freedom fighters attempting to overthrow the Sandinista government in Nicaragua. Personal testimony suggests that the CIA has organized courses in the techniques of torture for the police and armed forces of some of our client states. As one Honduran army sergeant has revealed,

> They [the CIA instructors] taught us psychological methods—to study the fears and weaknesses of a prisoner. Make him stand up, don't let him sleep, keep him naked and isolated, put rats and cockroaches in his cell, give him bad food, serve him dead animals, throw cold water on him [every half hour], change the temperature.[44]

And the question why torture? in our time is rendered the more bitterly upsetting by the realization that confessions and secrets can probably be more readily and reliably extracted by drugs than by pain. I say probably because we know that sodium pentothal as a truth serum is clumsy and difficult to control, but we don't know where the classified pharmacopeia of the CIA has led since its experiments with LSD in the 1960s. But whatever the status of truth serums, torture remains attractive because personal worth, while it certainly can be undermined by the humiliation of drug-induced confession, is much more satisfactorily attacked by the torturer's personal attention to the victim's pain.

We imagine that on the farther shore of the 1790s there was less respect for individual lives than we practice. We point to evidence such as the prevalence of capital punishment and the social and economic cruelties of rigid class systems. But Gilbert White and his contemporaries thought that the leaders of nations were morally obligated to respect the lives of their subjects and of one another. Thus White's quiet outrage not at the birth of the French Republic but at the new republic's execution of Louis XVI and the dishonor of his burial, "and his body flung into a deep grave without any coffin or funeral service performed."[45]

One outstanding example of this morality occurred early in 1806 when Charles James Fox, the British secretary of state for foreign affairs, was approached by a French adventurer who called himself Guillet de la Gevrillière and asked Fox's support for a plot to assassinate Napoleon. Fox not only refused, he placed Gevrillière in custody and warned his French counterpart, Talleyrand (and, through him, Napoleon), of the plot. One hundred years later, Thomas Hardy presented that scene in *The Dynasts: An Epic Drama of the War with Napoleon.*[46] He describes Fox as "astonished" by Gevrillière's proposal and has Fox say, half to himself, in the presence of his secretary,

> *Now what does strict state-honour ask of me?—*
> *No less than that I bare this poppling [boiling up,*
> *   bubbling] plot*
> *To the French ruler and our fiercest foe!—*

Fox's act (1806) and Hardy's dramatization (1906) bracket a century of at least the commitment to, if not the practice of, strict state honor. But now, in the era of 1984, state honor has undergone a sea change into superpower morality. The CIA has engineered or condoned several assassinations* and its plots to assassinate Castro (or to depilate his head and face and embarrass him into retirement) read like the antics of sinister Keystone Kops. The bombing raid on Tripoli in April 1986—all too clearly targeted on the life of Colonel Mu'ammar Qaddafi—can stand as the dark technological underside of the way the agents of our so-called security play with strict state honor.

Covert activities (including the encouragement of terrorism, the accommodation of torture, and diplomacy by assassination) are now justified and defended by advisers to the U.S. government as necessary to the security of the superpower and to its responsibilities to its allies and client states in the jungle of the modern world (where, after all, the other guys do the same). But what of our government's responsibility to its citizens and their individual and collective sense of personal worth? As instruments of policy, terrorism, torture, and assassination threaten not only the personal worth of the victims but also the personal worth of those in whose name such instruments of policy are condoned or employed. "For God's Justice, he who kills one man destroys the world."

When our anxieties about the morality of our superpower combine with our anxieties about the terminal potential of nuclear weaponry, the individual's sense of powerlessness (and, therefore, worthlessness) ranges from profound to staggering to unimaginable. This is even more sharply the case when we realize that large numbers of our fellow citizens and many in high office are

---

*Ngo Dinh Diem in South Vietnam; Jacobo Arbenz Guzmán in Guatemala; Salvadore Allende in Chile.

convinced, many violently, that covert activities are legitimate, that a nuclear war can be fought and won, and that those of us who believe otherwise are unpatriotic, idiotic, or naive. This public myopia has been nurtured by slack-minded talk about evil empires and Star Wars and, more particularly, by Pentagon talk (circa 1981) about strategies for fighting, surviving, and even winning a nuclear war. The key word in this strategy has been *decapitation*—the destruction of the enemy's command and control structure, assassination of his leaders and commanders by special forces and nuclear attack. At the same time, the strategy dictates that we protect our side from decapitation by supplying our leaders with phalanxes of bodyguards, by burying our command and control personnel under mountains, by hiding them at the bottom of the ocean, or by flying them high above the firestorms, the radioactive dust clouds, and the rubble. In short, we should protect those who would presumably have been responsible for the nuclear disaster in the first place. The unstated and devastating corollary is that the rest of us are worth nothing and can be left to shift for ourselves on the surface of the earth.

Personal privacy is, of course, an ambiguous state. The institutional privacy of solitary confinement is well known as a threat to sanity as is the extreme exposure of no privacy at all. Exquisite forms of solitary confinement combine the extremes: the light in the cell is always on, the eyes and ears of the guards are ever-present though the guards remain unseen. Another version of Big-Brother-Is-Watching is the legal nightmare of what the high-technology bureaucracies of our world have already done and might further do to invade, monitor, and record our lives, to test us for drugs, trace the flow of our money and credit, to eavesdrop on our politics and dissent. That civil libertarian nightmare depicts us as bleached worthless in the full glare of total exposure to publication. Conversely, we might ponder what the high-technology bureaucracies have already done to overpopulate our individual lives, to crowd our homes and workplaces and the stations in between with images and voices from all over the globe.

Gilbert White's privacy on the farther shore of the 1780s can strike us as phenomenal—cradled in a closed world of stasis and quietude—but within those apparent confines he led an intensely social life, in constant touch with his village and parish, his household animated by frequent visits by relatives and friends, his correspondence voluminous. White never seems to dwell on (or even imply) a sense of isolation. His writings reflect instead a continual participation in a lively, but by no means distracting, social and natural world.

In the overstated isolation of *Walden,* Thoreau structures his life not only as a book of hours but as a sequence of oscillations; the fifth chapter, "Solitude," swings toward the sixth, "Visitors," and the seventh, "The Beanfield" (and its isolation), gives way to the eighth, "The Village." Indeed, in the understatement of real life, the hermit of Walden Pond habitually took his midday dinner in Concord.

The pace of Thoreau's oscillation was measured by a three-mile walk. The pendulum of our oscillation between solitude and society can swing in an electronic split second; the distance traversed, magnified into the distance between the grid of intimacy (our individual Selbornes and Waldens and Concords) and the national grid of 220 million, the world grid of billions, the sights and sounds of the globe and its overcrowded electronic agora. The result of that oscillation can easily be what Leopold Bloom perceives as "lonechill," the individual isolated in "the cold of interstellar space."[47]

Altered modes of self-definition, ways of dressing against that cold, seem to be taking over in the decade of 1984. In 1975, 49.5% of a large sample of college freshmen identified being well-off financially as one of their primary goals; in 1986, the number had soared to 73.2%. In 1975, 64.2% thought that developing a philosophy of life was of significant importance; in 1986, 40.6%.

That 25% shift suggests self-definition by practical plan. One can't plan to develop a philosophy of life, and if one does so plan, part of the development, if it occurs, will be the realization that the original plan was naive, if not foolish. But one can plan to be well-off financially. One can outline and choose among the options—law school, business school, computer science, and forget the humanities and liberal arts. One can calculate how to "get on track," how to minimize "stress factors" such as marriage and children and other entangling alliances. This new breed of self-definers has been called "the Unromantic Generation" and described as a generation of "planners . . . not heartless, cold or unimaginative, they are self-preoccupied."[48] And, I would add, they are confident that they know their own minds; they can define their preferences for this or that life-style, for Perrier and white wine and condominiums; they can *prioritize* en route to life in the duty-free zone of anonymous affluence.

The word *life-style* carries the assumption that giving character to a life and having a style is just a matter of making the right initial choices in the Crystal Palaces—the consumer spaces that include colleges and universities—of our time. Life-style is to living a life what gimmicks and trends are to creating a work of art: mechanisms to attract notice and achieve celebrity.

The life-style mode of self-definition involves the expectation of simplified causalities, the lowest-common-denominator view encouraged by statistical generalities and read as demonstrating that all human behavior—social, economic, political, cultural—boils down to self-interest. So one should start there and head for those realms where wergild is calculated by cost-benefit analysis, where computers can tell us what the twenty-five-year-old graduate of the top-flight career school is worth (what his or her earning potential is over the next fifty years). To help us find our way in the wilderness of "stress factors" in the 1980s, there is an unending supply of personal-advice books: how to adjust to success (or failure), to alcoholism, to unruly children or aged parents, to midlife crisis, terminal illness, and old age.

The cult of self-definition by oversimplification doesn't stop with cost-benefit analysis and self-help books but expands to include the pleasures of a bipolar world with virtue in our camp and vice in theirs. It's a melodramatized world inhabited by a small band of true believers or patriots, besieged by billions of dolts, incompetents, and, in Lenin's phrase, "useful idiots" in addition to the enemy. This has, after all, been a century not only of massacre but also of absolute certainties and fundamentalisms (national, religious, Marxist, tribal) because modern fundamentalisms promise a sense of personal worth that will be proof against the challenges of moral, historical, and metaphysical doubt. In the light of the new fundamentalisms, the purities that should govern behavior are assured, and what Erik Erikson has called pseudo-speciation* takes command. Born again, the inerrantist becomes a religious pseudospecies, licensed to melodramatize and despise all the once-born opposition. Born again, the originalist becomes a constitutional pseudospecies, similarly licensed. Those of us who have been born only once seek the comfort of more subtle certainties and the license to embrace that most comforting of absolutes, the hatred of our enemies. The twentieth-century plague of fundamentalisms and neo-nationalisms reminds me that Ireland has, in the last 150 years, experienced two Devotional Revolutions: one after the Great Famine of the 1840s and another after the Troubles, the civil wars and strife of 1916–22 that preceded the establishment of the Irish Free State. In both cases, the revival of faith occurred not during the crisis but in the aftershock. In fact,

*The term denotes the fact that while man is obviously one species, he appears and continues on the scene split up into groups (from tribes to nations, from castes to classes, from religions to ideologies) that provide their members with a firm sense of distinct and superior identity—and immortality. This demands, however, that each group invent for itself a place and a moment in the very center of the universe where and when an especially provident deity caused it to be created superior to all others, the mere mortals.[49]

our time on this near shore of the 1980s could easily be characterized as a period of world-class aftershock.

For those in the upper echelons of celebrity, self-definition is liable to come not so much from personal-advice books and fundamentalisms as from the audience, from the celebrants and what they want to see and hear—what they want to consume. At the very top of the celebrity pyramid, self-definition is liable to be managed by a committee of agents, lawyers, accountants, public-relations consultants, speechwriters, masseurs, make-up people, acolytes, and bodyguards. Thus it's hard to believe that the first president to have a bodyguard was the sixteenth, Abraham Lincoln, who was living and working within a few miles of the Confederate enemy. Presidents now have battalions protecting them. The first president of the United States to employ a full-time speechwriter was the thirtieth, Calvin Coolidge. Judson Wellner managed the job single-handedly for Coolidge, but his position has evolved into a multitiered committee in the course of the last sixty years—a presence so readily assumed that a reasonably intelligent college sophomore could ask me, in the good faith of 1982, who Lincoln's speechwriters were for the Gettysburg Address.

When these new modes of self-definition (cost-benefit analysis and market research) are projected into caricature, it is as though the self were being defined so that it can be imitated by a computer, as though the whole tangled question of artificial intelligence were to be resolved not by creating a humanly intelligent and responsive machine but by turning a human being into a machine so that it can be imitated by a machine. It's Alan Turing's game in reverse: trying not to create a computer that can fool a human being into thinking it human, but trying to create a human being who can fool another human being into thinking it a computer.

*   *   *

When I turn from self-definition by cost-benefit analysis, pseudo-speciation, and market research to enter what Keats called "the vale of Soul-making"[50] where many of us would prefer to labor, I find that the mystery inherent in the proposition "it is not natural to be human" still abides. Wordsworth, for all of his fascination with the growth and history of his own mind, continued to cling to the eighteenth-century assumption that growth would culminate in a fixed maturity. Once the season of growth was accomplished, the fully fledged poet would find himself on a plateau where he would be employed—as Spenser and Milton had been before him—in the service of "the enthusiastic and meditative imagination." Wordsworth didn't achieve this growth without cost. After he felt that he had arrived, around 1798, the moments of "celestial light" he had experienced in his childhood and youth came less and less frequently and then ceased altogether, no longer available except through the indirection of recall. Wordsworth lamented this as the loss of the primary source of his creativity. Coleridge, in answer, said that he shared a similar sense of loss, but asserted that the joy of the creative imagination comes from within the soul. Coleridge thus implies that joy can be reentered and realized through further spiritual growth. In the next generation, Keats could face calling "the world . . . the vale of Soul-making" without the sense of loss consequent on the assumption of fixed maturity. Keats seems to have been comfortable, as Wordsworth wasn't and Coleridge was only partially, with the prospect of open-ended growth. Not that Keats didn't have a sense of sorrow and pain in the mature world; that much is obvious in the figurative resonance of *vale,* as in "vale of tears." But for Keats, as for subsequent generations, the assumption that the soul was to be made and remade throughout life was a challenge rather than a distress.

That vale where the making takes place has been, and remains, a realm of mystery where the aides to navigation are as undependable as they are numerous.

During the last several decades, we have been urged in a

variety of ways to improve our responsiveness to what William James called "the inner feelings, and . . . the whole inner significance of lives that are different from our own."[51] We have been urged (and taught to urge ourselves) not to be elitist, racist, or sexist. The urgings have produced a new set of thou-shalt-nots— negative imperatives in the service of James's positive ethical principle and, as negatives tend to be, ambiguous guidelines for the cleansing and purification of the self. I can so readily surprise in myself the forbidden impulse:

> *I too knotted [knitted] the old knot of contrariety,*
> *Blabb'd, blush'd, resented, lied, stole, grudg'd,*
> *Had guile, anger, lust, hot wishes I dared not speak,*
> *Was wayward, vain, greedy, shallow, sly, cowardly,*
> *   malignant,*
> *The wolf, the snake, the hog, not wanting in me.*[52]

These lines from "Crossing Brooklyn Ferry" partially review what Whitman called the "dark patches," which we presumably share.

In some moods, I wonder what it means to profess this study of literature if not to feel, at times, elitist, conservative, authoritarian, to be committed to what Matthew Arnold called "the best that is known and thought in the world"[53] and not always to be patient and temperate in its service. And why, when my elbows are surprised by the world, do these momentary blips of racism and sexism make their grotesque gestures from the wings? Why does the dark, impassive face in the subway conjure images of mugging and assault? Why do the nervous Arabic-speaking travelers at the security check in Heathrow spell hijackers? Why do the nifty hips in the slick skirt prompt a quickly suppressed whistle? Whitman felt that most of us must surprise those gestures in ourselves, and I cannot think that they invalidate and make a mockery of our attempts to improve our perception of others, our sense of "the inner significance of other lives." Quite the contrary, the dark patches, recognized for what they are, may confirm and spur our enterprise by grounding it in the shared earth of our humanity and not in the purities and abstractions so dear to the thought police.

Personal worth and self-esteem may seem precarious to most of us as we confront the sharpening sense of our isolation and powerlessness on this near shore. But I wonder whether Whitman and Thoreau were more secure on the shifting sands of their shore or whether it was that much easier for White and Wordsworth and Coleridge to establish a working and coordinated self. Different, certainly, but they too must have had those periods when the self seems an unruly committee with an undependable chairman. There must have been then, as there is now, room for tentativeness and self-doubt in the complex interaction between the personal enterprise of taking appropriate pride in one's talents and the social enterprise of realizing the significance of other lives and, by reciprocity, one's own.

6.
How Are We Housed?

· ·

In exploring the question of how we are housed, I came to think of being housed as involving a sequence or hierarchy of edges or boundaries, physical and social. At the center, there is the physical house, located on its site and in its neighborhood, and set in turn in increasingly larger units of man-made and natural surround. There is also the family of those housed, set in the context of neighborhood and the larger contexts that reach out toward nation and community of nations. The question thus expands to include consideration of how near at hand or far away those boundaries seem to be—whether they're nearby and can be seen and touched or whether they seem remote, beyond all possibility of contact; whether they're oppressive and disturbing or supportive and reassuring.

When Gilbert White looked up from his worktable at The Wakes in the village of Selborne, how did he see himself as housed? What was the place of his habitation? Writing in 1875, one memoirist describes the "plain room," with White's bookcase and thermometer still in place, as White's "study." But the concept of a private study postdates White by a generation. He would have regarded that room as a small parlor, one of the public spaces of the house where he and his guests would gather; where he also would work on his sermons, his *Naturalist's Journal,* his correspondence, and some of his experiments as naturalist; and where he would keep part of his collection of curiosities of natural history and archeology.

A generation later, Wordsworth's wife and sister would be concerned that "William's little parlour" at Dove Cottage was more and more frequently invaded by the press of family and visitors in that small house. Their concern was eventually alleviated by the move to the much larger house, Rydal Mount, where "William's study," complete with Brussels carpet, meat safe, sofa, and two writing desks was finally a securely private space. At The Wakes, White spent much of his indoor working time in a small parlor on the second floor that overlooked his gardens, until he added a large new parlor on the ground floor with low-silled windows that opened directly onto the garden. This lowering of the house to ground level was an eighteenth-century development in England.

> People began to feel that the main rooms of a house should be in touch with the outside world—not just by views through the windows, although increasing attention was paid to these, but also by means of having the rooms at ground level, with low-silled or actual French windows opening straight into the garden.[1]

White had anticipated his great parlor and the lowering of his house with earlier alterations to the inner garden, by "levelling my grass-plot and walks at the garden-door, & bringing them down to the level of the floor of my house" (i.e., down two feet).[2] From the perspective of his worktables in those two parlors, White would have perceived his gardens as integral parts of the house, as outside rooms: the inner garden with its perennial border immediately behind the house, flanked by vegetable gardens and orchards, with the outer or wild garden beyond, seven acres of small fields laid out in grass walks defined by high hedges with urns to mark moments of interest on the route and a giant carpenter's cutout of Hercules at the far end under the Hanger, the abrupt wooded hill that overlooks the village street of Selborne. Eleven acres all told—a smallholding, lands cultivated, not for an entire income as does a farmer, but to supplement the resident's income. The gardens were the natural historian's workrooms. They were also relatively public spaces, especially the wild garden with its parklike walks and the access to the commons land above on the Hanger that it provided to the village as well as to White and his household.

Care and management of these bachelor spaces, indoors and out, was the cooperative enterprise of White and his assistants: a gardener-groom-handyman; a "weeding woman"; at least one, sometimes two, maids for "parlour and kitchen"; and extra help for gardens and fields recruited as necessary, usually from the poor who were always with Selborne, and with late-eighteenth-century rural England. In 1780, the household was expanded when White's brother's widow moved in as housekeeper. The village and parish of Selborne, and at times one or two neighboring parishes, were in White's pastoral care. The villagers apparently cherished him and certainly served him as laboratory assistants, collecting and observing for the *Naturalist's Journal.* When young, White traveled widely on horseback in the Selborne-London-Oxford triangle and so often that his friend John Mulso called him the "Hussar Parson." As he grew older, he traveled less, and his naturalist's range was reduced to Selborne and the twelve adjacent and neighboring parishes, a radius of four and a half or five miles. In the closing decades of his life, his contact with the outside world took the form of occasional trips to see his brothers in London, to visit his college at Oxford, and his aunt in East Sussex. There were frequent visits to and from local families, extended visits from his four brothers and two sisters and their families, from a horde of nieces and nephews, and visits from other friends and fellow workers in the vineyards of natural history. There were four weekly newspapers to be kept up with, and there was, of course, a voluminous correspondence. That which survives suggests that White was, with characteristic modesty, in touch with the principal natural historians of his day and that he was a firm member of that community of knowledge.

The domestic economy of The Wakes combined a high order of self-sufficiency with dependency on the outside services of the village butcher and miller, local farms for milk, butter, and cheese, wood- and peat-cutters, itinerant fishmongers, truffle hunters, and so forth. The village, in turn, was an almost closed agrarian economy, exporting hops (its principal cash crop), some wheat and barley, and a little wool spun in cottage industry. Cooking at The Wakes was done over a wood fire; heating was also by wood in fireplaces, though normally only the kitchen and parlors were heated; entries like the one for 20 November 1787, which cited "ice in the pantry and chambers," were common. Plumbing consisted of a fairly dependable draw well; wastes were removed by hand-carried buckets and deposited in a sump beyond the garden. Light was provided by fire, rushlights, oil lamps, and candles. Food was stored in the cellar (where things didn't freeze), which was also adequate for the "wine vault" and for storage of what White called his "provisions" (not-so-perishable foods such as apples, potatoes, onions, and root vegetables). Food was also kept in the pantry, with its grilled opening to the outside, which would keep perishables quite well in the cool seasons.

Throughout the year, White and his household and parish were largely dependent on what was in season in the immediate surround. White and his servants raised and stored and preserved a wide variety of fruits and berries and vegetables,* and the

---

*The crops included apples, apricots, crabapples, nectarines, peaches, pears, plums, barberries (for jam), cherries, European cranberries, currants, gooseberries, grapes, raspberries, strawberries, whortleberries, filberts, walnuts, artichokes,

Hampshire growing season, thanks to White's studied husbandry and constant use of hotbeds and hand glasses (bell jars or small glazed frames for the protection of plants), was almost year-round (cabbages in December, turnip greens in January, cucumbers by mid-April). White made his own malt and beer and some wine; he kept poultry, pigeons, bees, and at least three horses. In season, he bought hogs from local farmers and put them down in salt. From London came hams and twenty-five- to thirty-pound shipments of salt fish several times each winter; coffee and tea; select wines; brandy, rum, and gin by the gallon; books and stationery and other refinements.

White's *Naturalist's Journal* (1768–93) includes daily entries of temperature, wind, weather, and voluminous notations on the "manners," the "life and conversation" of the fauna and flora of the local ecology. The effect is an overwhelming emphasis on the procession of the seasons—time governed not by clocks and calendars but by the infinite shadings of event in the natural and village world, endless recurrence but always with variations. As he put it, "New occurrences still arise as long as any inquiries are kept alive."[3] The kingdom of England and the worlds of politics and international relations were there, but they seem remote from White's perspective—unless the Royal Navy's guns at Spithead, what the navy called "the king's bedchamber," twenty-five miles away to the south, rattled his windows while celebrating

---

asparagus, beans (French, kidney, and broad), cabbages, cantaloupes, carrots, cauliflower, celeriac, celery, cress, cucumbers, endive, leeks, lettuce, maize, mustard, onions, parsley, parsnips, peas, potatoes, radishes, salsify, sea kale, skirrit, "spinage," squash, turnips, white broccoli, and wild rice. Notable for their absence were tomatoes—introduced into England as decorative, but possibly poisonous plants in 1596, their primacy as edible fruit only began to emerge in the 1830s. Barley, hay, oats, rye, sainfoin, and wheat were harvested with sickle or scythe and threshed with a flail. Food was preserved by dessication (beans, some fruits such as currants and apricots); making preserves (jams, jellies, etc.) with sugar; pickling; salting; and smoking. Preserving foods and meats by canning was developed by the French chef Nicolas-François Appert between 1795 and 1809; tin cans, 1823; stamped cans, 1847.

the accession of the king. The marginalia of the *Journal* does include back-dated entries, noting under 19 October 1781 the "ill-fated day" of Cornwallis's surrender at Yorktown and noting under 21 January 1793 that Louis XVI was beheaded. The beginning of the war with France that followed also merits an entry. But most of the items from the beyond are accounts of unusual or extraordinary natural phenomena that filter through to him from the weekly newspapers and from his correspondents: earthquakes, storms, volcanic eruptions off Iceland, drastic melts of snow and ice in the Carpathians.

From our perspective, this stationary man lived in an almost unbelievably closed and static world, all the news postdated by weeks or months. As his friend John Mulso said, "the access" to Selborne was (as it still is) "inscrutable." But from White's perspective, Selborne wasn't remote and inaccessible. His was a world open, animate, full of light and air (and rain and drought) and rhythm, and permeated by music:

> When I hear fine music I am haunted with passages therefrom night and day; and especially at first waking, which, by their importunity, give me more uneasiness than pleasure: elegant lessons [pieces for performance] still tease my imagination, and recur irresistibly to my recollection at seasons, and even when I am desirous of thinking of more serious matters.[4]

But White's world had boundaries other than those created by its physical isolation; it was a world held strictly to a circumference and a measure. Like his contemporaries, he assumed that the achievements of the classical world were unique, that those achievements had established standards of absolute value against which the arts, letters, morality, and politics of the present should be measured and judged. The physical contexts that were White's habitation and habituation had changed so little from those of Greece and Rome that the absolute dominion of the classics could comfortably preside. Indeed, the physical design of The Wakes, particularly its plumbing and heating arrangements, could have benefited from the example of the sophisticated systems in the villas that dotted the countryside of Roman Britain in the third and fourth centuries A.D. and that survived into White's time as ruins interesting to the antiquarian in search of coins (rather than tips on domestic technology). That neoclassical reverence for the classical world not only established circumferences that were supportive and comforting, it also brought with it a stern warning: "High civilization, once achieved, can be lost."[5]

When, fifty-two years after White's death, Thoreau looked up from his worktable at Walden Pond, or when he looked back on that table, cabin, and pond from the retrospect of Concord several years later, how did he see himself housed? Housed in his clothes, he was also clothed against the weather by his cabin, which in turn was contained by the larger house of Walden Pond.

> Like the wasps, before I finally went into winter quarters in November, I used to resort to the northeast side of Walden, which the sun, reflected from the pitch-pine woods and the stony shore, made the fireside of the pond.[6]

Beyond the house of the pond, there was the walking radius of wood- and farm-land and the dominating presence of Concord, a country village over ten times the size of Selborne (whose population in 1783 was 313, plus 363 in the rest of the parish).

But numbers in this case say very little. By comparison to Selborne, Thoreau's Concord was a metropolis. It was the home of a vigorous intellectual and cultural community in addition to its Yankee assemblage of farmers and merchants and manufacturers of rubber goods, harnesses and underwear—not to mention Thoreau's father's pencil factory. Concord had developed a lively tradition of public discussion in its town meetings and its lyceum. The rhythms of its life in the 1840s and 1850s were still agrarian, but they were no longer those of an economy based on subsistence farming and casual barter. Those rhythms were still in place in the hinterlands, but Concord's was a cash economy undergoing the radical stimulus of the railroad and telegraph. Concord wasn't Boston—"the Hub," "the Athens of America," twenty miles away—but Concord was heard and felt there more powerfully than any other village in New England. For all his disclaimers, Thoreau was a member of that influential chorus. Boston, in turn, wasn't just the capital of Massachusetts but also the economic, political, religious, and cultural capital of New England and the Northeast—a hive of crusaders and reformers preaching abolition of slavery, women's rights, temperance, and vegetarianism or Grahamism, together with concentrations of educators, bankers, merchants, industrialists, shipping magnates, and the ruling Brahmins.

The closure and relative stasis of the way White was housed, and his consonance with natural rhythms, were no longer present and available as the given conditions of life in Concord. That closure, stasis, and consonance were available only through the artifice and discipline of a two-year sojourn at Walden Pond—or rather through the artifice and discipline of the book *Walden,* which doesn't describe two years of "life in the woods" anything like as much as it creates that life and the genius of the place, Walden Pond. Thoreau wasn't a stationary man immersed in the rhythms of the gardens that housed him but an odd-job man walking the periphery of a cash economy, making pencils in his father's factory, living with Emerson, working as his caretaker and handyman, earning money as a freelance surveyor. That beanfield near Walden Pond with its "seven miles" of bean rows was a one-shot attempt to raise a cash crop with a minimum investment of time (and a seriocomic return on his money, "Leaving a pecuniary profit . . . of $8.71½").[7] On another level the beanfield is presented as an experiment to test Carlyle and Emerson's theory that manual labor was a stimulus to the life of the mind. In any event, "labor of the hands, even when pursued to the verge of drudgery, is perhaps never the worst form of idleness."[8]

After the Walden experiment, Thoreau moved steadily toward more public worlds: in the realm of letters, chiefly natural history and social criticism, and in that increasingly turbulent realm of political reform, the crusade for the abolition of slavery. Before and during the Walden sojourn, Thoreau's audience was Concord and the Concord Lyceum; after 1848, his lectures and essays took him out into New England and gave him tentative and partial admission to the house of letters, to the threshold of firm entry when he was invited in 1862, toward the end of his foreshortened life, to prepare a series of essays for *The Atlantic Monthly*.

The 1850s were marked by an increasing stridency of tone in Thoreau's social and political criticism. Two undercurrents seem to have combined to urge this increase. The millennial expectations of the reformers were suspended and frustrated: slavery continued as legal fact and moral affront. And "the prophets," Thoreau said, "are all employed in excusing the ways of men."[9] Meanwhile, rapid technological change was threatening seismic social and political change. The earth was shifting under the conservative feet that he wanted to plant so firmly. The intellect of all America was being "macadamized for the wheels of travel to roll over."[10] And no matter how shrill his voice, how trenchant his words, that intellect didn't hear, or didn't heed, or if it heard and heeded, unaccountably continued to languish in paralysis of the will.

Thoreau's stridency was applauded in radical abolitionist circles, but it wasn't regarded as parlor-safe in the houses of literate New England. It wouldn't do to enter "A Plea for Captain John Brown," which ambiguously condoned violence in the service of the antislavery cause on the eve of that worthy's execution for the violence of Harper's Ferry. And so Thoreau was put away in a closet in the house of letters. That closet was gradually opened, thanks to a tepid interest in his "nature writings" in the 1880s (nature writing was regarded as parlor-safe, provided Darwin was absent). The vigorous revival of interest in his social criticism awaited the Chicago Renaissance of the 1890s. And so Thoreau passed from the threshold of provincial New England recognition and emerged forty years later from Emerson's shadow and entered the hall of the masters by way of brawling middle America and its stockyard wealth.

The two worktables in this Williamstown study have small Oriental rugs as covers: literally, in order to save the rugs from further battering on the floor; figuratively, in order to remind me of those seventeenth-century Dutch interiors where "the two great discoveries of the Bourgeois Age,"[11] privacy and domesticity, were achieved. The magic carpet of the computer/printer is poised in dialogue with the Oriental beneath it. In support of this island of privacy are five thousand or so books and a thousand-odd file folders stuffed with reading notes and class notes and all sorts of writings, from closet poetry and fiction to various public voices. The mini floppy disks in their boxes have only been at work three years, but they encode more and more words. A clutter of two-dimensional objects animates the walls. "PEOPLE MATURE TOO," the billboard complains in the photograph of the dark mass of the Guinness Brewery complex in Dublin. And as I begin to list the objects, I pause to reflect that the conglomeration on the walls says something about the timespace of our travel and recall. There are maps of Dublin (circa 1855) and of Inishbofin (1892), and photographs of Inishbofin harbor, of a small bronze relief set in the wall of a side chapel in the ruined cathedral on the Rock of Cashel, of the interior of King's College Chapel, Cambridge, a 1930s postcard of Tintern Abbey, a photograph of a woman with camera beneath a statue of Sainte Avoye in her chapel near Auray in Brittany, and a poster-photograph of the Brooklyn Bridge. There are other objects: a wooden mask from

Nigeria, a brass rubbing of a medieval knight (devout), a grand-
daughter's colored-pencil sketch of autumn leaves, a reproduction
of George Caleb Bingham's "Fur Traders on the Missouri," a
watercolor of two fish sculptures (one Nicaraguan, one modern
folk art). Overhead, there's a model of Ithiel Town's lattice-truss
covered bridge (1820). That isn't the lot, but it will do to suggest
the timespace we take for granted as the condition of our perspectives, not just as pictures on the walls but as available to our
walkabout with camera and notebook in hand.

The mist-concealed Apennines of poem 210 and the "slant of
light" in a cathedral nave (258) were available to Emily Dickinson
in the ubiquitous sepia prints on the walls of well-dressed Am-
herst homes but not to her walking about. Or contrast the clearly
defined concentric circles of Gilbert White's peripatetics: Selborne at the center, the walking and horseback circles around
Selborne in the middle; Oxford, London, the South Downs in
Sussex, and the Channel at the outermost orbit.

For Thoreau, the real center was at Concord and the pretend
center at Walden Pond, a mile and a half to the south.

> Wherever I sat, there I might live, and the landscape radiated
> from me accordingly.[12]

Even when he contemplated the afterglow of a journey toward
the outer circumference,

> I wanted only to be set down in Canada and take one honest
> walk there as I might in Concord woods of an afternoon.[13]

Thoreau's outer circumference was east to Boston, southeast to
Cape Cod, south to Staten Island, west to Mount Greylock and the
Berkshires, north to Quebec and Montreal, northeast to Katahdin
and the Maine woods. At the very end of his life, he journeyed
west to Minnesota, to the headwaters of the Mississippi and a
Sioux encampment. This trip was summed up in a journal entry
for 11 May 1861: "Set out for Minnesota via Worcester" (Worces-

ter is twenty-two miles southwest of Concord, a comfortable day's walk for a healthy man). Thoreau remained in the Concord orbit by conscious choice, a reactionary choice made by a man trained as a classicist, a self-made naturalist and a self-styled eighteenth-century liberal, a would-be stationary man, out of step in nineteenth-century America and not entirely welcome in the parlor-safe havens of Concord and Boston.

Seated at this worktable I can, of course, try to describe "the landscape that radiates from me accordingly." My study faces east from the second floor of a house set down in a hollow 640 feet above sea level. From the windows and the skylight of this house and study in summer, the horizon lines are pushed up by deciduous trees. In winter, the horizon lines (except those established by the white pines to the north) decline a few degrees, and we can catch glimpses of the hills beyond. The house is surrounded by the asymmetry of its L-shaped lawn and its amoeboid flower gardens; there is no longer sufficient sun-space for vegetables. The lawn flows into other lawns without much fence or screen on what amounts to an eighteen-family island, bounded south, east, and north by two streams, Buxton Brook and Hemlock Brook, and shut in by the town's Westlawn Cemetery up the hill to the west. It's even more of an island now that the bridge over Hemlock Brook that was our access has given in to the age on its plaque, 1910. The "temporary" detour circles up through the cemetery to exit between the white gateposts that glimmer at night like the ivory gate "Without a flaw," as Virgil said, "and yet false dreams are sent / Through this one by ghosts to the upper world."[14]

This creek-bottom cul-de-sac sits on the periphery of Williams College in the village of Williamstown. College and village have their political identity only by inclusion in the Town of Williamstown. The township in turn is geographically enisled in a bowl formed by the Taconic Mountains to the west and southwest, the Berkshire Hills to the south, the Greylock massif east and southeast, and the southern foothills of the Green Mountains to the north.

This island township has its own wayward microclimate, oblivious to the weather forecasts computerized in Albany, New York, thirty miles to the west, or in Springfield, Massachusetts, in the Connecticut Valley fifty-five miles to the southeast. According to conventional wisdom, weather systems on this continent generally move on axis from west to east. The mountains that define this valley (2.4 miles to the east, 1.8 miles to the west) are on axis north to south with east-west ridges like thresholds 1.6 miles to the north and 4.6 miles to the south. "A meteorological toilet bowl" is the received witticism about this extinct lake bottom (Lake Bascom disappeared when the last glacier withdrew). Like many of the microclimates in this country, ours was once monitored by a one-man weather station, until the Nixon administration, in a fit of cost cutting, decided that only macroclimates and the sites of major airports were of interest to its Commerce Department. Shutting down the one-man stations banned the clutter of wayward microclimates from the computer loops. Something in this should, as Thoreau once said, "serve a parable-maker one day."[15]

My neighbors are a mix of types and classes: a retired steeplejack and his wife; an art-museum custodian and his wife, a registered nurse, and their two daughters; a grandfather who doubles as bartender and motel nightclerk, his wife, and a daughter who cleans for several families we know in town (and brings back the news) and mothers her only child, a daughter; a young woman who owns and manages several boutiques; a somewhat older woman pursuing a career as a professional writer; a professor of mathematics and his wife; and twelve other families scattered across that range. Gentrification has set its seal on eight of the eighteen houses down here, and many of our neighbors probably couldn't afford to buy their houses from themselves in today's real-estate market, as we probably couldn't. All the signs promise further gentrification in this out-of-the-way cluster of what were once low-cost, affordable houses. These houses themselves displaced a scattering of small houses, the cabins of what was once a black ghetto. One of those cabins, once enlarged and twice refurbished, remains.

In its way, this island constitutes a neighborhood, neighborly in its manners and behavior, informed both by the impulse to affirm others and lend a hand and by the necessary contraries of irritations, jealousies, and gossip. Not an ersatz neighborhood like a condominium or some other variation of contemporary barracks life, this is an organism that cuts its own lawns, shovels its snow, and changes over time.

Up in the village, there is a similar mix of types and classes but with a greater display of affluence and, in the case of one neighborhood, more poverty and dereliction. The college dominates village life and is the principal employer. There are the inevitable town-gown fault lines, enlivened by seasonal outbreaks of conspiracy theory. From September to May, there is the noisy presence of two thousand handsome and intelligent young men and women, most of them affluent, and this creates certain distortions. For some of us, the two thousand represent eternal youth and complicate the processes of our aging. The merchants, and many townspeople, find them an arrogant and irritating bunch, but the students are amusing too and a fairly consistent, usually gratifying, surprise in person and in the classroom.

I am, of course, gown, but I move about on a first-name basis in town with merchants and shopkeepers and bankers and public servants and with those who help us out with our carpentry and painting and plumbing and electrical and landscape problems. In a closet way I am town as well—my mother (1895–1982) was born in a boarding house for the families of textile workers in North Adams, five miles to the east; her father (1872–1922) was born in an ironmaster's house in Lanesboro, fourteen miles to the south; her mother (1873–1954) was born twenty-eight miles down-country in West Stockbridge. But I stay in the closet because I've been in residence here only since 1951, and my childhood roots (the Gifford ones that count locally) are in and around Schenectady, thirty-seven miles to the west.

There are fracture zones other than town and gown. The French-Canadian church remained French-speaking until twenty years ago and still regards itself as the church of the poor and downtrodden. The Irish-Catholic Saint Patrick's houses the rich. The town is bedroom for owners, managers, and other high-level employees of industries and businesses in northern Berkshire County. Increasingly, there are the affluent more-than-visitors among us, retirees, second-home and weekend-home people who see Williamstown as a haven "away from it all" but with the many amenities created by the college, by two impressive art museums, by a lively tradition of summer theater, and by music here in the winter and nearby in the summer. A strange expression, "to get away from it all." Some of us live here year-round under the impression that this is where it all is.

Many of us feel, probably mistakenly, that these affluent immigrants will eventually take over and hold us hostage, as the hordes of tourists do when they dispossess us on weekends and turn our village into a quaint boutique during the peak seasons: summer, fall (foliage), winter (skiing). Tourists anywhere tend to be a bother to the locals because they don't speak the language, because they mess up traffic patterns and crowd the shops and sidewalks, and because they're always so rich (having prepared to indulge themselves by saving up at home). In sum, all these outlanders and intruders make us feel more native than we actually are.

Our village, town, and county are "outside," as Daniel Shays, preaching rebellion two hundred years ago, said they would be as long as the state capital is in what he called "merchant- and lawyer-infested Boston." There the capital remains, and there, when they think of western Massachusetts, they think of the place where the voters are, in the growing megalopolis of the Connecticut Valley, a little more than an hour to the east of us. As well-conditioned outsiders, we don't expect our bridge to be fixed any time soon; if the time ever comes, we expect to battle once again a Boston-based department of public works that wants to treat this little cul-de-sac to a bridge appropriate to an interstate highway. But that outsider status and experience has its rewards—in the intuitive sympathy that informs the traveler from Williamstown when he visits the outsider places of other geographies: Cornwall, Wales, Ireland, Brittany, Provence, Catalonia, the Basque country, and many of the corners of the Third World.

One tourist, that professed or professional outsider Thoreau, had a transcendental and mocking brush with this enisled college and town when he climbed Mount Greylock during a walking tour in 1848 and spent the night in the lee of the observatory that Williams College students had erected on the summit in 1830. Thoreau remarks that the college "building might be seen by daylight gleaming far down in the valley." He continues,

> It would be no small advantage if every college were thus located at the base of a mountain, as good at least as one well-endowed professorship.* It were as well to be educated in the shadow of a mountain as in more classical shades. Some will remember, no doubt, not only that they went to the college, but that they went to the mountain. Every visit to its summit would, as it were, generalize the particular

---

*I held two of those "well-endowed professorships" in turn, one in English and another in American Studies. I wasn't aware of Greylock's close competition, though I did know that Melville had dedicated *Pierre: Or the Ambiguities* "to GREYLOCK'S MOST EXCELLENT MAJESTY" with remarks that ironically identify his neighbors as blocks of wood and Greylock as remote and indifferent, a local companion of Shelley's remote Mont Blanc:

> Nevertheless, forasmuch as I, dwelling with my loyal neighbours, the Maples and the Beeches, in the amphitheatre over which his central majesty presides, have received his most bounteous and unstinted fertilisations, it is but meet, that I here devoutly kneel and render up my gratitude whether, thereto, The Most Excellent Purple Majesty of Greylock benignantly incline his hoary crown or no.

information gained below, and subject it to more catholic tests.[16]

Never mind that the college buildings cannot be seen from the summit of Greylock and vice versa; that bit of poetic license doesn't upset me, but it does remind me that, unseen from here, Greylock is still one of the many horizons of my world. That in turn reminds me of the difficulties I have mapping those multiple and shifting horizons and locating a center among them. White could confidently locate the center of his world and trace the circumferences of its edges. Thoreau had some trouble with his centers—was it Concord or Walden Pond or the Celestial Kingdom?—and the edges were for him less securely determined, thanks to the swirl and fluidity being created by railroads, telegraphs, steamships, and all their hustling progeny.

If I look up from my worktable and try to define the edges and circumferences of my worlds, the walls of this study dissolve. The circumferences project beyond the farthest imaginable horizons before I can chart location or direction or diameter or the speed of their regression. Even in this haven, this outside, we are not stationary people or sojourners in Arcadia, despite what the affluent immigrants and other visitors might think. Instead, we are urban nomads, people of what David Jones has called "the shapeless cosmopolis and of the megalopolitan diaspora."[17] When immigration and tourism threaten to overwhelm, our impulse is to declare once again that we are country people with our own special brand of calm and considerate understanding, quite the opposite of the harried intelligence of the city dwellers. But our urbanity, or rather the suburbanity we share in the coast-to-coast suburb of this country, betrays us into this world without edges, this city intelligence, which we share with the interlopers. (Only the ghettos remain urban in the old-fashioned sense, and rural simplicity is at least a generation ago.)

In 1951, the telephone at my elbow had a three-digit number with a telephone operator to handle every call, whether local or national, at the manual switchboard in a storefront near the post office downtown. Today, the reach of this instrument is extraordinary: eleven digits will fetch any corner of this country; thirteen digits and the fetch is global. But the intermediary presence of a telephone operator has faded into a shadow world outside of town.

The computer keyboard under my fingers was made in Japan. It uses mini floppy disks "made in Japan and assembled in the U.S.A." Power comes out of the wall to run this machine and the letter-quality printer that tractor-feeds paper made in Canada. That power also runs a host of other things all over the house: lights and television and hi-fi and radios and clocks and ovens and cooking pans and the thirty-odd electric motors that power the labor-saving network of this house.* That power comes unseen from an electrical utility that generates and sells power to us and buys and sells power from and to other utilities in an arrangement called the New England Power Pool. The pool is in turn an interlocking and overlapping system of grids and confusions that derive from the differing regulatory policies of the six New England states and from the contrasting long- and short-term profit motives of the several utility companies involved.

The hydroelectric station at Shelburne Falls on the Deerfield River, less than twenty-five miles to the east of us, could supply (and on emergency occasions has supplied) the electricity needs of this geographically isolated pocket. But there is a nuclear-energy plant at Rowe, ten miles this side of Shelburne Falls. Why there, where it's not needed locally? Because that nuclear plant

---

*Four for the furnace; two for the workshop; six in the kitchen for the odd jobs of squeezing, blending, and chopping; one each for the refrigerator and the freezer; one in the dishwasher; one in the washing machine; one each in the two vacuum cleaners; one in the sewing machine; one each for the record turntable, tape deck, and VCR; two for the solar-exchanger pumps; one for the weed cutter; one for the hair dryer; one for the convection oven; one in a large fan; one in a small electric heater; and that doesn't count the compact-disc player or the battery chargers for the lawn mower, edger, and car.

was one of the first and, in case of accident, Rowe was appropriately remote from population centers of any political significance. The not-in-my-backyard chorus wouldn't have been very large and could safely have been overruled. The electric grid is organized in the same way. When grid-wide power shortages occur, the chances are that backwater towns like ours will get blacked-out or browned-out first.

Most of the technology and energy that sustains my home is located offstage in a circumferenceless space of power and manufacturing and service stations, in distribution and disposal systems that have their edges not only outside the house and village but also outside the state, the region and, more and more frequently, the nation. The repair services that keep the power coming out of the wall and the electronic signals coming over the wires are headquartered and dispatched from centers a two-hour drive away from here, their voices full of astonishment and disbelief when we've been cut off by a storm they haven't seen or felt. An exception is the wood, our primary source of winter heat, that now awaits stacking in its three-cord mound beneath my study window. It comes from a woodlot two miles away. I can visit that woodlot in a walking afternoon as I cannot even identify, let alone visit, the sources of the electricity that comes out of the wall or of the natural gas that powers the kitchen stove. That woodlot edge is only an arbitrary and highly qualified exception to the rule that the dependencies of this household cannot begin to be defined in terms of the edges and contacts that were so clearly available to White's perception and less clearly to Thoreau's. That may be why he had to assert his independence so vigorously.

Last spring, another edge, another contact was suddenly removed: the twice weekly home delivery of milk and eggs stopped. A link with the past was cut, and therefore the past was evoked. In the 1920s, the milkman made daily rounds from his farm on the plateau above the lake where we spent the summers. He dipped the milk from the forty-quart can with a pint measure.

I don't remember the year when he shrugged in complaint, but state law would henceforth require him to bottle and cap his milk with the label Raw prominent. (There was much fear of contracting tuberculosis from raw milk in the 1920s.) In town, the horse-drawn vans of the dairyman and the baker and the iceman made their daily rounds; the fruit and vegetable cart called in season; the butcher's wagon came three times a week, but his meat was not dependable; the fishmonger was a Friday regular. In addition to all those shops that paused at our door, there was the corner grocery a three-minute walk away. What remains as the edges dissolve in this village sixty years later? Two small supermarkets, each two automobile miles away, and one gourmet food and produce store one mile away. All three offer year-round meats, fish, fruits, and vegetables without regard to what's in season, and therefore all three blur the edges of space and time that might otherwise limit and define our world.

The stock image of New England village life is of a tight-knit, gossipy combination of neighborly comfort and tyranny. On occasion, that image fits. But the anonymity and edgelessness of modern urban life is everywhere in the fabric of this subrural, suburban life. The village contacts dissolve, and the remoteness of the they on whom the dailyness of our home lives depends means that we have little or no influence on the choices being made in our name, the anonymous policies designed to serve us. If this were a tight-knit village in a regional world, the tyranny of that anonymity and remoteness might well constitute the conditions for rebellion. Daniel Shays and his Berkshire County contemporaries thought so in 1787, when the remoteness of the state authorities in Boston and the confiscatory taxes they demanded sparked rebellion. But the passivity induced by the comfort and leisure of our urban dependencies renders such an observation ludicrous.

And so, without edge or circumference, is there no margin to our lives, no room for marginalia? Again, are we on the fringe or at the center? This house in this village, my center, is on the fringe of the nation, if it exists for the nation at all. The economy of this household is on the fringe of political economy, hardly a factor in the wealth of nations.

But I am centered, for all of that want of circumference. As a human being, I am more or less midway in the mammalian scale between the smallest of the shrews and the great blue whale, and perceptually I move about in a timespace midway between that of the atoms and that of the stars, realms so remote that I can't perceive them without the speculative mediation of instruments. Centered. And orbiting on the fringe of this "placeless cosmopolis."[18]

If from this microcosm I set out in search of the macrocosm, the concentrated presence of what Joyce called this "wilderness of inhabitation,"[19] what better place to seek it than on Manhattan Island? There all human scale is transcended in an apotheosis of urbanity. Congenial spaces are shuffled about or hidden in the concentration of conspicuously affluent (or conspicuously dilapidated) habitats. In the lobby of the World Trade Center or the atrium of the Trump Tower, I am impressed by spaces that make me feel small and anxious with agoraphobia. Why, in contrast, do the naves of the great medieval cathedrals, for all their size and for all the affluence they represent, still strike us as human in scale, as spaces that enhance instead of diminish our sense of personal dignity and stature?

There is no ready answer, but when I consider the edges of the World Trade Center, I find some suggestions. The edges of a medieval cathedral are right where the architecture of wall and glass and buttress and pillar and vault say they are, from both the outside and the inside. The twin towers of the World Trade Center seem, from across the river, to declare themselves as discrete and self-contained, even if they are too heavy for that end of the raft. But up close, the two buildings assert another edge in the winds of the microclimate they create. Looking up at one of the corners, the flanks of the building recede and disappear until only a vertical ribbon of steel remains. The approach seems to be on foot, but it is really by mechanism from indeterminate demographic edges by subway, bus, taxi, private car, limousine, helicopter. The inside is even more enigmatic. Without electricity for heating and cooling, the building would be uninhabitable. On warm days, the towers would become passive solar collectors designed to slow-cook their inhabitants, and on cold days, the radiant heat loss from all that glass and the drafts generated by those vertical wind tunnels would paralyze the hands. Without electricity, the buildings would also be unworkable; elevators are an absolute necessity, as are pumps for air and water and sewage, not to mention lights, since most of the buildings' spaces are lightless as well as airless interior rooms. Without electronic communications equipment, the inhabitants of the towers would be without the contacts indispensable to their work.

The Trade Center's electrical energy requirements equal that of an American industrial city of eighty to a hundred thousand, and that electricity is hardly generated in-house. At what edges, near or remote, are the sources of its other requirements: the water, the office and computer supplies, the cleaning and maintenance materials, the food and transport and shelter for the round-the-clock shifts of its temporary inhabitants, none of whom live in? And at what edges are the waste products generated in the twin towers to be dumped? Pope's great quip about Blenheim Palace applies here and with a vengeance: " 'Tis very fine, but where d'ye sleep and where d'ye dine?"*

The towers are anything but self-contained as architecture. The sources from which come all the energies and things necessary to their functioning have to be housed somewhere, but that somewhere remains unseen; the sumps where all the garbage,

---

*In Pope's time, the grand dining salon at Blenheim was roughly a quarter of a mile from the kitchens.

sewage, and trash go are obscure. And, microcosm to macrocosm, the same can be said for Manhattan Island and for New York City. Its edgelessness is a major ingredient in its broth of creativity and excitement. Everything from everywhere comes here, is here. And edgelessness is a major contributor to the play of anxiety and depression the city generates. Everything dissipates here. In this nucleus of the great East Coast megalopolis, everything comes from and with promise and goes to and for waste.

If Fernand Braudel is right that cities are luxuries, economically parasitic on their countrysides, then this supercity in the countryside of the Boston to Washington, D.C., megalopolis may be approaching the ultimate flamboyance of luxury and parasitism. The superpower state that houses it may prove, in its turn, to be approaching its own brand of ultimates.

Applicants for taxi-driver licenses in London must apprentice themselves for two years in order to acquire what their slang calls "the knowledge" of the labyrinth of London's six thousand streets and how to thread it. But in practice, that Gordian knot is reducible to an elegant mnemonic simplicity in contrast to what "the knowledge" of New York City's labyrinthine circulatory systems would be. I'm speaking of the comprehensive knowledge of all the influxes and outfluxes that support that island's incredible capacity to stimulate and sustain the undifferentiated appetite of a nation and a world and its corresponding capacity to produce and channel dilapidation and waste.

The city in its superscale is a bleak house, functioning with no apparent regard for the inner significance of the individuals, families, and neighborhoods it contains. The end result is a proliferation of special interest groups—tenant and block and neighborhood associations, parent-teacher associations, unions, political clubs, and endless group-protection bureaus (for women's rights, gay rights, children's rights, the rights of the poor and battered and homeless) all attempting to alleviate the inhumanity of superscale, and fated, as reform institutions so frequently are, to reinforce that inhumanity with the cacophony of their demands.

Once back home, the contrast with the megalopolis initially highlights the intimate scale of this house, neighborhood, and village and the ways in which they shelter, nourish, and center us. But as the contrast fades, I realize that the megalopolis infiltrates even here with its suggestion of the placeless where the edges dissolve. This remote corner of Massachusetts thus becomes at once exciting, because everything converges here to irradiate us, and disorienting, because everything radiates from or rather recedes from here. The result is an oscillation that centers us now, decentralizes us then. All around us, the fabulous play of technologies and their energies mediate to center us, to bring us close to the objects our eyes would see, the sounds our ears would hear, the timespaces far and near that we would enter. At the same time, those technologies and energies intervene to separate us from the sights, sounds, timespaces we desire to touch and inhabit. And so we oscillate between the center and the fringe, between the close-up and the big picture. When I turn to Whitehead's dictum, "We think in generalities but we live in detail," that too seems to be in continuous counterpoint with its contrary: our perceptions are locked in generalized separation from their objects, even as our thoughts strive to focus on detail.

Ever-present as another version of this paradox is our independence as individuals. We enjoy a radical independence that Gilbert White and his contemporaries never could have imagined. But our dependencies on others, whom we will never see or know, for the goods and services that sustain our independence have increased exponentially since the late eighteenth century, as have our vulnerabilities. We find ourselves in the midst of independence that is, in fact, the fruit of our dependence.

Given these paradoxes and our consequent vulnerability, it is no wonder that pessimists and other realists cite the iron law of physics: if something can happen it will. They then apply it to intense human uncertainties, such as the uncertainties of the fractured environment and of war and peace. But that may be metaphorical misapplication, because that law pertains to the realms of the atoms and the stars.

Here in this midrealm of our habitation, the iron law of technology does, however, apply: the more complex or energy-intensive a technology is, the more vulnerable and potentially dangerous and destructive it is. In the close-up of the home and workplace, a power tool is more vulnerable to breakdown and potentially more dangerous or destructive than a hand tool; as the chainsaw is to the axe, the automobile to the bicycle, the backhoe to the shovel. In the big picture, there are similar disparities: between an atomic power plant and a hydroelectric plant, between a heat-seeking or laser-guided missile and David's slingshot, between the Strategic Defense Initiative and Achilles's shield. Our century has born ample witness to the operation of this iron law, from the *Titanic* and World War I to Three Mile Island, the *Challenger* disaster, Chernobyl, and the *Valdez* oilspill in Prince Edward Sound. And in my case, a distant rumble of thunder can remind me that a computer file is much more vulnerable (if not more dangerous) then a card index; one brief surge or lapse of the power that comes out of the wall, and this page greets oblivion.

The workplace, too, has lost its edges to the simultaneously mediating and separating presences of our technologies and their energies. In 1798, the workplace was at home or nearby: in the workshop on the ground floor of the master craftsman's house, in the barns and fields of the hide and hoard outside the farmer's door, or just over the way in the walking distances of villages and city neighborhoods. Half a century later, in the world that jarred against Thoreau and that Dickens was satirizing in *Hard Times,* separation and concentration had taken over. In factory towns, the owners and managers had moved to houses on the hill, away from the hands who were being standardized toward the mono-skills of machine operators and assembly-line workers. And the hands were being kept track of not in the extended household of the master's three-generation family—plus journeymen and apprentices or agricultural laborers—but in what Dickens lampooned as "tabulations," what Marx raged at as the statistical inhumanities with which capitalism sought to measure the minimal amenities provided for the workers and their families.

The factories and offices continued to change: toward division of labor, toward the standardized efficiencies dictated by Frederick W. Taylor's time studies (stopwatch analysis of a worker's patterns of movement), toward the centralization of the assembly line, toward amenities like Muzak and more congenial spaces, toward safer and healthier working conditions but also toward more complex (and potentially more dangerous) technologies, more hazardous substances.

The transportation revolution (railroad, streetcar, bus, automobile, airplane, and helicopter) was to further change the relation between the home and the workplace by encouraging the commuter separation of the two toward the polarization of suburban sprawl and urban concentration. This polarization reflects our tendency to perceive work and leisure as mutually exclusive states in the rhythms of our lives. That polarization was institutionalized with the introduction of that most modern of amenities, the vacation with pay. Together, geography and time encouraged a sharp separation between the presumably free and personal time of leisure and the captive, homogenized, round-the-clock time of the factory and office—or, for the owners and managers, between the peaceful moral sanctuary of the home and the amoral arena of competitive violence that is their workplace. The separation undermines what William Morris called "work-pleasure" by insisting that everyday life is an alternation (daily, weekly, yearly) between the often boring and unrewarding conformity of the workplace and the anarchic leisure of "let the good times roll."

In the world of 1984, the workplace is continuing to change as automation and robotics take over manufacturing and workers retire to the air-conditioned sanctuaries of the computerized control room. But dangers lurk even there, as the monitors on duty at the control panels of the nuclear-energy plant are dazed to somnolence by the hypnotic play of dials and indicator lights ("Why not switch off the alarm buzzers so we can get some sleep"). But if these are dangers, there are also exciting prospects of a new decentralization: the stockbroker plugged into the appropriate computer terminals in his Adirondack lodge, complete with bass fishing at the door, can be as immediate a presence on the New York Stock Exchange as the broker in his Wall Street office. The researcher at his computer terminal in this village might as well be in the Library of Congress. Chambered beneath their Colorado mountain, command personnel guard the keys to a world-class range of missiles. Action at a distance. And the assembly-line worker's turn to decentralize will come, as the Illinois corn and soybean farmer's already has: prepare the soil and plant and spray with herbicides and pesticides in spring and early summer and head for the Minnesota lakes; return for harvest in the fall and pack up and head for Florida. And yet, in spite of this new opportunity to decentralize, the prediction is that by the year 2020, seventy-five percent of the population of the United States will be concentrated in fifty-mile-deep strips of megalopolis on the East and West coasts and an additional fifteen percent in a megalopolis on the shores of the Great Lakes. If so, we are faced with a new version of the energizing and destabilizing asymmetry between decentralized sprawl and superconcentration as the edges that once provided our parents or grandparents with circumference continue to dissolve in both directions.

*   *   *

The over-militarized world in which we live presents us with outstanding examples of the edgelessness of our habitations, not only in the increasing capabilities of terrorists worldwide, but also—and more devastatingly—in the way the inconceivable, full-scale modern war, is now conceived. In Geneva, by apparent agreement of the superpowers, "battlefield nuclear weapons" are defined as weapons with a maximum range of three hundred miles. The killing zone of a battlefield presided over by those weapons would be almost six hundred miles deep, Boston to Detroit, London to John o'Groat's. Clearly, in some once-upon-a-time, the term battlefield[20] implied edges as at Agincourt (750 yards wide, three-hundred-plus yards deep) and at Waterloo (three miles wide, half a mile deep), but edges began to dissolve on the Somme in 1916. The five-by-twenty-mile field of that battle was only a sector in the 485-mile siege line that ran from the Channel to Switzerland. And while the battles at Agincourt and Waterloo occurred between sunup and sundown on a single day and thus had edges in time, the Battle of the Somme began at 7:30 A.M. on 1 July 1916 and petered out inconclusively on 18 November of that year. At El Alamein in 1942, the front extended sixty-odd miles from the Mediterranean to the Qattâra Depression. The killing zone ruled by artillery was ten miles deep; that ruled by ground-support aircraft was twenty to thirty miles deep. The battle began on the night of 23 October 1942 and was over by 4 November. If things on that field during those twelve days reached toward the intolerable, one could at least imagine reaching some sort of edge eight or ten miles to the east beyond which there was relative safety and quiet. (I say imagine, because the latitude of being able to consider escape from the battlefield was at least one part of what enabled us to stick it out.) Back in Alexandria and Cairo, one could be off the field altogether, though subject to the urban harassment of sporadic air raids.

But in a battle zone six hundred miles deep, the edge that might be reached would be an unimaginable three hundred miles away from anything that could be called the front. The whole concept of front and rear, combat zone and rest area or safety zone would dissolve in a twilight zone of edgeless terror, where time would exist only as sleepless suspension.

And where would one locate that other edge called the firebreak between nuclear weapons and conventional arms? At the end of World War II, that edge seemed clear enough, but now conventional arms themselves reach toward the superlethal. At El Alamein, the Germans dropped fifty-pound bombs at random to harass us and make us keep our heads down (but we had the cold comfort of hearing them coming). In Vietnam, the B-52s carpet-bombed from unheard-of heights with five-hundred-pound bombs to pulverize the earth and concuss those who escaped dismemberment and death. Add napalm and phosphorus and poison gas and antipersonnel devices designed to frustrate the farthest skill of modern surgery, and the looming question is whether a small nuke would be any worse. Where is the edge between the tolerable and the terror in that edgeless timespace?

That question is, of course, unanswerable, just as the experience, were it to come, wouldn't conform to our imaginings. In trying to imagine the big picture, we will have neglected the close-ups, and it is in the up-close that we are most aware of how we are housed. We can imagine living in a house like The Wakes or camping out in a cabin on the shore of Walden Pond. But unless we were playacting, we would inevitably bring our technology with us, and that would dismantle the enclosure that was the given in Selborne, the construct at Walden Pond. From those places, as from here, the sense of the edges and boundaries that both define and confine us would dissolve. We would find ourselves, as we are, in these highly permeable envelopes we call our houses, our neighborhoods, and our world.

Epilogue

A Haydn quartet on the radio has just finished the breakfast hour. It was composed in 1799 and intended for performance by live players who could modulate their playing to the resonances of the spaces within which they performed, as this hi-fi version performed in a sound studio and perfected by computer cannot. Even so, it will do, and I dare say it would have staggered the sixty-seven-year-old Haydn's imagination to have heard it. Sixty years ago, an eight-year-old wound a careful coil of wire on a mailing tube to complete his crystal set; that night, the single earphone on his pillow whispered to him in the dark. That, too, would have stunned Haydn, just as the distance from these loaded and calibrated speakers and the FM tuner to that tinny earphone fading in and out as the feeler wire stumbled around on the crystal gives me pause. And yet that extraordinary set of contrasts—live music to crystal set to hi-fi—seems perfectly natural to the enterprise of continuing to learn how to hear.

That phrase *seems perfectly natural* reminds me that I can perceive no closure to the circling and repetitive phases of these essays. And when I think I've approached one, there's always an accident. The other day, I read that the average annual income in Tanzania in 1984 was slightly lower than the average annual income in the Mohawk Valley in 1776, an interruption that reminded me that I know very little about the real contrasts between my modes of living and perceiving and those of the contemporary Tanzanian or the Colonial American. I can try to imagine, but I always wind up at square one of an abiding anxiety that history or natural history is not an artifact of time or income, not a thing made in the past and therefore subject to closure but an ever-present exercise in self-making and self-knowing, an exercise that seeks, through an interminable discipline of retrospect, some sort of communion with those on farther shores, whether of Tanzania (1984), Walden Pond (1845), Selborne (1793), Nether Stowey (1798), or the Mohawk Valley (1776).

However revolutionary, even cataclysmic, the changes in our modes of perception between 1798 and 1984, William James's question still obtains: have those changes improved our sensibility "to the inner feelings, and to the whole inner significance of lives that are different from our own?"[1] The answer: not markedly. Our sense of the enigmatic complexities and simplicities of our own lives and of lives different from our own remains much the same, shared with those who lounged on the farther shore of 1798. That one-and-the-sameness with the past suggests that these essays may well be overstating the distance from here to those farther shores, and I should somersault to the conservative (in the true sense of the word) perception that it isn't that far at all. Homer still speaks out "loud and bold" as he did to Pope and Gilbert White and Keats and Thoreau. He may say something slightly different to us, but our translators and hearing aids aren't so bad that we can't still listen. In short, now that I've overstated the discontinuities, I must reverse direction and emphasize the continuities of the outward beholding and of the outward to which we are beholden—the ever-shifting, unchanging givens of history and nature that are the stuff of our knowings and makings and arts.

High up in the back of a 1940 lecture hall, the first-year graduate student struggled to visualize relativity theory: the billiard player on the moving train sends the cue ball perpendicularly from side to side, cushion to cushion, of the table; from A_1 to B_1 to A_1. The observer on the ground outside the moving train watches the cue ball describe a triangular course, A_1 to B_2 to A_3. In the same period of time, the two observers, one stationary on the ground, the other in the moving train, see the cue ball travel two different distances at, therefore, two different speeds. But if a beam of light is substituted for the cue ball and a system of mirrors for the billiard table, the apparent differences of distance and speed must dissolve because the speed of light is constant, and the moving and stationary observers see apparently contrasting phenomena relative to and subsumed in that one constant.

Given that metaphoric model, Gilbert White sees Homer from the rock of that farther stationary shore. I see Homer from this moving shore, all quicksand. There are seas between us. But the apparently contrasting phenomena of his Homer and Thoreau's and mine may also be relative to and subsumed in the lifelong enterprise of half-creating, half-perceiving a shared humanity that all three of us could still call Homer.

Notes
· · · · · · · ·

Introduction

1. J. Shawcross, ed., *Biographia Literaria* (London, 1907), 2: 218.

2. Oliver Sacks and Robert Wasserman, "The Case of the Colorblind Painter," *New York Review of Books,* 19 November 1987, 32.

3. See Lynn Barber, *The Heyday of Natural History: 1820–1870* (London, 1980), passim.

4. David Jones, Preface to *Anathemata* (London, 1955), 15–16.

5. Henry David Thoreau, *Walden* (1854; reprint, ed. Sherman Paul, Boston, 1960), 2.

6. Gilbert White, *The Natural History of Selborne* (1789; reprint, London, 1971), 80.

7. Stephen Jay Gould, "This View of Life," *Natural History* 92 (April 1983): 21.

8. John Keats to George and Thomas Keats, 21, 27 [?] December 1817.

9. Mulso to White, 23 August 1756, Rashleigh Holt-White, *The Life and Letters of Gilbert White of Selborne* (London, 1901), 1: 88.

10. White to Pennant, 2 January 1769, Holt-White, *Life and Letters of Gilbert White*, 1: 166.

11. Thoreau, *Walden*, 200.

12. Henry David Thoreau, *The Maine Woods* (Boston, 1864), 64.

13. William Butler Yeats, *Explorations*, sel. Mrs. W. B. Yeats (New York, 1962), 263.

1. The Mighty World of Eye

1. Coleridge, *Biographia Literaria*, 1: 202.

2. Tate Gallery, *Landscape Britain, 1750–1850* (London, 1973), 124.

3. Mark Girouard, *Life in the English Country House* (New York, 1980), 210.

4. Thomas West, *Guide to the Lakes* (Kendal and London, 1778). Also see Victoria and Albert Museum, *The Discovery of the Lake District*, (London, 1984), 14.

5. Richard A. Muller, "An Adventure in Science," *New York Times Magazine*, 24 March 1985, 34, 36.

6. William H. Gass, "The Face of the City," *Harper's* 272 (March 1986): 39.

7. William Wordsworth, "Tintern Abbey," lines 100–102.

8. The text subsequently appeared under Wordsworth's name as *A Description of the Scenery of the Lakes in the North of England . . . with Additions and Illustrative Remarks upon the Scenery of the Alps* (London, 1822).

9. G. M. Hopkins, "To what serves Mortal Beauty?" (1918), lines 1–2.

10. Erwin Panofsky, "Style and Medium in the Motion Pictures," *Critique* 1 (January–February 1947): 5–28.

11. Philip Caputo, *A Rumor of War* (New York, 1978), 100, 255, 297.

12. Leo Tolstoy, *War and Peace*, trans. Louise and Alymer Maude, ed. George Gibian (New York, 1966), 1133–34.

13. Holt-White, *Life and Letters of Gilbert White*, 1: 326.

2. The Mighty World of Ear

1. White, *Natural History of Selborne,* 44.

2. Entry for 6 December 1787, *Gilbert White's Journals,* ed. Walter Johnson (London, 1970), 300–301.

3. White, *Natural History of Selborne,* 101.

4. Quoted in Oliver Sachs, "The Revolution of the Deaf," *New York Review of Books,* 2 June 1988, 27.

5. Jean Jacques Rousseau, *Confessions,* trans. J. M. Cohen (1781; reprint, London, 1953), 19.

6. Katharine C. Balderston, ed., *Thraliana: The Diary of Mrs. Hester Lynch Thrale (Later Mrs. Piozzi); 1776–1809* (Oxford, 1942), 1: 161.

7. John Stuart Mill, "Thoughts on Poetry and Its Varieties" (1833, revised, 1859).

8. William Wordsworth, "Scorn not the Sonnet; Critic, you have frowned," lines 2–3.

9. Edgar Allen Poe, "The Philosophy of Composition," *Graham's Magazine,* 28 (April 1846): 163–67.

10. Julian Jaynes, *The Origin of Consciousness in the Breakdown of the Bicameral Mind* (1976; reprint, Boston, 1982), 25.

11. William James, *Principles of Psychology,* 1: 237.

12. Stephen Jay Gould, "A Triumph of Historical Excavation," *New York Review of Books,* 27 February 1986, 9.

13. W. H. Auden, "September 1, 1939," lines 70–71.

14. Sigmund Freud, *The Interpretation of Dreams,* trans. A. A. Brill (New York, 1938), 183.

15. Quoted in Richard Ellmann, *James Joyce* (New York, 1982), 716n.

16. Arthur Power, *From an Old Waterford House* (London, n.d.), 67.

17. James Joyce, *Finnegans Wake* (New York, 1939), 122.22–23.

18. Ibid., 353.22.

19. Ellmann, *James Joyce,* 543n.

20. Virgil, *The Aeneid* 6.894.

3. The Mighty World of Timespace

1. Joyce, *Finnegans Wake,* 419.5–8.

2. James Joyce, *Ulysses* (New York, 1986), 17.1006.

3. Sir Thomas Browne, *Christian Morals,* Part III, xix.

4. William Paley, *Natural Theology, or Evidences of the Existence and Attributes of the Deity* (London, 1802).

5. Philip Larkin, "Church Going" (1955), lines 49–52.

6. Williams Wordsworth, *The Prelude* (1850), book 3, lines 60–63.

7. Quoted in Mary Moorman, *William Wordsworth: The Early Years, 1770–1803* (London, 1957), 430.

8. Ralph Waldo Emerson, "Nature," chap. 1 in *Nature* (Boston, 1836).

9. Nathaniel Hawthorne, *The Ancestral Footstep,* Standard Library Edition (Boston, 1882–91), 2: 488–89.

10. Entry for 24 April 1859, *The Journal of Henry D. Thoreau,* ed. Bradford Torrey and Francis H. Allen (Boston, 1906), 12: 159–60.

11. Entry for 8 May 1852, *Journal of Thoreau,* 4: 41.

12. Entry for 13 February 1859, *Journal of Thoreau,* 11: 446.

13. Thoreau, *Walden,* 68.

14. White, *Natural History of Selborne,* 135.

15. Ernest Hemingway, *The Green Hills of Africa* (New York, 1935).

16. St. Augustine, *Confessions* XI: 20 (26).

17. White, *Natural History of Selborne,* 167.

18. Ibid., 239.

19. Herman Melville, *Moby-Dick* (1851: reprint, New York, 1967), 469.

20. See Mark Girouard, *The Return to Camelot: Chivalry and the English Gentleman* (New Haven, Connecticut, 1981).

21. William Butler Yeats, "The New Faces," in *The Poems*, ed. Richard J. Finneran (New York, 1983), 211.

22. Coventry Patmore's *The Angel in the House* (1854) was expanded by the inclusion of several sequels, *The Espousals* (1856), *Faithful Forever* (1860), and *The Victories of Love* (1862).

23. Herbert Asquith, "The Volunteer" (1915), lines 1–2, 11, 16.

24. Henry David Thoreau, *A Week on the Concord and Merrimack Rivers* (Boston, 1849).

25. Thoreau, *Walden*, 58.

26. Ibid., 62.

27. Ibid.

28. See John Henry Raleigh, *The Chronicle of Leopold and Molly Bloom: Ulysses as Narrative* (Berkeley, California, 1977).

29. Joyce, *Ulysses*, 17.1005–6, 17.1246, 17.1055–56.

30. Jaynes, *Origin of Consciousness*, 30.

31. Entry for 27 March 1857, *Journal of Thoreau*, 9: 306.

32. Marcel Proust, *Du Coté de chez Swann*, vol. 1 of *A la recherche du temps perdu* (Paris, 1926), 68.

33. John Berger, *Pig Earth* (New York, 1979), 163.

34. David Jones, *In Parenthesis* (1937; reprint, New York, 1963), 15–16.

35. Martin Amis, "A Blast against the Bomb," *The Observer* (London), 19 April 1987, 17.

36. Andrew Marvell, "To His Coy Mistress" (1681), lines 45–46.

37. *The American Heritage Dictionary of the English Language*, ed. William Morris (Boston, 1970), 1012.

38. George Eliot, *Middlemarch* (1871–72; reprint, Boston, 1956), 361.

39. James, *Principles of Psychology*, 1: 609–10.

40. Walt Whitman, "Song of Myself" (1855, 1881), line 232.

41. Michel de Montaigne, *The Essays of Montaigne*, trans. E. J. Trechmann (London, 1935), 2: 336.

42. Fernand Braudel, *The Mediterranean and the Mediterranean World in the Age of Philip II,* trans. Siân Reynolds (New York, 1972), 1: 369.

43. Thoreau, *Walden,* 36.

44. William Faulkner, *Light in August* (1932; reprint, New York, 1950), 32.

45. Fernand Braudel, *The Perspective of the World,* vol. 3 of *Civilization and Capitalism: Fifteenth to Eighteenth Century,* trans. Siân Reynolds (New York, 1984), 367, 583.

46. Braudel, *Perspective of the World,* 583.

47. Ibid., 584.

48. Ibid., 316.

49. J. H. Plumb, *Georgian Delights* (Boston, 1980), 12.

50. Braudel, *Perspective of the World,* 316; see also the schematic maps of travel times in France in 1765 and 1780, 316–17.

51. Plumb, *Georgian Delights,* 12.

52. Entry for 18 July 1837, *The Greville Memoirs: A Journal of the Reign of Queen Victoria from 1837 to 1852* (London, 1885), 1: 11.

53. Walt Whitman, "Passage to India " (pub. 1870; dated, 1871), lines 2–7.

54. Henry Adams, *History of the United States during the Administration of Thomas Jefferson,* ed. Earl N. Harbert (New York, 1986), 107.

55. Thoreau, *Walden,* 36.

56. David Jones, *Epoch and Artist* (London, 1959), 142.

57. Joyce, *Ulysses,* 7.735.

58. Evan S. Connell, *Son of the Morning Star* (San Francisco, 1984), 392.

4. Quantity and Scale and the Confetti of Numbers

1. Hermione Hobhouse, *Prince Albert: His Life and Work* (London, 1983), 100.

2. William Wordsworth, in a sonnet in *Poems Composed or Suggested during a Tour in the Summer of 1833* (London, 1833).

3. Charles Dickens, *Bleak House* (1852–53; reprint, Boston, 1956), 64–65; see also 301.

4. Richard D. Altick, *The Shows of London* (Cambridge, Massachusetts, 1978), 499.

5. George Dangerfield, *Victoria's Heir* (New York, 1941), 70.

6. *The Art-Journal Illustrated Catalogue: The Industry of all Nations 1851* (London, 1851), xxi. In facsimile, *The Crystal Palace Exhibition: Illustrated Catalogue* (New York, 1970).

7. Samuel Johnson, *The Rambler,* No. 60, 13 October 1750.

8. Herman Melville, "A Utilitarian View of the *Monitor*'s Fight," in *Battle-Pieces and Aspects of the War* (New York, 1866).

9. Jones, *In Parenthesis,* 37.

10. Hugh Kenner, *The Counterfeiters* (1968; reprint, New York, 1973), 127.

11. William Blake, *The Marriage of Heaven and Hell* in *The Poetry and Prose of William Blake,* ed. David V. Erdman (New York 1970), 35.

12. See the essay entitled "Thoughts on Poetry and Its Varieties" (London, 1833; revised 1859) and chapter 5 of Mill's *Autobiography* (London, 1873).

13. Charles Dickens, *Hard Times* (1854; reprint, New York, 1966), 2.

14. Emile Zola, *The Experimental Novel* (Paris, 1880).

15. Dickens, *Hard Times,* 96, 118.

16. Ralph Waldo Emerson, "Fate " (reprint, Boston, 1957), 337.

17. White, *Natural History of Selborne,* 27.

18. Citing Mrs. Loudon's *The Entertaining Naturalist* (London, 1850) in Barber, *Heyday of Natural History,* 128–29.

19. Dickens, *Hard Times,* 75.

20. Robert Browning, *The Ring and the Book* (London, 1868–69), book 10; lines 292–95.

21. *The New International Encyclopedia* (New York, 1904), 18: 515.

22. Daniel J. Boorstin, *The Americans: The Democratic Experience* (New York, 1973), 172.

23. (Paris, 1812), followed by *Essai philosophique sur les probabilités* (Paris, 1814).

24. Adolphe Quetelet, *Sur l'homme et le développement de ses facultés, où essai de physique sociale* (Brussels, 1835).

25. Quoted by Emerson in *Complete Works* (Boston, 1903–04), 6: 342.

26. Emerson, "Swedenborg," in *Complete Works,* 6: 109.

27. Emerson, "Fate," 337.

28. Retold in Robert J. Seidman, *One Smart Indian* (New York, 1977), 9–12.

29. Thoreau, *Walden,* 1.

30. Ibid., 222.

31. Ibid., 58.

32. Joyce, *Ulysses,* 17.2008.

33. Ibid., 12.1481–85.

34. Ibid., 8.978.

35. Ibid., 13.1217.

36. David Jones, *The Dying Gaul* (London, 1978), 58.

37. Joyce, *Ulysses,* 18.879.

38. John Stuart Mill, *Principles of Political Economy* (London, 1848).

39. John Keegan, *The Face of Battle* (New York, 1976), 307.

40. Associated Press, in *North Adams Transcript,* 1 December 1986, 2: 3–6.

41. Chapter 4, paragraph 5 of the treatise "Sanhedrin" of the *Mishnah.*

42. Wilfred Owen, "Insensibility," in *The Poems of Wilfred Owen,* ed. Edmund Blunden (New York, 1931), 64–65.

43. From a letter in possession of Sir Nevil Macready, The White House, Odiham, Hampshire.

44. Robertson Davies, *Fifth Business* (1970; reprint, New York, 1977), 73.

45. Ibid., 123.

46. Ibid., 76.

47. William Butler Yeats, "Lapis Lazuli" (1938), lines 21–24.

5. Personal Worth and Self-Esteem

1. Samuel Johnson, *The Rambler,* No. 60, 13 October 1750.

2. Wordsworth, "Tintern Abbey," line 61.

3. Wordsworth, *The Prelude,* book 1, line 301.

4. William Wordsworth, "Prospectus" to *The Recluse* (1814), lines 40–41.

5. William Wordsworth, "Preface" to *Lyrical Ballads* (London, 1802).

6. Coleridge, "To William Wordsworth: Composed on the Night [7 January 1807] after His Recitation of a Poem on the Growth of an Individual Mind," lines 3 and 45.

7. Quoted in Moorman, *Wordsworth: The Early Years,* 436.

8. Quoted in Mary Moorman, *William Wordsworth: The Later Years, 1803–1850* (1965; reprint, London, 1968), 266.

9. Byron, *Childe Harold's Pilgrimage* (London, 1816), canto 3, line 20.

10. Ibid., line 47.

11. Herman Melville, *Pierre* (1852; reprint, New York, n.d.), 476.

12. Robert W. Buchanan, an unsigned review of *The Ring and the Book* in *The Atheneum,* 20 March 1869, 399–400.

13. Browning, *The Ring and the Book,* 1: 1370.

14. Buchanan, review in *The Atheneum,* 399–400.

15. George W. S. Trow, *Within the Context of No Context* (New York, 1981), 7.

16. Quoted in *Penthouse* (December 1986).

17. Trow, *Within the Context,* 50.

18. Ibid., 51.

19. *American Heritage Dictionary,* 216.

20. Ellen Goodman in *North Adams Transcript.* 4 December 1985, 4.

21. *American Heritage Dictionary,* 1521.

22. John Milton, "Lycidas" (1637) lines 70–72.

23. Byron to Lord Holland, 25 February 1812, *Lord Byron: Selected Letters and Journals,* ed. Leslie A. Marchand (Cambridge, Massachusetts, 1982), 58.

24. Hawthorne to William D. Tichnor, his publisher, 27 June 1855, *Letters of Hawthorne to William D. Tichnor* (Boston, 1910).

25. John Berger and Jean Mohr, *A Fortunate Man* (London, 1967), 99.

26. Edgar Allan Poe, "The Philosophy of Composition," *Graham's Magazine,* 28 (April 1846): 163–67.

27. Nathaniel Hawthorne, "Writings of Aubépine," prefatory to "Rappaccini's Daughter," *Democratic Review* (December 1844).

28. See Girouard, *Return to Camelot,* chapter 18.

29. Kirk Douglas, *The Ragman's Son: An Autobiography* (New York, 1988), 268. The story is repeated with variations on 475.

30. Norman Mailer, *Marilyn* (New York, 1973).

31. Richard Schickel, *Intimate Strangers: the Culture of Celebrity* (New York, 1985), 197–98.

32. Molly Haskell, *New York Times Book Review,* 30 October 1983, 9.

33. *The New International Encyclopedia* (New York, 1904), 9: 406.

34. Ezra Pound, "Hugh Selwyn Mauberly: Life and Contacts" (1919) lines 80–85.

35. Nathaniel Hawthorne, *The Scarlet Letter* (1850; reprint, Boston, 1960), 201.

36. James Joyce, *A Portrait of the Artist as a Young Man* (New York, 1964), 171.

37. Rybczynski, *Home: A Short History of an Idea* (New York, 1986), 77.

38. *The New International Encyclopedia; The Encyclopaedia Britannica,* 11th ed. (Cambridge, England, 1910–11).

39. Dr. Allodi, quoted in the *New York Times Magazine,* 17 August 1986, 20.

40. William L. Shirer, *The Rise and Fall of the Third Reich: A History of Nazi Germany* (1960; reprint, New York, 1968), 375.

41. Primo Levi, *Survival in Auschwitz* (1959; reprint, New York, 1961), 36.

42. Ibid., 81.

43. Primo Levi, *The Drowned and the Saved* (New York, 1987), 27.

44. Honduran Sergeant Florencio Caballero quoted in James Le Moyne, "Testifying to Torture," *New York Times Magazine,* 5 June 1988, 62.

45. Entry for 21 January 1793, *Gilbert White's Journals,* 422.

46. Thomas Hardy, *The Dynasts,* part 2, act 1, scene 1.

47. Joyce, *Ulysses,* 17.1249, 17.1246.

48. Bruce Weber, "Alone Together: The Unromantic Generation," *New York Times Magazine,* 5 April 1987, 22, 25.

49. Erik Erikson, *Gandhi's Truth: On the Origins of Militant Nonviolence* (New York, 1969), 431.

50. "Call the world if you Please 'the vale of Soul-making.'" John Keats to George and Georgiana Keats, 14 February–3 May 1819, entry of 21 April.

51. William James, *Human Immortality: Two Supposed Objections to the Doctrine* (Boston, 1898), 39, n10; repeated as a refrain with variations on 37 and 44.

52. Walt Whitman, "Crossing Brooklyn Ferry" (originally "Sun-Down Poem," 1856; retitled circa 1860), lines 71–74.

53. Matthew Arnold, "The Function of Criticism at the Present Time" in *Essays in Criticism* (London, 1865).

6. How Are We Housed?

1. Girouard, *English Country House,* 214.

2. Entry for 25 October 1773, *Gilbert White's Journals,* 73.

3. White, *Natural History of Selbourne,* 249.

4. Ibid., 264.

5. Jasper Griffin, Introduction to *The Oxford History of the Classical World* (Oxford, 1986), 2.

6. Thoreau, *Walden,* 164.

7. Ibid., 112.

8. Ibid., 108.

9. Henry David Thoreau, "Life Without Principle," *Atlantic Monthly* (October 1863).

10. Ibid.

11. Rybczynski, *Home,* 77.

12. Thoreau, *Walden,* 56.

13. Quoted in Henry Beetle Hough, *Thoreau of Walden* (New York, 1956), 172.

14. *The Aeneid,* trans. Robert Fitzgerald (New York, 1983), 191–92.

15. Thoreau, *Walden,* 112.

16. Thoreau, *A Week on the Concord,* 154.

17. Jones, *Epoch and Artist,* 122.

18. Jones, *Dying Gaul,* 58.

19. Joyce, *Ulysses,* 17.1022.

20. See Keagan, *The Face of Battle.*

Epilogue

1. James, *Human Immortality,* 39 (n10), 69.